핵심 고급 단어
SAving Time
SAT Vocabulary

아이생각
www.ithinkbook.co.kr

[만든 사람들]
기획 … 실용기획부
진행 … 최정은
집필 … 박기혁, 박종범, 송승룡
표지 디자인 … 권득남
편집 디자인 … 파인에디팅

[책 내용 문의]
도서의 내용에 대한 궁금한 사항이 있으시면,
디지털북스 홈페이지의 게시판을 통해서 해결하실 수 있습니다.
디지털북스 홈페이지 www.digitalbooks.co.kr

[각종 문의]
영업 관련 … digital@digitalbooks.co.kr
기획 관련 … period@digitalbooks.co.kr
전화 번호 … (02)447-3157~8

※ 잘못된 책은 구입하신 서점에서 교환해 드립니다.
※ 이 책의 일부 혹은 전체 내용에 대한 무단 복사, 복제, 전재는 저작권법에 저촉됩니다.

머리말

글로벌 무대로 도약하려는 학생들에게 SAT는 하나의 중요한 통과의례가 되었다. 영어에 대한 대략의 개념만 잡혀도 무난한 점수가 나오는 여타 시험과는 다르게, SAT는 고급 어휘의 습득이 상당히 중요하다. 전문 교과 지식의 체계가 잡힐 만큼 어휘가 뒷받침되어야 하는 것이다.

그러나 국내 여건상 SAT에 정통한 단어장이 많지 않은 실정이다. 이에 뜻있는 저자들이 모여 본서를 마련하게 되었다.

이 책으로 공부함에 있어서 특별히 다음을 명심하기 바란다.

1. 어근 관념을 확실히 하라.
복잡한 단어 암기의 제1원리는 어근을 포착하는 것이다. 한자에서 핵심인 부수를 이해하면 기억이 오래 가는 것과 마찬가지이다.

2. 예문을 숙지하라.
단순히 단어만을 암기하는 것은 능률이 오르지 않는다. 맥락(예문)과 아울러 보아야 또 다른 맥락(시험) 속에서 발휘할 수 있다.

3. 다소 까다로운 단어들도 보라.
단어장을 훑는 중에 쉬운 단어는 거듭해 보게 되고, 어려운 것은 그냥 넘어가는 경향이 있다. SAT 고득점 달성의 관건은 어려운 단어를 많이 알고 있는지의 여부라 해도 과언이 아니다.

여러분은 한 개의 parabola antenna를 가지고 있다.
그 내면의 초점으로 정신을 집중하라.
이제 우리가 한 개를 더 준다.
extro; extra.
무수한 지식의 parallel들을 모은 후 진리의 빛줄기 한 개를 만들어라.
시간축이 훨씬 짧은 hyper hyperbola가 완성된다.

by 박기혁, 박종범, 송승룡

목차

어근 활용 예제   p.09

언어 감각이 있는지 스스로 확인합시다.

주어진 어근의 용례를 보고 한 단어의 의미를 추론하는 작업을 합니다. 10문제 중 5문제 이상을 못 맞히면 이 책을 일단 덮고 반성해야 합니다. 단어를 보는 안목, 나아가 언어 전반의 이해력과 감수성을 의심해 볼 만합니다.
한편, 10문제 모두 맞힌 학생도 자만해서는 안 될 것입니다. 미처 몰랐던 어근과 접사들을 습득하여 보다 고급의 어휘들로 재무장해야겠습니다.

어근과 접사   p.15

단어를 먼저 이해하고 효율을 추구합시다.

어근의 학습을 한다 함은 한 단어에 대해 제대로 이해부터 하자는 것입니다. 기계적인 단순 암기에 지연된 시간은 독해와 문법 학습의 감소라는 심각한 기회비용으로 이어집니다. 근본과 계통을 알고서 쉽게 그리고 빨리 습득해야 합니다.
최소 비용, 최대 효과라는 경제 원칙을 단어 학습에 적용하는데 어근과 접사가 큰 역할을 합니다. 10개의 접두사와 10개의 어근, 10개의 접미사가 조합하여 만들 수 있는 단어의 수는 1,000개입니다. 30단위의 수고로 1,000단위의 결과물을 획득하니 일종의 수지맞는 거래입니다.

day by day I   p.59

철저히 SUBROUTINE을 하는 시간.

이따금 낯익은 단어가 나오지만 여전히 생소해 보이는 많은 단어들이 있을 것입니다. day 단위로 학습하고 하루쯤 지나 연습문제를 풀며 확인 점검을 해봐야 합니다.

day by day II   p.211

마침내 UPGRADE된 나를 발견하는 시간.

여기 나온 단어는 이른바 고급 단어입니다. 에세이 등에서 고급 단어를 많이 구사하면 좋은 인상을 남길 수 있습니다. 남들과 차별화되고 싶고 선택 받고 싶으면 차분하게 꾸준히 외우십시오.

외연과 내포   p.333

미묘하지만 엄연한 차이를 설명해 줍니다.

단순히 유의어라 하여 대용했을 때 원어민이 느끼는 위화감을 우리 학생들은 못 느끼는 것이 큰 문제입니다. 하나의 외연으로 묶이지만 각기 내적으로 함축하는 바가 다른 단어들이 있습니다. 그 뉘앙스를 포착하여야 실전에서 또 실생활에서 어이없는 실수를 면할 수 있습니다. 작문을 대비하는 차원에서도 이러한 내실 있는 학습이 중요합니다.

부록

전문용어 100선   p.362

전문용어를 알아야 진정한 프로페셔널입니다.

Multi multa; nemo omnia novit. 많은 것을 아는 사람은 많지만, 모든 것을 아는 사람은 없습니다. 하지만 적어도 우리는 남보다 더 많은 것을, 더 심화된 것을 아는 부류가 되어야 하겠습니다.

연습문제 정답   p.367

이 책에 대하여

SAT를 준비함에 있어서는 매개가 되는 언어의 이해가 우선이고 그러면서 방대한 어휘 습득이 관건입니다. 이 책은 어휘 학습 과정 중에 면밀한 분석과 추론 능력까지 익히게 하여 SAT 체질을 만들어줍니다.

본 교재의 저자들은 원어민의 시각에서 수험 대비에 유효한 어휘들을 모으고, 그것을 일선 교육 환경에서 터득한 원리에 입각하여 짜임새 있게 범주화하였습니다. 또한 원활히 소화해내는 방식을 시사해주는 것에도 역점을 두었습니다.

어휘 습득을 제한된 용기에 물건을 수납하는 개념에 빗대어 볼 수 있겠습니다. 수납의 요령은 계통대로 분류해 놓고 적당한 식별 기능이 장치되어 있어 겉으로만 보아도 인지하기 좋게 만드는 것입니다.

결국, 마구잡이식이 아니라 유의미하게 수납하도록 유의미하고 적절한 환경을 제공하는 것이 본서의 핵심 취지입니다. 저자가 강조한 3가지를 다시 한 번 강조합니다.

    계통을 이해하고 유연하게 활용하라는 의미에서
    ▶ **어근과 접사의 학습을 권합니다.**

복잡한 단어를 형태소 분석해 보면 의외로 다 알 만한 단어들의 조합입니다.

벌레(虫)가 집 천장(宀)에 더듬이만 살짝 대고도 매달려 있기 위해 반드시(必) 필요한 끈끈이하면 꿀(蜜)이 떠오릅니다. 원래 형성자이지만 honey-splashed의 형상화라고도 볼 수 있겠습니다.
splash, flash, hush, blush, rush
좀처럼 허락되지 않아 애틋하고 때로 격하게도 보이는
몰래 떠나는 밀월(蜜月) 여행.
바로 연상되지요? 계통적으로 관련 있는 단어들이 전달하는 힘입니다.

기억에 개연성을 부여해주는
▶ **예문을 숙지하십시오.**

단순히 단어만을 암기하는 것은 재미도 없고 능률도 오르지 않습니다. 꼭, 예문과 같이 숙지하십시오. 자꾸 따라붙는 예문이 구속(shackle)하는 것 같아도 나중에는 쏟아지는 한 줄기 광선(shaft)이 되어 강한 영감을 줄 것입니다.

형상 기억 합금 아시죠? 형상 기억(shape memory)이란 특정 온도가 되면 본래의 모양으로 되돌아가는 현상입니다. 단어도 특별히 잘 어울리는 환경이 있습니다. 다음에 비슷한 환경에 처하게 될 때 잠재된 기억 속에서 해당 단어가 떠오를 것입니다.

이제는 미루지 말고
▶ **다소 까다로운 단어들도 학습하십시오.**

단어를 외우다보면, 익숙한 단어만 눈길을 주고, 어려운 것은 일단 거슬리니까 외면하는 경향이 있습니다. 낯선 단어는 그것을 몇 번 써보며 발음기호대로 따라 발음도 해보십시오. 감각과 지력을 다 동원하여서라도 반드시 어려운 단어와의 장벽을 허물고 고급 단계로 진일보해야 합니다.

근본부터 익히고 예문으로 강화하며 고난도 코스로 이행하라는 것이 요지였습니다.
반드시 이것을 실천하여 고득점 획득과 합격의 위업을 달성하기 바랍니다.

디지털북스

SAving Time
SAT Vocabulary

어근 활용 예제

어근 활용 예제

Intro

SAT 고득점을 위해 어휘를 외우기 전 반드시 짚고 넘어가야 할 것이 어근과 접사이다. 이들은 단어 생성의 기본 단위이고, 이 중 어근은 단어의 구성에 있어 가장 중요한 부분이다. 따라서 어근과 접사만 잘 알아도 단어 암기에 필요한 노력을 상당부분 절약할 수 있다.

이 책에서는 1. 시·공간·수의 표현 2. 관계나 상태의 표현 3. 품사 전환 표시 4. 기타의 네 가지로 범주화하였다.

본격적 학습에 들어가기 전 가볍게 퀴즈를 풀어 보고 어근과 접사의 효용 가치를 절감하자.

01   bi, bin 둘

예시 bi + nomial 항, 부분 = binomial : (수학) 이항식

biennale
① 격년 행사
② 음악 축제
③ 계간 잡지

02   ante 이전

예시 ante + meridian 정오의 = antemeridian : 오전의

antechamber
① 회의실
② 대기실
③ 연회장

03   quasi 유사한, 준(準)

예시   quasi + tax 세금 = quasi-tax : 공과금

quasi-equilibrium
① 유사분열
② 준평형
③ 불균형

04   extra 외부로

예시   extra + terrestrial 지구의 = extraterrestrial : 외계의

extracurricular
① 과외의
② 도망하는
③ 비범한

05   sub 아래

 sub + contract 계약 = subcontract : 하도급 계약

subtropical
① 적도의
② 극지방의
③ 아열대의

06　rupt 깨다

예시　dis 분리 + rupt = disrupt : 분열시키다

erupt
① 방해하다
② 분출하다
③ 분쇄하다

07　after 이후

예시　after + crop 수확 = aftercrop : 그루갈이

afterthought
① 상념
② 연속
③ 재고, 반성

08　trans 건너, 저리로

예시　trans + current 흐르는 = transcurrent : 횡단하는

transplant
① 변형
② 이식
③ 흡수

09   pon, pos 놓다

예시   op 적대적 + pon + ent(*n.*) = opponent : 적수, 상대편

deposit	① 예치하다 ② 휴대하다 ③ 들어 올리다

10   cide 살해

예시   gen(o) 생식자 + cide = genocide : 특정 집단 학살

herbicide	① 제초제 ② 살충제 ③ 자살

정답   01. ①   02. ②   03. ②   04. ①   05. ③   06. ②   07. ③   08. ②   09. ①   10. ①

SAving Time
SAT Vocabulary

어근과 접사

어근과 접사

1. 시간 · 공간 · 수

1) 시간

ante
이전
- ante + cede 나아가다 = **ante**cede 선행하다
- ante + date 날짜 = **ante**date 소급시키다

pre
이전
- pre + cept 잡다 = **pre**cept 교훈
  *경험하기 전에 이해하고 뜻을 잡는다는 의미
- pre + clude 닫다 = **pre**clude 방해하다
  *사전에 무엇을 못하도록 차단한다는 의미

pro
이전
- pro + pit 알리다 + ous (a.) = **pro**pitious 길조의
- pro + gen 출생 + itor 만드는 사람
  = **pro**genitor 선조, 어버이

after
이후
- after + thought 생각 = **after**thought 재고, 반성

epi
이후
- epi + logue 담화 = **epi**logue 맺음말
- epi + taph 새기다 = **epi**taph 비문, 묘비명

post 이후	■ post + graduate 졸업하다 = **post**graduate 대학 졸업 후의, 대학원의 ■ post + mort(em) 죽다 = **post**mortem 사후의

re 다시	■ re + spect 바라보다 = **re**spect 존중하다 ■ re + spir(e) 호흡하다 = **re**spire 호흡하다

2) 공간

ac ~을 향해(접근)	■ ac + credit 신용 = **ac**credit 신용하다 ■ ac + cess 나아가다 = **ac**cess 접근

ad ~을 향해(접근)	■ ad + vert 돌리다 = **ad**vert 언급하다

af ~을 향해(접근)	■ af + firm 단단한 = **af**firm 단언하다 ■ af + flux 흐르다 = **af**flux 유입

ag ~을 향해(접근)	■ ag + gress 나아가다 + ive (a.) = **ag**gressive 공격적인

an ~을 향해(접근)	■ an + nul 영(zero), 없음 = **an**nul 취소하다 ■ an + nounce 말하다 = **an**nounce 발표하다

as ~을 향해(접근)	■ as + simil 같다 + ate (v.) = **as**similate 동화하다
by 가까이	■ by + way 길 = **by**way 샛길, 옆길
circum 주위에	■ circum + vent 내보내다 = **circum**vent 포위하다 ■ circum + stance 입장 = **circum**stance 환경
de ~부터, ~아래	■ de + train 열차 = **de**train 열차에서 내리다 ■ de + lete 글자 = **de**lete 지우다
dia 통해서	■ dia + gnos 알다 + sis (n.) = **dia**gnosis 진단 ■ dia + therm 열 + y (n.) = **dia**thermy 투열요법
e 밖으로, ~로부터 떨어져	■ e + merge 잠기다 = **e**merge (수면 위로) 떠오르다 ＊잠겨 있다가 밖으로 나온다는 의미 ■ e + mit 보내다 = **e**mit 방출하다
em, en 안으로	■ en + velop 나아가다 = **en**velope 봉투 ■ em + bark 범선 = **em**bark 싣다

enter ~중에, 안에	■ enter + tain 지속하다 = **enter**tain 즐겁게 해주다 ■ enter + prise (비밀 등을) 캐내다 　= **enter**prise 모험심, 기업 경영

epi 접촉하여	■ epi + dermis 피부 = **epi**dermis 표피 ■ epi + center 중심 = **epi**center 진앙, 중핵

ex 밖으로	■ ex + pel 힘을 주다 = **ex**pel 쫓아내다 ■ ex + ped 다리 + ent (a.) = **ex**pedient 편의적인

extra 외부로	■ extra + terrestrial 지구의 = **extra**terrestrial 지구 밖의 ■ extra + judicial 재판의 = **extra**judicial 재판권 외의

im 속으로	■ im + bib(e) 마시다 = **im**bibe 흡수하다 ■ im + migrate 이동하다 = **im**migrate 이주해 오다

intra ~이내, 안에	■ intra + mural 벽의 = **intra**mural 건물 내의 ■ intra + party 정당 = **intra**party 정당 내의

inter ~중에, 사이에	■ inter + cept 잡다 = **inter**cept 가로채다 ■ inter + loc 말 + tion (n.) = **inter**locution 대화, 회담

mid
중간에

- mid + summer 여름 = **mid**summer 한여름
- mid + cult 문화 = **mid**cult 중류 문화

off
벗어나서, 밖에

- off + line 선, 경계 = **off**line 온라인상이 아닌
- off + stage 무대 = **off**stage 사생활의

on
~에

- on + shore 육지 = **on**shore 육지에서
- on + side 변 = **on**side 규정 구역 내의

para
옆에

- para + lel 나아가다 = **para**llel 평행의
- para + graph 쓰다 = **para**graph 단락

per
통과하여

- per + vas 통과하다 + ive (a.) = **per**vasive 침투하는
- per + ferv 열 + id (a.) = **per**fervid 열렬한

peri
주위에

- peri + spher 구 모양의 + y (n.) = **peri**phery 주위, 주변
- peri + scope 관찰용 기구 = **peri**scope 잠망경

pro
앞으로

- pro + pel 힘을 주다 = **pro**pel 추진하다
- pro + scribe 쓰다 = **pro**scribe 금지하다, 추방하다
  *백성들 앞에 금지 대상을 쓴다는 말에서 유래한 의미

re 뒤로	■ re + tract 끌다 = **re**tract 취소하다 ■ re + serve 봉사하다 = **re**serve 보류하다 ＊대기시켜 두었다가 나중에 봉사한다는 말에서 유래
retro 뒤로	■ retro + flex 구부리다 = **retro**flex 뒤로 굽은 ■ retro + gress 나아가다 = **retro**gress 퇴보하다
sub 아래	■ sub + scribe 쓰다 = **sub**scribe 서명하다 ■ sub + tract 끌다 = **sub**tract 빼다, 감하다
super 상위의	■ super + vis 보다 + or 행위자 = **super**visor 감독자 ■ super + sede 나아가다 = **super**sede 대신하다
tele 멀리 떨어져	■ tele + path 느끼다 + y (n.) = **tele**pathy 텔레파시 ■ tele + graph 쓰다 = **tele**graph 전신, 전보
trans 건너, 저리로	■ trans + plant 심다 = **trans**plant 이식하다 ■ trans + scribe 쓰다 = **trans**cribe 복사하다
under 밑에	■ under + estimate 평가하다 = **under**estimate 과소평가하다 ■ under + water 물 = **under**water 수중의

| **with** 뒤로 떨어져 | ■ with + draw 당기다 = **with**draw 철수하다
■ with + hold 붙들다 = **with**hold 억제하다 |

3) 수량과 규모

| **demi** 반 | ■ demi + god 신 = **demi**god 반신반인
■ demi + tint 색조 = **demi**tint 중간색 |

| **hemi** 반 | ■ hemi + sphere 구 = **hemi**sphere 반구체
■ hemi + cycle 원 = **hemi**cycle 반원형 |

| **semi** 반 | ■ semi + annual 1년의 = **semi**annual 반년마다의
■ semi + classic 고전 = **semi**classic 준고전적 작품 |

| **mon(o)** 하나 | ■ mono + archy 통치자 = **mon**archy 군주 정체
■ mono + graph 쓰다 = **mono**graph 특수연구서, 전공논문
＊하나의 분야만 연구해서 쓴 것의 의미 |

| **uni** 하나 | ■ uni + lateral 측면의 = **uni**lateral 한편의, 일방적인
■ uni + voc 소리 + al (a.) = **uni**vocal 단조롭게 말하는 |

| **bi, bin** 둘 | ■ bi + ling(ual) 언어의 = **bi**lingual 2개 국어의
■ bi + partisan 당파적인 = **bi**partisan 양당의 |

tri 셋	■ tri + pod 발 = **tri**pod 3각대 ■ tri + phibia 서식자 = **tri**phibian 육해공 3군의
dec, deci 십	■ dec + ade 시대 = **dec**ade 10년간 ■ deci + mal 단위의 = **dec**imal 십진법의, 소수의
cent, hect 백	■ cent + enni 년 + al (a.) = **cent**ennial 100년제의 ■ hect + gram 그램 = **hect**ogram 100그램
mill(e/i) 천(분율)	■ milli + gram 중량 단위 = **milli**gram 1/1,000그램 ■ mill(en) + um 집 = **mill**ennium 천년 왕국
kilo 천	■ kilo + stere 입방(세제곱)미터 = **kilo**stere 1,000입방미터
myria 만, 무수히 많은	■ myria + pod (연결형) 발 = **myria**pod (지네 등) 다족류
olig 소수의	■ olig + archy 정치체제 = **olig**archy 과두정치 ■ olig + poly 다수, 시장 = **olig**opoly 과점

poly
다수의
- poly + gamy 결혼, 결합 = **poly**gamy 일부다처
- poly + mer 물체, 형체 = **poly**mer 복합체

prot(o)
첫째의, 원래의
- prot + agonist 투쟁자 = **prot**agonist 주창자
- proto + type 형태 = **proto**type 원형, 시제품

extra
지나친
- extra + vag 방랑하다 + ant (a.) = **extra**vagant 낭비하는
- extra + sens 감각 + ry (a.) = **extra**sensory 초감각의

hyper
너무 많은
- hyper + bola 올가미 = **hyper**bola 쌍곡선
- hyper + trophy 영양, 발육 = **hyper**trophy (기관, 조직의) 이상 비대

hypo
아주 작은, 적은
- hypo + glycemia 혈당증 = **hypo**glycemic 저혈당의
- hypo + derm 피부 = **hypo**dermic 피하의

micro
작은
- micro + scope 관찰용 기구 = **micro**scope 현미경
- micro + organism 유기체 = **micro**organism 미생물

macro
큰
- macro + economics 경제학 = **macro**economics 거시경제학
- macro + cosmos 우주 = **macro**cosm 대우주

magni 굉장한	■ magni + fic 만들다 + ent (a.) = **magni**ficent 장대한 ■ magni + tude 성질, 상태 = **magni**tude 광대함
mega(l) 큰	■ megal + mania 심취 = **megal**omania 과대망상증 ■ mega + trend 흐름 = **mega**trend 시대의 조류
omni 모든	■ omni + pot 힘, 에너지 + ent (a.) = **omni**potent 전지전능한
out 외부로, 넘어서는	■ out + do 행하다 = **out**do 능가하다 ■ out + pace 발걸음 = **out**pace 앞지르다
over 지나친	■ over + flow 흐르다 = **over**flow 넘쳐흐르다 ■ over + dose 1회 복용량 = **over**dose 과잉복용
pene 거의	■ pene + insul 자르다, 섬 = **pen**insula 반도 ■ pene + tra 통과, 통행 + ate (v.) = **pene**trate 관통하다
ultra 넘어	■ ultra + modern 현대적 = **ultra**modern 초현대적인, 최첨단의 ■ ultra + sonic 음파의 = **ultra**sonic 초음파의

under
보다 적은

- under + weight 무게 = **under**weight 중량 미달
- under + buy 사다 = **under**buy 싸게 사다

2. 관계나 상태

1) 부정

a(n)
아닌, 없는

- a + moral 도덕의 = **a**moral 도덕성이 없는
- a + archy 정치체제 = **a**narchy 무정부주의

dis
아닌, 없는

- dis + soci 사교 + ate (v.) = **dis**sociate 분리하다
- dis + arm 무장 = **dis**arm 무장해제하다

il
아닌, 없는

- il + liter 글자의 + ate (a.) = **il**literate 문맹의
- il + leg 법 + al (a.) = **il**legal 불법의

im
아닌, 없는

- im + material 유형의 = **im**material 무형의

in
아닌, 없는

- in + cred 신뢰 + ous (a.) = **in**credulous 쉽사리 믿지 않는
- in + equit 동등 able (a.) = **in**equitable 불공평한, 불공정한

ir
아닌, 없는

- ir + revers 돌리다 + ible (a.) = **ir**reversible 순환할 수 없는

mis
잘못된

- mis + nom 이름 = **mis**nomer 잘못된 명칭
- mis + hap 우연한 일 = **mis**hap 불행한 일

non
아닌, 없는

- non + age 연령, 고령 = **non**age 미성년

un
아닌, 없는

- un + ortho 옳은 + dox 생각, 교리
  = **un**orthodox 정통이 아닌

2) 가치와 판단

anti
~에 반하여

- anti ~에 반하여 + sept 수용하다 + ic (a.)
  = **anti**septic 살균의
- anti + rust 녹 = **anti**rust 녹을 방지하는

bene
좋은

- bene + vol 의지 + ent (a.) = **bene**volent 자비심 많은
- bene + dict 말 = **bene**dict 축복하다

contra
~에 반하여

- contra + cept 수용하다 + tion (n.) = **contra**ception 피임
- contra + ban(d) 금지 = **contra**band 밀수품

| **dys** 나쁜 | ■ dys + function 기능 = **dys**function 기능장애
■ dys + peps 소화 + ia 병 = **dys**pepsia 소화 불량 |

| **eu** 좋은 | ■ eu + phoria 감정 = **eu**phoria 행복감
■ eu + logy 말 = **eu**logy 찬사 |

| **mal** 나쁜 | ■ mal + adjusted 조정된 = **mal**adjusted 조정이 잘못된
■ mal + vol 의지+ent (a.) = **mal**evolent 악의 있는, 사악한 |

| **mis** 싫어하다 | ■ mis + gamy 혼인 = **mis**ogamy 결혼을 싫어함
■ mis + anthro 사람
= **mis**anthrope 인간을 싫어하는 사람, 염세가 |

3) 상호 관계

| **ab** ~로부터 떨어져 | ■ ab + duct 끌어내다 = **ab**duct 유괴하다
＊부모의 보호권인 가정에서 밖으로 끌어낸다는 의미
■ ab + solve 해결하다 = **ab**solve 해제하다, 용서하다
＊해결해서 밖으로 석방하다는 의미 |

| **auto** 자신, 스스로 | ■ auto + crat 정치 + ic (a.) = **auto**cratic 독재의
■ auto + nym 이름 = **auto**nym 본명, 실명 |

co
함께

- co + ord 질서, 서열 + ate (a.)
  = **co**ordinate 조화되다, 조정하다
- co + heir 상속인 = **co**heir 공동상속인

col
함께

- col + labor 일 + tion (n.) = **col**laboration 합작
- col + loqu 대화 + al (a.) = **col**loquial 일상 회화의

com
함께

- com + mun 사회, 공동체 = **com**mune 교제하다
- com + bine 덩굴 = **com**bine 결합하다

con
~와 함께

- con + vene 오다 = **con**vene 소집하다
- con + cur 발생하다 = **con**cur 동시에 일어나다

self
자신

- self + sufficient 충분한 = **self**-sufficient 자급자족하는

sym
~와 함께, 같은

- sym + pose 놓다 + um 장소 = **sym**posium 토론회
  *다양한 의견을 한자리에 두는 장소의 의미
- sym + metry 측정 = **sym**metry 좌우대칭, 균형
  *측정하니 양쪽이 같다는 의미

syn
~와 함께

- syn + chron 시간 + ize (v.)
  = **syn**chronize 동시에 일어나다

4) 기타

ambi
양쪽의
- ambi + val 가치 + ent (a.) = **ambi**valent 양면가치의
- ambi + dexterity 손재주 = **ambi**dexterity 양손잡이

amphi
둥근, 양쪽의
- amphi + theater 극장, 활동 무대 = **amphi**theater 원형경기장
- amphi + bi 둘 + ous (a.) = **amphi**bious 이중성의

be
~이 되다
- be + friend 친구 = **be**friend 친구가 되다
- be + fall 떨어지다 = **be**fall 일어나다

hetero
다른
- hetero + dox 생각, 주의 = **hetero**dox 이단의
- hetero + gamete 생식체 = **hetero**gamete 이형 배우자

homo
같은
- homo + gene 유전자 + ous (a.) = **homo**geneous 동질의
- homo + centric 중심의 + ic (a.) = **homo**centric 같은 중심을 가진

meta
변화
- meta + bol 움직이다 + ism (n.) = **meta**bolism 신진대사
- meta + morphosis 이상 변이 = **meta**morphosis 변형

neo
새로운
- neo + natal 출생의 = **neo**natal 신생아의
- neo + classic 고전 + ism (n.) = **neo**classicism 신고전주의

pseudo
가짜의

- pseudo + nym 이름 = **pseudo**nym 가명
- pseudo + cyesis 임신 = **pseudo**cyesis 상상임신

3. 품사 전환 접사

1) 명사화

◆ 행위자

cian
기술자, 예술가

- magic 마술 + ian = magi**cian** 마술사
- music 음악 + ian = musi**cian** 음악가

ist
특수한 일을 하는 사람, 학자

- noct 밤 + amble 걷다 + ist = noctambul**ist** 몽유병자
- phil 좋아하는 + anthrope 인간 + ist = philanthrop**ist** 박애주의자, 자선가

man
특정 대상을 다루는 사람

- air 공중 + man = air**man** 비행사

wright
재주가 있는 사람

- play 연극 + wright = play**wright** 극작가
- ship 배 + wright = ship**wright** 배 만드는 목수

◆ 여성

enne
여성
- comedy 희극 + enne = comedi**enne** 여성 희극배우
- equestrian 기수의 + enne = equestri**enne** 여성 기수

(str)ess
여성
- seam 꿰매다 + stress = seam**stress** 여성 재봉사

ette
(일하는) 여성
- usher 안내원 + ette = usher**ette** 여성 안내원
- major 소령, 장 + ette = major**ette** 여성 악대장

ine
(남자를 전제로 한 이름의) 여성
- hero 주인공 + ine = hero**ine** 여자 주인공
- clement 온화한 + ine = Clement**ine** (여자이름)

trix
(남자를 전제로 한 이름의) 여성
- aviate 비행하다 + trix = avia**trix** 여성 비행사
- testate 유언 남기고 죽은 사람 + trix = testa**trix** 여성 유언자

◆ 장소

arium
부속 장소
- aqua 물 + arium = aqu**arium** 수족관
- frigid 몹시 추운 + arium = frigid**arium** 냉욕장

ary
장소

- infirm 허약한 + ary = infirmary 양호실
- libr 책 + ary = library 도서관

orium
장소

- sanat 병 고치는 + orium = sanatorium 요양소
- audit 듣다 + orium = auditorium 강당, 방청석

ory
장소

- reposit 두다 + ory = repository 저장소, 창고

◆ 행위, 과정 등

ade
행위, 행동

- block 막다, 봉쇄하다 + ade = blockade 해상봉쇄
- para 펼치다 + ade = parade 행렬

age
과정

- marry 결혼하다 + age = marriage 결혼
- pilgrim 순례하다 + age = pilgrimage 순례

ation
동작, 상태

- dur 지속 + ation = duration 지속, 계속
- ab 벗어난 + err 실수 + ation = aberration 탈선, 과오

cy
것

- truant 무단결석하다 + cy = truancy 무단결석
- liter(a) 글자 + cy = literacy 읽고 쓸 줄 앎

ism 주의, 체계	■ pan 널리 + the 신 + ism 주의 = pan**ism** 범신론, 다신교
ship 기술, 자격	■ showman 흥행사 + ship = showman**ship** 흥행술 ■ penman 문인 + ship = penman**ship** 서법, 필적
ment 하기	■ move 움직이다 + ment = move**ment** 움직임
ure 하기	■ seize 붙잡다 + ure = seiz**ure** 붙잡기

◆ 직업

ant, ent 행위자	■ superintend 감독하다 + ent = superintend**ent** 감독자
eer 행위자	■ sonnet 14행시, 단시 + eer = sonnet**eer** 소네트 시인
er, or 행위자	■ mental 정신의 + or = ment**or** 교사 ■ peddle 행상하다 + er = peddl**er** 행상인

ite
(집단 중의 한) 사람

- social 사교계의 + ite = social**ite** 사교계의 명사
- labor 노동당 + ite = labor**ite** (영국) 노동당원

ry
방법, 학문

- dentist 치과의사 + ry = dentist**ry** 치과학
- chemist 화학자 + ry = chemist**ry** 화학

◆ 생산물, 일

ade
일

- crucifix 십자가상 + ade = crus**ade** 십자군
- masque 가면극 + ade = masquer**ade** 가장무도회

ery, ry
행동

- master 지배하다 + ery = mast**ery** 지배
- treach 배반하다 + ery = treach**ery** 배반

ment
결과, 상태, 수단

- in 안 + stru 만들다 + ment = instru**ment** 기구
- sedi 가라앉은 + ment = sedi**ment** 침전물

mony
결과, 동작

- harmonic 조화적인 + mony = har**mony** 일치
- matri 결혼 + mony = matri**mony** 결혼식

◆ 작은 것

cle
조각, 파편

- part 부분 + cle = part**cle** 조각
- icy 얼음의 + cle = ici**cle** 고드름

cule
작은 조각

- mole 그램분자 + cule = mole**cule** 분자
- minus 보다 작은 + cule = minus**cule** 극소의

ette
작은 것

- kitchen 부엌 + ette = kitchen**ette** 간이 취사장
- cigar 시가 + ette = cigar**ette** 궐련, 담배

let
조각, 작은 것

- plate 판 + let = plate**let** 혈소판
- pamph 출판 + let = pamph**let** 소책자

ling
새끼

- fledge 깃털이 다 나다 + ling = fledg**ling** 풋내기
- hire 고용하다 + ling
  = hire**ling** 부하, 돈만 주면 일하는 사람

◆ 학문명

logy
학문

- physio 자연의 + logy = physio**logy** 생리학
  *인체의 물리적 현상을 분석하는 학문
- ped 어린이 + logy = ped**ology** 소아학

ics
학문

- stat 정지 상태, 통계 + ics = stat**ics** 통계학
- ortho 제대로 + dont 이빨 + ics
  = orthodont**ics** 치과 교정학

◆ 상태

ance, ence
상태

- acquaint 알게 되다 + ance = acquaint**ance** 친분, 면식
- i 반대 + gno 알다 + ance = ignor**ance** 무지

ancy, ency
상태

- flip 가볍게 치다 + ancy = flipp**ancy** 경솔함
- in 안에 + surg 일으킨 + ency = insurg**ency** 반란

dom
상태

- king 왕 + dom = king**dom** 왕국
- martyr 순교의 + dom = martyr**dom** 순교, 헌신

ery, ry
상태

- treach 배반하다 + ery = treach**ery** 배반
- slave 노예의 + ry = slav**ery** 노예 신분

hood
연령층, 단체

- boy 소년 + hood = boy**hood** 소년기
- brother 형제 + hood = brother**hood** 친목단체, 형제애

ion
상태, 동작

- per 통과 + cept 수용 + ion = percept**ion** 견해, 지각력

ity
상태, 성질

- am 우호 + ity = amity 친선, 우호
- ver 진실 + ity = verity 진실

ness
상태, 성질

- happy 행복한 + ness = happiness 행복
- friendly 친절한 + ness = friendliness 친절

or
상태

- horrify 무서워 떨게 하다 + or = horror 공포
- stuporous 무감각한 + or = stupor 마비, 인사불성

ship
상태, 신분

- friend 친구 + ship = friendship 우정
- hard 힘겨운 + ship = hardship 고난

sion
상태, 동작

- apprehend 이해하다 + sion = apprehension 이해
- perverse 비뚤어진 + sion = perversion 곡해, (성)도착

th
상태

- long 긴 + th = length 길이
- wide 넓은 + th = width 폭

tion
상태, 동작

- part 나누다 + tion = partition 분할

tude
태도
- rect 바른 + tude = rectitude 정직
- atti 태도 + tude = attitude 태도

ty
상태, 성질
- felici 행복 + ty = felicity 행복
- obscure 분명치 않은 + ty = obscurity 애매함

◆ 기타

ing
재료
- line 안감을 대다 + ing = lining 안감
- stuff 채우다 + ing = stuffing (속을 채우는) 재료

ectomy
절제
- tonsil 편도선 + ectomy = tonsillectomy 편도선 절제
- appendix 충수, 맹장 + ectomy
  = appendectomy 맹장수술

itis
염증
- tonsil 편도선 + itis = tonsillitis 편도염
- arthr 이음매 + itis = arthritis 관절염

2) 형용사화
◆ 성질

al, an
~한, ~의
- epi 접촉하여 + derm 피부 + al = epidermal 상피(표피)의
- con 함께 + gen 탄생 + al = congenital 선천성의

ary
~한, ~의

- volunteer 자발적으로 나서다 + ary = voluntary 자발적인
- liter 글자 + ary = literary 문학의

able, ible
~할 수 있는

- intellig 이해력이 있는 + ible = intelligible 알기 쉬운
- alien 다른 곳으로 + able = alienable 양도 가능한

esque
~같은

- picture 그림 + esque = picturesque 그림 같은
- statue 조각 + esque = statuesque 조각 같은

etic
~한

- sym 함께 + path 감정 + etic = sympathetic 인정 있는
- a 없는 + path 감정 + etic = apathetic 냉담한

ic
~한

- Barbary 바르바리 (이교도 지역) + ic = barbaric 미개한
- arch 원시, 태고 + ic = archaic 고풍의

ical
~한

- iden 동일한 + ical = identical 동일한
- hypocrit 위선 + ical = hypocritical 위선적인

ine
~같은, ~의

- bovid 소과의 동물 + ine = bovine 소 같은
- div 신 + ine = divine 신의

| **ish** ~한, ~스러운 | ■ child 어린이 + ish = childish 유치한
■ Ireland 아일랜드 + ish = Irish 아일랜드 사람 같은 |

| **like** ~같은 | ■ life 실물 + like = lifelike 실물과 꼭 같은 |

| **ly** ~한 | ■ come 오다 + ly = comely 어여쁜
＊거부감 없이 매력 있게 다가온다는 뜻
■ sister 자매 + ly = sisterly 자매의 |

| **oid** 유사한 | ■ alkali 알칼리 + oid = alkaloid 알칼리성의
■ aster 별 + oid = asteroid 소행성의 별 |

| **ular** ~적인 | ■ pop 대중적인 + ular = popular 대중적인
■ capsule 캡슐 + ular = capsular 캡슐 모양의 |

◆ 충만과 결여

| **ful** 가득 찬 | ■ art 기술 + ful = artful 교묘한, 빈틈없는 |

| **ose** ~한 | ■ verbal 말의 + ose = verbose 장황한
■ grand 웅대한 + ose = grandiose 웅대한 |

ous
~스러운

- auto 스스로 + nomy 체제 + ous
  = autonomous 자치권이 있는, 자율적인
- melli 꿀 + flu 흐름 + ous = mellifluous 감미로운

ulent
~한

- turb 동요하다 + ulent = turbulent 거친

less
~이 없는

- joy 재미 + less = joyless 재미없는

◆ 상태

ate
~의

- ob 부정적 + dur 지속 + ate = obdurate 고집 센, 완고한

id
~한

- lux 빛 + id = lucid 빛나는

ile
~ 할 수 있는

- doc 생각 + ile = docile 온순한, 가르치기 쉬운
  *자신의 생각을 남에게 가르치기 쉽다는 의미

ous
~한

- malice 앙심 + ous = malicious 악의 있는
- sense 감각 + ous = sensuous 감각적인

| y ~한 | ■ wealth 부유 + y = wealthy 유복한
■ sun 태양 + y = sunny 밝게 비치는 |

◆ 경향

| acious ~한 | ■ ten 힘줄 + acious = tenacious 끈질긴
■ ver 진실 + acious = veracious 진실한 |

| ant, ent ~한 | ■ err 벗어난 + ant = errant 정도에서 벗어난
■ malign 악한 + ant = malignant 악성의 |

| ative ~한 | ■ talk 수다를 떨다 + ative = talkative 수다스러운
■ demonstrate 내색하다 + ative = demonstrative 노골적인 |

| ive ~한 | ■ recess 역행하다 + ive = recessive 퇴행(역행)의 |

| some ~을 좋아하는, ~의 성질을 가진 | ■ quarrel 싸움 + some = quarrelsome 싸움을 좋아하는
■ meddle 방해하다 + some = meddlesome 방해하는 |

3) 동사화

◆ ~하게 만들다

| **ate**
하다 | ■ equ 같은 + ate = equate 동등하게 하다
■ de 퇴보 + genera 종족 + ate = degenerate 퇴화시키다 |

| **en**
하다 | ■ bright 밝은 + en = brighten 밝게 하다
■ broad 넓은 + en = broaden 넓히다 |

| **(i)fy**
하다 | ■ null 무효의 + fy = nullify 무효로 하다
■ uni 하나 + fy = unify 통일하다, 통합하다 |

| **ize**
~화하다 | ■ ag 방향성 + grand 크게 + ize
= aggrandize 확대(강화)하다 |

◆ 행동하다, 진행하다

| **ble**
(작은 동작을
여러 번) 하다 | ■ fum 만지다 + ble = fumble 더듬다
■ mum 잠자코 있다 + ble = mumble 중얼거리다 |

| **age**
하다 | ■ scrim 싸우다 + age = scrimmage 난투하다
■ pill 약탈하다 + age = pillage 약탈하다 |

| **er** 하다 | ■ de 아래 + liver 자유롭게 + er = deliver 배달하다
＊억압에서 자유로운 상태 아래로 옮긴다는 의미 |

| **ish** 하다 | ■ burn 불타다 + ish = burnish 윤이 나다, 닦다
■ nour 기르다 + ish = nourish 기르다 |

4) 부사화

| **ly** ~하게 | ■ happy 행복한 + ily = happily 행복하게
■ speed 신속 + ily = speedily 빨리 |

| **ways** ~하게 | ■ side 옆 + ways = sideways 비스듬하게
■ length 길이 + ways = lengthways 길게 |

| **wise** ~하게, ~으로 | ■ clock 시계 + wise = clockwise 오른쪽으로
■ end 끝 + wise = endwise 똑바로 세워서 |

4. 기타

ACT-ART

act ~하다	■ re 서로 + act = re**act** 상호작용하다
agr(i/o) 벌판	■ agr + culture 경작 = **agr**iculture 농업 ■ agr + arian (a.) = **agr**arian 토지의
anthr 인간	■ phil 사랑하는 + anthr + ist 행위자 = phil**anthr**opist 박애주의자 ■ mis 싫어하다 + anthr + ope 사람 = mis**anthr**ope 염세가
aqua 물	■ aqua + naut 항해 + ics 학문 = **aqua**nautics 수중 탐사
arch (단체의) 장, 체제	■ arch + tect 만들다 = **arch**itect 조물주, 건축가 ■ auto 스스로 + arch = aut**arch** 독재자
art 기술	■ art + isan 행위자 = **art**isan 공예가 ■ art + fact 만들다 = **art**ifact 가공품

BELLI-BREV

belli
전쟁
- belli + cose 친근한 = **belli**cose 호전적인
- re 반대 + belli + on (n.) = re**belli**on 반란

biblio
책
- biblio + graphy 보여주기 = **biblio**graphy 저서목록
- biblio + poly 팔다 = **biblio**poly 서적판매

bio
생명, 일생
- bio + metry 측정법 = **bio**metry 수명측정법
- sym 함께 + bio + sis (n.) = sym**bio**sis 공생

brev
짧은
- brev + ity (n.) = **brev**ity 순간
- ab (v.) + brev + ate (v.) = ab**brev**iate 짧게 하다

CEDE-CUM

cede, ceed
가다, 내주다
- con 함께 + cede = con**cede** 인정하다
- inter 중간에서 + cede = inter**cede** 중재하다

cert
확실한
- cert + fic 만들다 + ate (v.) = **cert**ificate 증명서
- as (v.) + certain = as**cert**ain 확인하다, 확정하다

| **chron** 시간 | ■ ana 거스르는 + chron + ism 생각 = ana**chron**ism 시대착오
■ **chron** + cle 작은 = **chron**icle 연대기 |

| **cide** 죽이다 | ■ hom 사람 + cide = hom**icide** 살인
■ reg 왕 + cide = reg**icide** 왕의 시해, 반역 |

| **clar** 명백한 | ■ clar + fy (v.) = **clar**ify 명백히 하다
■ de 아래 + clar = de**clar**e 선언하다 |

| **cogn** 알다 | ■ re 다시 + cogn + ize (v.) = re**cogn**ize 인식하다
■ cogn + tion (n.) = **cogn**ition 인식 |

| **corp** 신체, 단체 | ■ corp + us (n.) = **corp**us 전집, 본체
■ corp + ate (v.) + ion 명사 = **corp**oration 법인 |

| **cum** 쌓다 | ■ cum + ula (v.) + tive (a.) = **cum**ulative 누적된
■ ac (v.) + cum + ulate (v.) = ac**cum**ulate 축적하다 |

DEM-DUCT

| **dem** 대중 | ■ dem + cracy 지배, 정치 = **dem**ocracy 민주주의
■ dem + graphy 기록 = **dem**ography 인구(통계)학 |

dict
말하다
- dict + ate 하다 = **dict**ate 명령하다
- mal 악한 + dict = male**dict** 저주하다

don, donat
주다
- donat + tion (n.) = **donat**ion 기부
- par 같다 + don = par**don** 용서하다
  *그전의 감정적 수준과 같도록 마음을 준다는 의미

derm
피부
- epi 바깥 + dermis = epi**derm**is 표피, 외피
- hypo 아래의 + derm + ic (a.) = hypo**derm**ic 피하의, 자극하는

duc, duct
이끌다
- con 함께 + duct = con**duct** 행하다
  *몸과 마음을 밖으로 즉 행동으로 끌어낸다는 의미
- e 바깥 + duc + ate (v.) = e**duc**ate 교육하다
  *인성이 바깥으로 나오게 한다는 의미

FAC-FIG

fac
행하다, 만들다
- bene 좋은 + fact + or 행위자 = bene**fact**or 은인
- fact + ory 장소 = **fact**ory 공장

fer
나르다
- trans 다른 곳으로 + fer = trans**fer** 운반하다
- fer + ry 장소 = **fer**ry 선착장

어근과 접사 49

fig
형성하다

- fig + ure (n.) = **fig**ure 형태
- fig + ment (n.) = **fig**ment 허구

GEN-GREG

gen(e)
출생, 생식

- gene + tics 학문 = **gen**etics 유전학

gnos
알다

- dia 통해서 + gnos + is (n.) = dia**gnos**is 진단
- a 없는 + gnos + tic (a.) = a**gnos**tic 불가지론자(의)

grad, gress
단계, 진보

- grad + ate (v.) + ion (n.) = **grad**uation 졸업
  *단계를 마친다는 의미
- di 옆으로 + gress = di**gress** 옆길로 샘

graph
기록하다

- phono 소리 + graph = phono**graph** 축음기

grat
감사

- grat + ful (a.) = **grat**eful 감사하는
- in 없는 + grat = in**grat**e 은혜를 모르는

greg
모으다

- greg + ari 동사 + ous (a.) = **greg**arious 군집의
- se 분리된 + greg 무리 + ate (v.)
  = se**greg**ate 분리하다, 격리하다

HOMO-JUS

homo
사람

- homo + cide 살해 = **homo**cide 살인
- homo + age 나이 먹다 = **hom**age 존경

iatr
치료

- psycho 정신병자 + iatr + y (n.)
  = psych**iatr**y 정신병 치료법
- pod 발 + iatr + y (n.) = pod**iatr**y 족병학

jus
법

- jus + ify (v.) = **jus**tify 변호하다
- ad (v.) + jus = ad**jus**t 조정하다, 조절하다

LAB-LYS

lab
일

- lab + or (n.) = **lab**or 노동
- col 함께 + labor + ate (v.) = col**lab**orate 합작하다

loc
위치

- loc + ation (n.) = **loc**ation 위치
- al (v.) + loc + ate (v.) = al**loc**ate 배치하다

lum
빛

- lum + in 안에 + ous (a.) = **lum**in**ous** 빛나는
- il 안에 + lum + nate (v.) = il**lum**i**nate** 비추다

lys
분해하다, 약해지다

- ana 전면적 + lys + is (n.) = ana**lys**is 분석
- para 옆 + lys + is 명사 = para**lys**is 마비
  *측면이 약해진다는 말에서 유래한 의미

MAN-MOV

man
손

- man + al (a.) = **man**u**al** 손으로 하는, 수동의
- man + mit 보내다 = **man**u**mit** 노예를 해방하다

mech
기계

- mech + anic 사람 = **mech**anic 기계공
- mech + anize (v.) = **mech**anize ~을 기계적으로 하다

mem
염두에 둔, 기억하는

- mem + ory (n.) = **mem**ory 기억
- com 함께 + mem + ate (v.) = com**mem**orate 기념하다

min
작은, 적은

- min + ute (a.) = **min**ute 미세한
- mini + ize (v.) = **min**imize 축소하다

mit, mis 보내다	■ sub 아래에 + mit = submit 순종하다, 제출하다 ■ e 밖 + mit = emit 방출하다
mov 움직이다	■ mov + ment (n.) = movement 이동 ■ re 다시 + mov 움직이다 = remove 옮기다

NAT-NYM

nat 출생하다	■ nat + al (a.) = natal 출생의 ■ in 속의 + nat = innate 타고난
nav 배	■ nav + y (n.) = navy 해군 ■ nav + ig (v.) + ate (v.) = navigate 항해하다
neo 새로운	■ neo + classic 고전주의의 = neoclassic 신고전주의의 ■ neo + natal 출생의 = neonatal 신생아의
nomen, nym 이름	■ pseudo 허위의 + nym = pseudonym 익명 ■ auto 스스로의 + nym = autonym 본명, 실명

OCU-ORTHO

ocu
눈
- oculus 눈 + ist 사람 = **ocu**list 안과의사
- bin 쌍 + ocular 접안경 = bin**ocu**lar 쌍안경

ortho
바른
- **ortho** + don 치아 + ist 사람 = **ortho**dontist 치열교정 의사
- **ortho** + ped 걷다 + ics 학문 = **ortho**pedics 정형외과

PHIL-PUT

phil
사랑하다
- **phil** + sophy 학문 = **phil**osophy 철학
- **phil** + anthropic 인류의 + ism 주의 = **phil**anthropism 박애주의

photo
빛
- **photo** + graph 그림 = **photo**graph 사진
- **photo** + synthesis 합성 = **photo**synthesis 광합성

plic, plex
접다, 만들다
- im 안 + plic + ate (v.) + ation (n.) = im**plic**ation 연루
- com 아주, 함께 + plex = com**plex** 복잡한

pon
놓다
- op 적의 + pon + ent (n.) = op**pon**ent 적대자
- post 뒤에 + pon = post**pon**e 연기하다

pop
사람

- pop + art 예술 = **pop**art 대중예술
- pop + ula (v.) + tion (n.) = **pop**ulation 인구

port
나르다

- trans 저쪽으로 + port = trans**port** 옮기다
- port + able ~할 수 있는 = **port**able 휴대용의

psych
정신

- psych + logy 학문 = **psych**ology 심리학
- psych + path 병 = **psych**opath 정신병자

pul
강요하다

- com 아주 + pul + ory (a.) = com**pul**sory 강제의
- re 되받아서 + pulse 힘쓰다 = re**pul**se 격퇴하다

pun
찌르다, 자르다

- ex 밖 + pun = ex**pun**ge 삭제하다
- acu 날카로운 + pun + ure (n.) = acu**pun**cture 침술, 침술요법

put
놓다, 생각하다

- re 다시 + put + ate (v.) + ion (n.) = re**put**ation 명성
  *후에 그 대상에 대해 다시 생각하게 한다는 의미
- com (여러 가지를) 함께 + put + er 행위자 = com**put**er 계산기

RAS-RID

ras
문지르다
- e 밖 + ras = e**ras**e 지우다
- ab 동사 + ras + ive (n.) = ab**ras**ive 연마제

rid
웃다
- rid + cul 동사 + ous (a.) = **rid**iculous 우스운
- de 아래를 (보고) + rid = de**rid**e 비웃다

SCRIBE-STRUCT

scribe, script
기록하다
- script + ure (n.) = **script**ure 성서
- circum 주변 + scribe = circum**scribe** 제한하다, 선으로 긋다

sens, sent
느끼다,
동의하다
- sens + ous (a.) = **sens**uous 감각적인
- dis 부정적 + sent = dis**sent** 반대하다

spir
호흡
- in 안에 + spir = in**spir**e 고취하다, 불어넣다
- con 함께 + spir = con**spir**e 공모하다, 작당하다

sta(g)
서다
- sta + tic (a.) = **sta**tic 정적인
- stag + ant (a.) = **stag**nant 불경기의

struct
짓다

- in 내부적으로 + struct = in**struct** 가르치다
  *사람의 정신을 지어준다는 의미
- ob 부정적 + struct = ob**struct** 가로막다

TACT-TRACT

tact, tang
만지다

- tang + ible ~할 수 있는 = **tang**ible 만질 수 있는
- tact + ile ~할 수 있는 = **tact**ile 촉각의

tain
붙잡다

- de 아래 + tain = de**tain** 붙들어 두다
  *자신의 발 아래 붙잡고 있다는 의미
- con ~을 가지고 + tain = con**tain** 함유하다

ten
가지다

- ten + ure (n.) = **ten**ure 보유
- in 안에 + ten = in**ten**t 의지

terr
땅

- terr + ain 장소 = **terr**ain 지형
- terr + ory 장소 = **terr**itory 영토

the
신

- a 없는 + the + ism 주의 = a**the**ism 무신론

therm
열, 온도

- hypo 아래에 + therm + ia 병 = hypo**therm**ia 체온저하
- dia 통해서 + therm + y 방법 = dia**therm**y 투열요법

tract
끌다, 움직이다

- ab 벗어난 + tract = ab**tract** 추상적인, 벗어난
- at 접근 + tract = at**tract** 유혹하다

URB-VIT

urb
도시

- urb + an (a.) = **urb**an 도시의
- urb + ane (a.) = **urb**ane 세련된

vene, vent
오다

- ad ~에 + vent = ad**vent** 출현
- con 함께 + vene = con**vene** 집합하다

vict, vinc
극복하다

- vict + im (n.) = **vict**im 희생자
- vinc + ible ~할 수 있는 = **vinc**ible 정복할 수 있는

vid
보다, 명백한

- vid + eo (n.) = **vid**eo 비디오
- e 밖 + vid + ence (n.) = e**vid**ence 증거

viv, vit
살아있는

- viv + id (a.) = **viv**id 생생한
- vit + al (a.) + ity (n.) = **vit**ality 생명력

SAving Time
SAT Vocabulary

day by day I

Day 1

01 antagonize

/ æntǽgənàiz /

동 적대감을 불러일으키다

syn face, confront, turn against, act hostile to

영영 make them feel angry or hostile towards something

예문 Japan's action over Dokdo Island ***antagonized*** Korean people further.
독도에 대한 일본의 행동은 한국 사람들에게 더 많은 적대감을 불러 일으켰다.

02 macro

/ mǽkrou /

명 거시적인

syn big, bulky, major

영영 relating to a general area, rather than being detailed or specific

예문 Many analysts take a ***macro*** view of the economy.
많은 분석가들은 경제에 대해 거시적인 관점을 가진다.

03 maladroit

/ mæ̀lədrɔ́it /

형 솜씨 없는, 재치 없는

syn inept, ham-handed, inadequate

영영 being clumsy or handling situations badly

예문 The stewardess I met on the flight to America was rather ***maladroit*** in serving the passengers on board.
미국으로 가는 비행기 안에서 만난 여 승무원은 기내 승객들에게 제대로 서빙하지 못했다.

04 bait
/ béit /

동 미끼를 놓다

syn decoy, lure

영영 deliberately put attraction on it

예문 The Eskimo Indian guide showed me how to **bait** the trap.
에스키모 인디안 안내인은 덫에 어떻게 미끼를 놓는지 보여주었다.

05 naive
/ nɑːíːv /

형 순진한, (너무 순진해서 조금) 모자란

syn innocent, ingenuous

영영 lacking experience and so too honest or kind

예문 I was so **naive** in believing his story to be true.
나는 그의 이야기가 사실인 것으로 믿을 정도로 순진했다.

06 cacophony
/ kəkáfəni /

명 불협화음

syn discord, dissonance

영영 a loud, unpleasant mixture of sounds

예문 The classroom was filled with a **cacophony** of sounds coming from various instruments.
그 교실은 다양한 악기들이 내는 불협화음이 가득했다.

07 obligate
/ ábləgèit /

형 의무를 지우다, 감사가 우러나게 하다

syn compel, force, oblige

영영 create a situation where someone has to do something

예문 Many senior Koreans feel **obligated** to those who have died in Korean War to save their country.
많은 한국인 고령자들은 한국동란 당시 나라를 구하기 위해 목숨 바친 이들에게 감사하는 마음을 가지고 있다.

08

paradox

/ pǽrədɑ̀ks /

명 역설적인 사람(상황), 역설

syn contradiction, anomaly, oddity, enigma

영영 involving two or more facts or qualities which seem to contradict each other

예문 The comments made by President was full of **paradox**.
대통령이 말한 것들은 모순으로 가득했다.

09

pacify

/ pǽsəfài /

동 달래다, 가라앉히다

syn placate, soothe, calm, comfort, coax

영영 succeed in making them calm or pleased

예문 The government of Monrovia tried to **pacify** the angry demonstrators that were staging anti-government protest.
몬로비아 정부는 반정부 시위를 벌이고 있는 성난 시위자들을 달래려고 노력했다.

10

feign

/ féin /

동 가장하다, ~인 척하다

syn pretend, disguise, assume, impersonate

영영 make other people think that they have it, although this is not true

예문 When the teacher came towards me to check my homework, I **feigned** an illness so that I might turn his attention away from checking it.
선생님이 나의 숙제를 확인하러 오셨을 때 주의를 딴 데로 돌릴 수 있도록 아픈 척 했다.

11

facet

/ fǽsit /

명 측면, 양상

syn aspect, side

영영 a single part or aspect

예문 As a scientist, you would have to look into all **facets** of a problem to solve it.
과학자로서 당신은 문제를 해결하기 위해 모든 면을 살펴봐야 한다.

12 fad
/ fæd /

명 (일시적) 유행

syn craze, fashion, trend, rage, vogue

영영 an activity or topic of interest that is very popular for a short time

예문 The Korean wave in dramas, movies and music has sparked a **fad** for everything that is Korean among young people in the Southeast Asian nations.
드라마, 영화, 음악에서의 한류는 동남아 국가의 젊은이들 사이에서 한국적인 것에 대한 유행을 불러 일으켰다.

13 habituate
/ həbítʃuèit /

타 길들이다

syn train, break in

영영 make used

예문 Once the students **habituate** themselves to wrong study habits, it is hard to correct that.
학생들이 잘못된 학습방식에 길들여지면 그것을 고치는 것이 힘들다.

14 embark
/ imbárk /

동 싣다, 탑승하다

syn board

영영 go on board a ship or aircraft

예문 The attendant **embarked** for France by a steamer.
그 승무원은 기선을 타고 프랑스로 향했다.

15 usurp
/ juːsə́ːrp /

동 찬탈하다, 약탈하다

syn supplant, seize, plunder

영영 take a position from someone in forceful manner, with an unjustifiable cause

예문 African military leaders have been **usurping** power in their countries by staging a coup d'etat.
아프리카의 군 지도자들은 쿠데타를 시도함으로써 그들 나라의 권력을 찬탈해왔다.

연습문제

I

1. June's ideas are often _____ because of her young age.
2. The listeners were bored but most tried to _____ polite interest.
3. I really feel _____ to the farmers who grow rice we eat every day.
4. If you miss one _____ of the problem, then you might never be able to solve it.
5. The mother's soft singing seems to _____ the baby.

/ facet / naive / obligate / pacify / feign /

II

1. craze, fashion, trend, rage, vogue = _____
2. decoy, lure = _____
3. discord, dissonance = _____
4. inept, ham-handed, inadequate = _____
5. face, confront, turn against, act hostile to = _____

/ maladroit / bait / antagonize / fad / cacophony /

Day 2

01 macroeconomics
/ mæ̀krou-i:kənάmiks /

명 거시 경제학

syn the study of large economic systems

영영 the branch of economics concerned with aggregates, such as national income, consumption, and investment

예문 *Macroeconomics* is an important field of academic studies that can help a government to manage its economy.
거시 경제학은 한 정부가 경제를 운용하는데 있어 도움을 줄 수 있는 중요한 학문 분야이다.

02 maculate
/ mǽkjulèit /

동 더럽히다, 반점(오점)을 남기다

syn dirty, defile

영영 mark with a spot or stain

예문 The bribe scandal, which surprised everyone, *maculated* the integrity of former prime minister.
모두를 놀라게 했던 그 뇌물 스캔들은 전 총리의 청렴함에 오점을 남겼다.

03 oblique
/ əblí:k /

형 (표현이) 완곡한, (경사가) 비스듬한

syn indirect

영영 not expressed directly or openly, making it difficult to understand

예문 When questioned by police, the prime suspect of a murder case gave *oblique* replies.
경찰에 의해 취조 받았을 때 살인 사건의 가장 유력한 용의자는 애매모호한 답변만 내놓았다.

04 quagmire
/ kwǽgmàiər /
명 수렁, 진창, 곤경
syn bog, morass

영영 a difficult or unpleasant situation which is not easy to escape from

예문 The child who was trapped by the mud slide was pulled out of the **quagmire** by rescuers.
진흙 산사태로 갇힌 그 아이는 구조대에 의해 수렁에서 건져졌다.

05 quaint
/ kwéint /
형 진기한, 이상한
syn novel

영영 attractive because it is unusual and rather old-fashioned

예문 Korean Folk Village is well known by its **quaint** thatched-roof houses.
한국 민속촌은 진기한 초가집들로 유명하다.

06 ramble
/ rǽmbl /
동 거닐다, 어슬렁거리다, 산책하다
syn walk, range, wander

영영 walk around in the countryside

예문 I saw some strange black men **rambling** in our neighborhood and reported it to police.
나는 우리 동네에 수상한 흑인이 돌아다니고 있는 것을 보고 경찰에 신고했다.

07 salient
/ séiliənt /
형 두드러진
syn projecting, prominent

영영 important and noticed easily

예문 It is said that a man's real personality becomes **salient** when he drives.
남자가 운전할 때 그의 참 성격이 드러난다고 한다.

08 sadistic

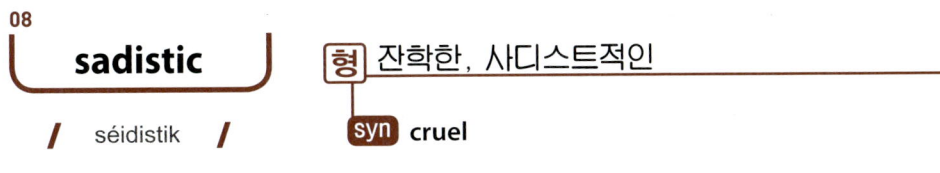

/ séidistik / 형 잔학한, 사디스트적인

syn cruel

영영 enjoying others' suffering or make them suffer

예문 The student thought their teacher had a ***sadistic*** nature because he enjoyed seeing his students struggle with the homework he gave out.
학생들은 그들의 선생님이 숙제로 학생들을 힘들게 하기 때문에 사디스트적이라고 생각했다.

09 tantalize

/ tǽntəlàiz / 동 감질나게 하다, 짜증나게 하다

syn tempt, torment

영영 promise others something that they might like, but break the promise at the end, which can make them feel really upset

예문 The teacher ***tantalized*** his students with the carrot and the stick but they were at their wits' end.
선생님은 당근과 채찍의 식으로 학생들을 애먹였는데 그들은 어찌할 바를 몰랐다.

10 tantamount

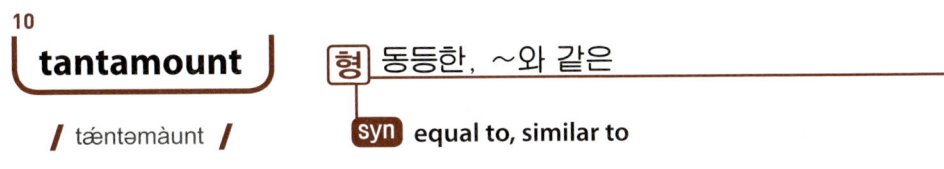

/ tǽntəmàunt / 형 동등한, ~와 같은

syn equal to, similar to

영영 comparing something to another that is bad, unacceptable

예문 The police thought the culprit's silence was ***tantamount*** to an admission of guilt.
경찰은 그 범인의 침묵이 곧 자신의 죄를 인정하는 것이라 생각했다.

11 unilateral

/ jùːnəlǽtərəl / 형 일방적인

syn single, solitary, sole

영영 decided by one individual or a group, without consulting others' opinion

예문 The EU has created its own currency, Euros, to stop the ***unilateral*** dominance of dollar currency in the international market.
유럽 연합은 국제 시장에서 달러화의 일방적 독점을 막기 위해 자체 통화인 유로를 만들어 냈다.

12 wafer
/ wéifər /

명 얇은 조각, 회로기판
syn slice

영영 a thin piece of something

예문 If you put some ice cream on the **wafer**, it will taste great.
만약에 웨이퍼위에 아이스크림을 얹으면 맛이 아주 좋을 거야.

13 wakeful
/ wéikfəl /

형 방심치 않는, 불면의
syn alerted, sleepless

영영 having difficulties sleeping or watching out for something

예문 I couldn't rest easy because I was **wakeful** over the unfinished project.
나는 끝내지 못한 프로젝트가 신경이 쓰여서 편하게 있을 수 없었다.

14 wane
/ wéin /

동 줄어들다, 감소하다
syn decline, diminish, weaken

영영 be reduced in size, number or in importance

예문 Some believe that the power of the United States is **waning** in the Pacific whereas China is emerging as the leading power in the region.
어떤 사람들은 태평양에서 미국의 힘이 줄어들고 있는 반면에 중국은 강자로 부상하고 있다고 생각한다.

15 connote
/ kənóut /

동 원뜻 외에 부수적 의미를 내포하다
syn imply, suggest

영영 suggest an idea in addition to the literal meaning

예문 The word 'home' usually **connotes** comfort and security.
'가정'이라는 말에는 보통 위안과 안전이라는 어감이 내포되어 있다.

연습문제

I

1. Stop trying to _____ me into granting your wishes; it's not going to work!
2. The cowboys of the Old West would _____ from town to town.
3. The black and white schemes _____ simplicity.
4. That may sound _____ but it works.
5. A _____ is a very thin piece of something.

/ connote / tantalize / ramble / wafer / quaint /

II

1. single, solitary, sole = _____
2. jutting, projecting, prominent = _____
3. decline, diminish, weaken = _____
4. alerted, sleepless = _____
5. walk, range, wander = _____

/ wane / unilateral / wakeful / salient / ramble /

Day 3

01 abash
/ əbǽʃ /

타 무안하게 하다, 당황하게 하다

syn embarrass

영영 cause to feel ashamed, ill at ease, or confused

예문 The students were **abashed** by the careless remark made by their homeroom teacher.
학생들은 그들의 담임선생님에 의해 행해진 부주의한 질문에 당황했다.

02 aberrant
/ əbérənt /

형 도리를 벗어난, 일탈적인

syn abnormal, out-of-line

영영 unusual and not socially acceptable

예문 The company is infamous for its **aberrant** manner of business practice.
그 회사는 도리를 벗어난 사업 관행으로 악명이 높다.

03 abhor
/ æbhɔ́:r /

동 혐오하다

syn loathe, abominate, execrate

영영 hate something very much, especially for moral reasons

예문 I **abhor** racism, as it stands against everything I believe in.
나는 인종차별주의를 내가 믿는 모든 것에 반하기 때문에 싫어한다.

04 callous

/ kǽləs /

형 냉담한

syn insensible, stony

영영 very cruel and showing no concern for other people or their feelings

예문 Years of hard struggle had made him a bit **callous** toward the feelings.
수년간의 고생은 그를 다소 냉담하게 만들었다.

05 calumniate

/ kəlʌ́mnièit /

타 비방하다, 중상하다

syn slander

영영 make false statements

예문 Rumors abounded that someone had **calumniated** her best friend behind her back.
누군가가 그녀의 절친한 친구를 뒷전에서 험담했다는 소문이 무성했다.

06 daunt

/ dɔ́ːnt /

동 겁먹게 하다, 기죽게 하다

syn intimidate

영영 make you feel slightly afraid or worried

예문 We should not let the threats made by terrorists **daunt** us from battling them.
우리는 테러리스트들의 협박에 겁먹고 물러나서는 안 된다.

07 decadence

/ dékədəns /

명 타락, 퇴폐

syn corruption

영영 the process or manifestation of moral or cultural decline

예문 Many people regard this century as a period of **decadence**.
많은 사람들은 금세기를 타락한 시기라고 본다.

08 factitious
/ fǽktíʃəs /

형 (진짜처럼 보이도록) 꾸며낸, 인위적인

syn sham, artificial

영영 artificial rather than natural

예문 He created **factitious** story of his past to draw others' sympathy.
그는 타인들의 동정심을 유발하려고 그의 과거에 대한 인위적인 이야기를 꾸며냈다.

09 fallacy
/ fǽləsi /

명 (많은 사람들이 옳다고 믿지만) 틀린 생각

syn mistake, error

영영 false or mistaken belief

예문 The Japanese people have developed a **fallacy** that they are the victims of World War II.
일본인들은 그들이 2차 세계대전의 희생자라는 잘못된 믿음을 가지게 되었다.

10 fecund
/ fíːkənd /

형 다산의, 비옥한

syn fertile

영영 supporting an abundance of offspring or new growth

예문 The Cholla province in the southwest region of Korea is well known for its **fecund** land for cultivating crops.
한국 남서부에 있는 전라도는 곡물 재배를 위한 비옥한 땅으로 잘 알려져 있다.

11 galvanize
/ gǽlvənàiz /

동 갑자기 활기를 띠게 하다, 아연도금을 하다

syn arouse, electrify, excite, stimulate

영영 cause one to take action, for example by making them feel very excited

예문 The president's speech was intended to **galvanize** his employees.
회장의 연설은 그의 직원들에게 활기를 불어넣기 위한 것이었다.

12. harrow
/hǽrou/

동 써레질하다, (정신적으로) 괴롭히다
syn torture, harass

영영 cause distress

예문 If you want to read the child's **harrowing** story of the escape from kidnappers, please click on here.
만약 그 유괴 당한 아이의 탈출을 다룬 아찔한 이야기를 듣고 싶다면 이곳을 클릭하세요.

13. illicit
/ilísit/

형 불법의, 통념에 어긋나는
syn illegal, unlawful

영영 not allowed by law or the social customs

예문 Although highly competent, Susan's company fired her for engaging in an **illicit** affair.
수잔은 비록 유능했지만, 불법적인 일에 관여했다는 이유로 회사는 그녀를 해고했다.

14. kaleidoscope
/kəláidəskòup/

명 만화경
syn pattern-forming tube

영영 a toy in the shape of a tube with a small hole at one end

예문 When I was a child, it was my great wish to get a **kaleidoscope** as a Christmas present.
어렸을 때 나는 크리스마스 선물로 만화경을 얻는 것이 큰 바람이었다.

15. kinetic
/kinétik/

형 운동의, 운동에 의해서 생기는
syn dynamic

영영 concerned with movement

예문 Everything around us carries **kinetic** energy.
우리 주변의 모든 것은 운동에너지를 지닌다.

day by day I 73

연습문제

I

1. It's a _____ that everyone needs the same amount of sleep.
2. He made everyone feel _____ with his dirty jokes.
3. The way she talks feels a little spooky that it _____ the people around her.
4. An ice cream and cool air conditioning is enough to _____ the students in the summer.
5. Although the schoolteacher seemed noble and proper, she had once been arrested for the use of _____ drugs.

/ abash / galvanize / illicit / daunt / fallacy /

II

1. loathe, abominate, execrate = _____
2. corruption, dissipation = _____
3. abnormal, out-of-line = _____
4. insensible, stony = _____
5. fertile, productive = _____

/ decadence / fecund / abhor / callous / aberrant /

Day 4

01 laconic / ləkánik /

형 말을 많이 하지 않는, 간결한

syn quiet, reserved

영영 not saying much except what he or she has to

예문 Married Korean males are famous for their **laconic** speech.
한국의 기혼 남성들은 말을 아끼는 것으로 유명하다.

02 magnanimity / mæ̀gnəníməti /

명 관대함, 담대함

syn generosity, tolerance

영영 kindness towards others even after being treated badly by them

예문 It is hard to accept others' criticism with **magnanimity**.
타인의 비난을 관대하게 받아들이기는 어렵다.

03 paleolithic / pèiliəlíθik /

형 구석기 시대의

syn of the Old Stone Age

영영 Paleolithic era describes the old stone age era

예문 The scholars are investigating how the **Paleolithic** era was started.
학자들은 구석기시대가 어떻게 시작되었는지 조사하고 있다.

04 sage

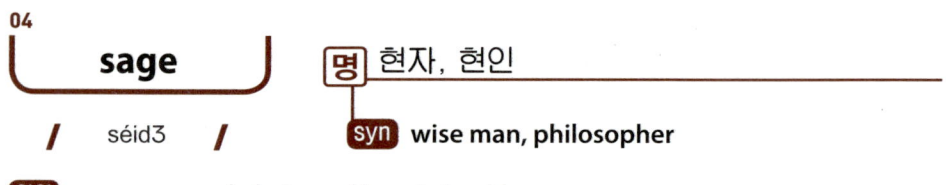

/ séidʒ /

명 현자, 현인

syn wise man, philosopher

영영 someone regarded wise and knowledgeable

예문 Confucius is considered as one of the greatest **sages** by many scholars in China
공자는 중국의 여러 학자들에 의해서 가장 훌륭한 현인들 중 한 사람으로 여겨진다.

05 taboo

/ təbú: /

명 금기

syn prohibition, ban, restriction

영영 something forbidden and to be avoided

예문 It was a **taboo** for a groom to see the face of his bride before the wedding in a certain culture.
한 문화권에서는 혼전에 신랑이 신부의 얼굴을 보는 것이 금기였다.

06 tacit

/ tǽsit /

형 말로 나타내지 않은, 무언의, 암묵적인

syn unspoken, agreed

영영 agreeing to doing something without saying anything

예문 Though no one mentioned a word, we had reached a **tacit** understanding.
누구도 어떤 말을 하지 않았지만 우리는 암묵적 합의에 도달했다.

07 tailored

/ téilərd /

형 맞추어진

syn custom-made

영영 making something adaptable for certain situation

예문 Our company strives to provide our clients with services **tailored** to meet their needs.
저희 회사는 고객들의 요구를 충족시키기 위해 맞춤식 서비스를 제공합니다.

08 ubiquitous
/ juːbíkwətəs /

형 어디에나 있는

syn everywhere, ever-present, pervasive

영영 seeming to be everywhere

예문 In a place like Phuket, Thailand, tourists seem to be **ubiquitous**.
태국의 푸켓과 같은 곳에서는 관광객들은 어디에나 있는 것처럼 보인다.

09 undue
/ ʌndjúː /

형 필요 이상의

syn excessive

영영 beyond being reasonable or appropriate

예문 The police were criticised for their **undue** use of violence in suppressing the demonstrators.
경찰은 시위대를 억압함에 있어 과도한 폭력을 사용해서 비난을 받았다.

10 unnerve
/ ʌnnə́ːrv /

동 안절부절못하게 하다, 지치게 하다

syn worry, tire

영영 trouble others by making others become restless

예문 The footprints of lions around our camping ground **unnerved** some tourists.
야영지 주변의 사자 발자국은 몇몇 여행객들을 안절부절못하게 했다.

11 unsurpassed
/ ʌnsərpǽst /

형 탁월한

syn unrivalled

영영 better or greater than anything else in comparison

예문 Messi has an **unsurpassed** talent in scoring goals and leading his team to the victory.
메시는 득점을 올리는 것이나 팀을 승리로 이끄는 데 있어 탁월한 능력을 가지고 있다.

12 vain

/ véin /

형 무익한, 허사인

syn **futile, useless**

영영 failing to achieve what one desires to do, being useless

예문 We tried to do everything to avert the disaster, but our effort was in **vain**.
우리는 그 재난을 피하기 위해 모든 것을 했지만 그 노력은 허사였다.

13 validate

/ vǽlədèit /

동 확실하게 하다, 입증하다

syn **prove, confirm**

영영 to prove and confirm

예문 I was held for a few hours at the airport because I had to **validate** my identity.
나는 공항에서 신원을 증명해야 했기 때문에 수 시간동안 잡혀 있었다.

14 valor

/ vǽlər /

명 용기, 용맹

syn **courage, braveness**

영영 being brave and showing courage

예문 The knights in medieval times had to prove their **valor** in battles.
중세시대의 기사들은 전투에서 그들의 용기를 증명해야 했다.

15 wanting

/ wántiŋ /

형 부족한, 불충분

syn **deficient, poor**

영영 lacking in required or necessary quality

예문 The presentation made by the sales department was **wanting** in many aspects.
판매부에 의해 만들어진 프레젠테이션은 여러 면에서 부족했다.

연습문제

I

1. Because of my muscular shoulders, I ordered a _____ jacket.
2. In the _____ era, people didn't know much about using tools.
3. I was delayed for a few hours at Immigration because I had to _____ my passport.
4. I disliked his _____ reply in the letter.
5. We tried in _____ to make him change his mind.

/ tailor / validate / paleolithic / vain / laconic /

II

1. prohibition, ban, restriction = _____
2. courage, braveness = _____
3. excessive, immoderate = _____
4. generosity, tolerance = _____
5. wise man, philosopher = _____

/ undue / magnanimity / valor / sage / taboo /

Day 5

01 abbreviate / əbríːvièit / 동 단축하다, 생략하다 syn shorten

영영 make something shorter

예문 The football association decided to **abbreviate** the names of players on their uniform as they were too long to be printed.
축구협회에서는 선수들의 이름이 너무 길다는 이유로 유니폼에 이름을 줄여 쓰기로 했다.

02 abduct / æbdʌ́kt / 동 납치하다 syn kidnap

영영 carry off or kidnap

예문 The rebel armies in Africa **abducted** children from their homes and forced them to become child soldiers.
아프리카 반란군들은 아이들을 그들의 집으로부터 납치하고 소년군이 되도록 강요했다.

03 abjure / æbdʒúər / 동 포기하다 syn give up, renounce

영영 give up or withdraw from certain things or realms

예문 By becoming a catholic priest, Alex had to **abjure** the life of dissipation.
천주교 사제가 된 알렉스는 무절제한 생활을 접어야 했다.

04 bashful
/ bǽʃfəl /

형 수줍어하는, 부끄러워하는

syn shy, feel abashed, awkward

영영 being shy and easily embarrassed

예문 When Laura stared at Sandro, he felt so **bashful** that he was trying to find a place to hide.
로라가 샌드로를 바라봤을 때 그는 너무 쑥스러워 숨을 장소를 찾으러 했다.

05 capacious
/ kəpéiʃəs /

형 널찍한, 큼지막한

syn spacious, vast, roomy

영영 being able to put a lot of things in one place

예문 The newly launched vehicle from Hyundai has **capacious** leg room that will add to the comfort of passengers.
현대에서 새로 출시된 자동차는 탑승자의 안락함을 더해줄 충분한 다리 공간을 가지고 있다.

06 dauntless
/ dɔ́:ntlis /

형 겁 없는, 용감한

syn fearless, bold

영영 confident and brave

예문 The patient who was diagnosed with the lymphoma was **dauntless** in fighting the disease.
림프종에 걸린 그 환자는 투병을 함에 있어 용감했다.

07 dazzle
/ dǽzl /

동 눈부시게 하다, 황홀하게 하다

syn impress, amaze, overwhelm

영영 impress others with qualities, make oneself look attractive

예문 The stage lighting at a rock concert **dazzles** the eyes of the audience.
록 콘서트의 무대 조명은 관중으로 하여금 눈부시게 만든다.

08 debilitate

/ dibílətèit /

syn weaken

동 (심신 등을) 쇠약하게 하다

영영 cause mind or body to weaken and make it unstable

예문 The illness had **debilitated** my father so much that he could no longer walk.
그 병이 나의 아버지를 너무 쇠약하게 만들어서 그는 더 이상 걸을 수 없었다.

09 eccentric

/ ikséntrik /

syn odd, strange, peculiar, quirky

형 보통과 다른, 별난, 괴짜인

영영 behaving in a strange way

예문 People thought Andy Warhol's **eccentric** behavior is what characterized him as an artist.
사람들은 앤디 워홀의 괴짜 행동이 그에게 주어진 예술가로서의 특징이라고 생각했다.

10 efface

/ iféis /

syn rub out, erase

타 지우다, 없애다

영영 meaning to remove or destroy a particular subject so that its trace won't be witnessed again

예문 A loved one's departure is always hard for the surviving family as the memory shared together is hard to be **effaced**.
같이 공유했던 기억들이 지워지기 어렵기 때문에 사랑하는 이의 죽음은 항상 남은 유족들에게 힘들다.

11 famish

/ fǽmiʃ /

syn starve

동 굶주리게 하다

영영 be or make very hungry

예문 I am so **famished**. Do you have any food left?
배가 너무 고파. 남은 음식 없니?

12 hapless
/ hǽplis /

형 (명사 앞에 옴) 불행한, 불운한

syn unfortunate

영영 feeling unlucky and not well

예문 A first love can be overwhelming to those who feel **hapless** in their marriages.
첫사랑은 결혼생활에서 불운함을 느끼는 이들에게 아주 크게 다가 올 수 있다.

13 illimitable
/ ilímitəbl /

형 무한의, 끝없는, 광대한

syn unlimited, infinite, endless

영영 having no boundaries

예문 As Einstein and other scientists suspect, the universe is vast but not **illimitable** in size.
아인슈타인이나 다른 과학자들이 의심하다시피 우주는 광대하지만 크기에서 무한한 것은 아니다.

14 illusory
/ ilúːsəri /

형 환영의, 환상에 불과한

syn illusive, fantasy

영영 seeming to be false or impossible

예문 A rosy future promised by the mayor was only **illusory**.
그 시장이 약속한 장밋빛 미래는 환상에 불과했다.

15 jovial
/ dʒóuviəl /

형 명랑한, 유쾌한

syn merry, jaunty

영영 being happy and behaving in an upbeat manner

예문 The atmosphere at the meeting was **jovial** because of the record profit the company has made.
회사가 창출한 기록적인 이윤 덕택에 회의의 분위기가 아주 밝았다.

day by day I 83

연습문제

I

1. I was _____ by the lights of the oncoming cars.
2. Overindulgence _____ character as well as physical stamina.
3. Because of the work that had to be done, I had to _____ the trip to Europe.
4. My child was _____ by the terrorist.
5. The director decided to _____ the original three-hour screenplay.

/ debilitate / dazzle / abjure / abbreviate / abduct /

II

1. shy, fell abashed, awkward = _____
2. unlimited, infinite = _____
3. starved, ravenous = _____
4. odd, strange, peculiar, quirky = _____
5. merry, jaunty = _____

/ eccentric / illimitable / jovial / famish / bashful /

Day 6

01 abate /əbéit/
동 감소시키다, 배제하다, 중지하다
syn reduce, rule out, stop

영영 soften something or become conciliatory

예문 We hoped the storm would ***abate*** soon so that we can head out into the sea on our ship.
우리는 태풍이 줄어들어서 배를 타고 바다로 나갈 수 있게 되기를 바랐다.

02 barometer /bərámətər/
명 기압계, (여론 등의) 지표
syn meter, indicator

영영 one that indicates fluctuations

예문 Infant mortality is the ***barometer*** that indicates the economic status of a country.
유아 사망률은 한 나라의 경제 지표가 될 수 있다.

03 catalyst /kǽtəlist/
명 촉매(제)
syn catalyzer

영영 a person or thing that makes certain process to accelerate

예문 The production of T-model by Ford Motor Company acted as a ***catalyst*** for a new era of transportation.
포드 자동차 회사측의 T모델 생산은 새 교통시대를 여는 촉매제 역할을 하였다.

day by day I 85

04

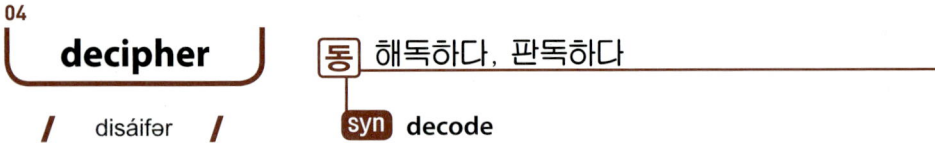

decipher

/ disáifər /

syn **decode**

동 해독하다, 판독하다

영영 to translate from secret writing

예문 The allied forces tried to **decipher** the secret transmission among German submarines during world war II.
세계 2차 대전 중 연합군은 독일군 잠수함들 사이의 비밀 통신을 해독하려고 노력했다.

05

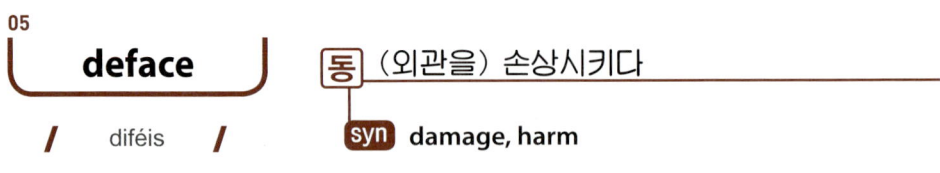

deface

/ diféis /

syn **damage, harm**

동 (외관을) 손상시키다

영영 to destroy or mar the face or surface of something

예문 The cliffside where hundreds of rock climbers climb has been **defaced** by countless nails and ropes left behind.
수많은 암벽 등반가들이 오르는 절벽은 남겨진 수많은 못들과 밧줄들에 의해 훼손되었다.

06

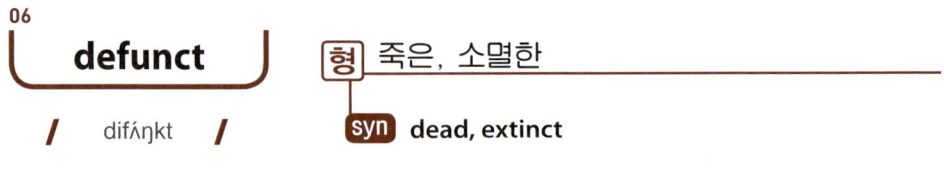

defunct

/ difʌŋkt /

syn **dead, extinct**

형 죽은, 소멸한

영영 not existing or functioning any further

예문 The government investigators sought to examine the illegal activities of the **defunct** NGO.
정부 조사관들은 현존하지 않는 비정부 단체들의 불법 활동을 조사하려고 했다.

07

germane

/ dʒə(:)rméin /

syn **appropriate, pertinent, relevant**

형 관련이 있는, 적절한

영영 connected or related to something in important aspects

예문 Your issue is not really **germane** to the present conversation.
당신의 안건은 현재 대화에 적절하지 않습니다.

08 hindrance

/ híndrəns /

명 방해, 장애물

syn obstacle, obstruction, hurdle

영영 a thing that makes doing something impossible

예문 The expensive price of I-phone acted as an **hindrance** in buying it.
비싼 가격이 아이폰의 구매에 장애물로 작용했다.

09 humility

/ hjuːmíləti /

명 겸손, 굴욕감

syn modesty, shame

영영 not acting too proud, acting humbly

예문 The life of Nelson Mandela taught me a lesson of **humility**.
넬슨 만델라의 삶은 나에게 겸손이라는 교훈을 가르쳐 주었다.

10 hypocrite

/ hípəkrit /

명 위선자

syn fake

영영 a person who pretends to possess qualities that he or she does not have

예문 We call a person who pretends to be good but isn't, a **hypocrite**.
우리는 착한 척 하지만 사실은 그렇지 않은 사람을 위선자라고 한다.

11 immoderate

/ imádərət /

형 지나친, 과도한

syn extreme

영영 overly excessive

예문 **Immoderate** drinking of alcohol can damage the liver.
과도한 음주는 간을 손상시킬 수 있다.

12 quadruple
/ kwadrú:pl /

형 네 배의

syn related with four

영영 four times bigger

예문 The star is **quadruple** the size of earth.
그 별은 지구 크기의 4배다.

13 rectify
/ réktəfài /

동 교정하다, 바로잡다

syn correct

영영 make something correct or satisfactory

예문 The engineers suggested new ways to **rectify** the problem.
기술자들은 문제를 해결하기 위한 새로운 방법들을 제안했다.

14 scrutinize
/ skrú:tənàiz /

동 세밀히 조사하다

syn examine, inspect

영영 examine something very carefully so that nothing is left out

예문 I had to **scrutinize** the documents before passing them on to the director.
나는 그 서류들을 사장님에게 보내기 전에 세밀하게 검사해야 했다.

15 denote
/ dinóut /

동 외연 표시하다, 지표가 되다

syn indicate, represent

영영 stand as a symbol for something

예문 Red eyes **denote** strain and fatigue.
빨개진 눈은 긴장과 피로를 의미한다.

연습문제

I

1. _____ is the foundation of all virtues.
2. I want to _____ my error before it is too late.
3. We hoped the storm would _____ soon so we could go out.
4. If you _____ a library book, you will have to pay a hefty fine.
5. He said that he would be by my side, when he was actually talking bad behind my back. I hate such a _____ .

/ abate / hypocrite / rectify / deface / humility /

II

1. extreme, unrestricted = _____
2. four times = _____
3. decode, break = _____
4. obstacle, obstruction, hurdle = _____
5. examine, inspect = _____

/ quadruple / hindrance / immoderate / scrutinize / decipher /

Day 7

01 belligerent
/ bəlídʒərənt /

형 교전 중인, 호전적인

syn **hostile, aggressive**

영영 hostile and aggressive to a certain thing

예문 The man seemed unnecessarily **belligerent** and impetuous.
그 남자는 불필요하게 호전적이고 성급한 것처럼 보였다.

02 benign
/ bináin /

형 자비로운, 친절한, 온화한

syn **charitable, mild**

영영 kind and gentle

예문 His intentions are always **benign**, though poorly communicated at times.
비록 잘 표현되지 않지만 그의 의도는 항상 선한 것이다.

03 delusion
/ dilúːʒən /

명 망상, 잘못된 생각

syn **misconception, misapprehension, hallucination**

영영 an erroneous or mistaken opinion or idea

예문 The communists are under **delusion** that their nuclear weapons can make them more powerful.
공산주의자들은 핵무기가 자신들을 더 강하게 할 것이라는 잘못된 생각을 가지고 있다.

04 electoral
/ iléktərəl /

형 선거의, 선거인의

syn shy, feel abashed, awkward

영영 of everything that has to do with an election

예문 Gerrymandering is the process of manipulating *electoral* boundaries for political gain.
게리멘더링은 정치적인 이득을 위해서 선거구를 조작하는 것이다.

05 elicit
/ ilísit /

동 도출하다, 이끌어내다

syn draw forth, evoke

영영 make others respond or react to your action or persuasion

예문 A census is intended to *elicit* information on the population distribution.
인구조사는 인구분포에 관한 정보를 이끌어 내기 위한 것이다.

06 eloquent
/ élәkwәnt /

형 웅변의, 설득력 있는

syn silver-tongued, moving, powerful, persuasive

영영 expressing or showing very strongly though without words

예문 A famous lecturer needs to possess an *eloquent* speech in order to draw students' interest.
유명한 강사는 학생들의 관심을 끌기 위해 설득력 있는 말을 할 수 있는 능력을 가지고 있어야 한다.

07 flamboyant
/ flæmbóiәnt /

형 이색적인, 대담한, 현란한

syn florid, ornate, showy, dashing, glamorous

영영 being very stylish, presentable and easy to be noticed

예문 Mariah Carey, an American female pop-singer, is known for her *flamboyant* life style.
미국의 여성 팝 가수 머라이어 캐리는 그녀의 화려한 생활로 유명하다.

12. laudable
/ lɔ́:dəbl /
형 칭찬할 만한, 건전한
syn commendable, noble

영영 something that deserves to get praised

예문 His service in helping the disabled was **laudable**.
장애인들을 돕는데 있어서 그의 봉사는 칭찬 받을 만한 것이었다.

13. legible
/ lédʒəbl /
형 읽어볼 수 있는, (글이) 잘 보이는
syn identifiable, obvious, apparent

영영 clear to read

예문 The writing on the blackboard was just **legible** enough.
칠판 위의 글씨는 간신히 읽을 수 있을 만 한 정도였다.

14. lethargic
/ ləθá:rdʒik /
형 혼수상태의, 활발치 못한
syn a state of torpor

영영 being in a powerless state, lacking in energy

예문 The students looked rather **lethargic** after their lunch.
학생들은 점심 후에 조금 둔감해진 것처럼 보였다.

15. nominal
/ námənl /
형 유명무실한, 이름 뿐인
syn titular, formal, purported

영영 to have a particular status, but not really having what it's supposed to have

예문 We were asked to pay a **nominal** fee to enter the art exhibition.
우리는 미술 전시회 관람을 위해 명목상 소정의 입장료를 내도록 요청받았다.

연습문제

I

1. The army interpreter tried to _____ information from the captured soldier.
2. Body balance is _____ when riding a unicycle.
3. His behaviour of doing the chores and getting good grades in school was _____ but his parents never gave him good comments.
4. Let's look at a _____ situation in which Carol gets invited to a party.
5. Winston Churchill was an _____ speaker.

/ eloquent / elicit / imperative / hypothetical / laudable /

II

1. florid, ornate, showy, dashing, glamorous = _____
2. a state of torpor = _____
3. audacious, impolite = _____
4. imaginary, assumed = _____
5. misapprehension, hallucination = _____

/ hypothetical / impertinent / lethargic / delusion / flamboyant /

Day 8

01 capricious
/ kəpríʃəs /

형 변덕스러운, 잘 변하는

syn unpredictable, changeable

영영 determined by chance or impulse and changing easily

예문 Alicia's **capricious** nature has made it difficult for her boyfriend to be in a relationship with her.
알리시아의 변덕스러운 성격은 남자친구로 하여금 그녀와의 관계를 유지하기 어렵게 만들었다.

02 defame
/ diféim /

동 명예를 훼손하다, 모욕하다

syn insult, affront, offend

영영 injure or destroy the reputation by slander

예문 If a person has **defamed** you on groundless facts, you are entitled to sue the person to get compensation.
만약 어떤 사람이 당신을 근거 없는 사실로 명예 훼손했다면 보상 받기 위해 그 사람을 고소할 수 있다.

03 elucidate
/ ilúːsədèit /

동 명료하게 하다, 해명하다

syn explain

영영 make it clear for others to understand

예문 It took her countless lectures to **elucidate** Saussure's linguistic theories.
소쉬르의 언어 이론을 이해하기 위해 그녀는 수많은 강의를 수강해야 했다.

04 fervor

/ fə́:rvər /

명 열기, 열정

syn zeal, passion

영영 sincerity and passion in doing something

예문 Dr. Martin Luther King Jr.'s speech, "I have a dream", is a powerful one as he speaks it with a **fervor**.
마틴 루터 킹 박사의 "I have a dream" 이라는 연설은 그의 열정으로 인해 강렬한 것이 된다.

05 immeasurable

/ imézərəbl /

형 헤아릴 수 없는, 엄청난

syn incalculable

영영 being of great importance, not able to count

예문 The economic value of 3D industry is **immeasurable**.
3D 분야의 경제적 가치는 이루 헤아릴 수 없다.

06 impending

/ impéndiŋ /

형 방금 일어날 것 같은, 임박한

syn imminent, looming

영영 being about to happen, very close

예문 Weather forecasters warned of an **impending** Tsunami from the earthquake in Indonesia.
기상예측자들은 인도네시아에 지진으로 인한 쓰나미가 올 것이라고 경고했다.

07 jubilant

/ dʒú:bələnt /

형 기쁨에 넘치는

syn delighted, overjoyed, beatific

영영 extremely pleased, more than just being happy

예문 We all had a **jubilant** celebration at our high school reunion.
우리는 고교 동창회에서 아주 기쁜 만남을 가졌다.

08 judicial

/ dʒuːdíʃəl /

형 사법의, 재판의

syn judiciary, legal, official

영영 related to the court of law and judgement process

예문 The American *judicial* system has long been criticized as a faulty one.
미국의 사법 체제는 오랫 동안 결함 있는 것으로 비판 받아왔다.

09 maltreat

/ mæltríːt /

동 학대하다, 혹사하다

syn ill-treat, abuse

영영 mistreat in a cruel way

예문 Many Japanese soldiers *maltreated* American and Australian prisoners of war during World War II.
제2차 세계 대전 중 많은 일본군들은 미국과 호주 출신 전쟁 포로들을 학대했다.

10 negate

/ nigéit /

동 부정하다, 효력이 없게 하다

syn deny, nullify

영영 not want to admit one's own fault or reject certain situation

예문 He strongly *negated* the charge that he was involved in the illegal dealings with the Mafia.
그는 마피아와 불법적인 거래를 한 혐의를 강하게 부인했다.

11 normative

/ nɔ́ːrmətiv /

형 표준의, 규범적인

syn prescriptive

영영 about creating certain standards or rules

예문 It is not easy to be *normative* when judging politicians.
정치가들을 평가할 때 기준을 세우는 것은 쉽지 않다.

12. obtrude
/ əbtrúːd /
동 강요하다, 내밀다
syn force, extend

영영 forcefully make others do something

예문 We tried to ignore him but he still **obtruded** his ideas on us.
우리는 그를 무시하기로 했지만 그는 여전히 자신의 생각을 우리에게 강요했다.

13. officiate
/ əfíʃièit /
동 직무를 수행하다, 임무를 다하다
syn correct

영영 carry out or be in charge of an official duty

예문 Former prime minister was **officiating** the funeral for ex-president of Korea, Mr. Moo-Hyun Roh.
전 국무총리가 노무현 전 대통령의 장례를 집행하고 있었다.

14. ominous
/ ámənəs /
형 불길한, 전조의
syn fateful, foreboding

영영 something bad being about to happen

예문 Numerous companies are redirecting their investments away from Japan to developing countries as recent economic signs in Japan are getting more **ominous**.
수많은 회사들이 최근 일본 내 경제지표가 불길한 조짐을 보여주고 있어 그들의 투자를 일본으로부터 개발도상국들로 돌리고 있다.

15. prudence
/ prúːdns /
명 신중, 조심, 검약
syn caution, discretion, frugality

영영 a careful approach in a decision or an action

예문 It is best to exercise **prudence** in judging who has committed the hideous crime.
누가 그런 끔찍한 범죄를 저질렀는지 판단함에 있어 신중을 기해야 한다.

연습문제

I

1. Her behavior is so _____ that I can never guess what she will do next.
2. There is no reason to _____ the man simply because you do not agree with him.
3. I felt that some disaster and upheaval might have been _____ .
4. She strongly _____ the fact that she was in an affair.
5. His words need to be _____ for clarification.

/ elucidate / capricious / impending / defame / negate /

II

1. incalculable, inestimable = _____
2. intense heat, zeal, passion = _____
3. prescriptive, dogmatic = _____
4. delighted, overjoyed, beatific = _____
5. perform one's duty = _____

/ normative / jubilant / immeasurable / officiate / fervor /

Day 9

01 nostalgia
/ nɑstǽldʒə /

명 향수
syn homesickness

영영 an affectionate feeling for the good things of the past

예문 A lot of old Korean generation have the **nostalgia** for the era of ex-President, Jung-Hee Park.
많은 한국의 기성세대들은 전 박정희 대통령에 대한 향수에 젖어 있다.

02 optimum
/ áptəməm /

형 최적의
syn optimal

영영 a level of state that can be achieved at its best

예문 The rocket was at its **optimum** condition for the launching.
그 로켓의 발사를 위한 최적의 조건이 갖추어져 있었다.

03 primeval
/ praimíːvəl /

형 원시(시대)의
syn prehistoric, primitive

영영 going back further than ancient

예문 There are some parts of Australian rainforests that have still been untouched and remained **primeval**.
호주 열대 우림의 몇몇 지역들은 아직도 훼손되지 않고 원시 그대로 남아 있는 곳도 있다.

04 sequester

/ sikwéstər /

동 격리하다, 은퇴하다

syn seclude, retire

영영 segregate one from a group of the others

예문 Child molesters should be **sequestered** from the society as their existence itself is of no benefit for others.
아동 성추행자들은 그들 존재 자체가 다른 사람들에게 유익하지 않아 사회로부터 격리되어야 한다.

05 severity

/ səvérəti /

명 엄격, 가혹

syn rigor, harshness, plainness

영영 employing extreme measures in a situation

예문 The **severity** of cold weather is about to lessen in late April.
혹독한 추운 날씨가 4월 하순에는 수그러들 전망이다.

06 sinister

/ sínəstər /

형 불길한, 재수 없는

syn threatening, evil, menacing

영영 looking evil or bad

예문 The man standing around the corner gave me a **sinister** look when I passed him by.
길 모서리에 서있는 남자는 내가 그를 지나칠 때 나에게 기분 나쁜 눈길을 주었다.

07 transcend

/ trænsénd /

동 능가하다, 초월하다

syn surpass, exceed

영영 go beyond normal limits and boundaries

예문 We must **transcend** our greatest weakness in order to achieve our dream.
우리는 꿈을 이루기 위하여 우리의 가장 큰 단점을 뛰어넘어야 한다.

08 trifle
/ tráifl /
명 하찮은 것
syn plaything

영영 something that carries little significance or value

예문 I don't want to be portrayed as a negative person by complaining about the **trifles**.
나는 사소한 것들에 대해 불평하는 것으로 부정적인 사람으로 비춰지기 싫다.

09 unison
/ júːnəsn /
명 일치, 조화
syn unity, harmony

영영 two or more things to be done at the same time

예문 The girls all called out the name of the teacher in **unison**.
소녀들은 그 선생님의 이름을 한 목소리로 불렀다.

10 unstop
/ ʌnstáp /
동 (막힌 것을) 뚫다, 마개를 뽑다
syn drill, dig, pierce

영영 make something free from being blocked

예문 I had to **unstop** the kitchen basin as leftover food blocked the drainage.
남은 음식물이 배수로를 막았으므로 부엌 싱크대를 뚫어야 했다.

11 volition
/ voulíʃən /
명 자유의지, 결단력
syn resolution

영영 one's own will

예문 My friend, Brandon, volunteered to serve in Iraq on his own **volition**.
내 친구 브랜든은 이라크 군복무를 자원했다.

12. voracious

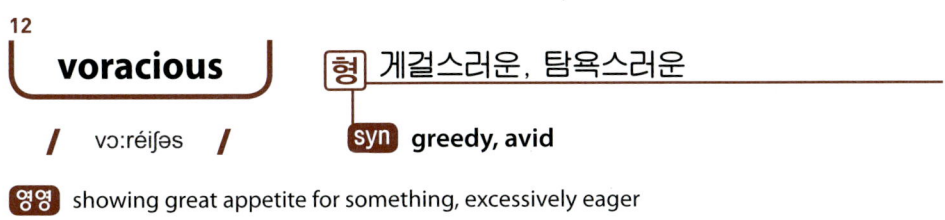

/ vɔːréiʃəs /

형 게걸스러운, 탐욕스러운

syn greedy, avid

영영 showing great appetite for something, excessively eager

예문 The piranha living in Amazon rivers is a fish known for its **voracious** appetites.
아마존 강들에 사는 피라냐는 게걸스러운 식욕으로 잘 알려져 있는 물고기이다.

13. wistful

/ wístfəl /

형 탐내는, 동경하는, 사색하는

syn regretful, yearning

영영 sad or regretful for something that they couldn't do

예문 Looking at photos from my college days made me feel **wistful** and nostalgic.
대학 시절의 사진들을 보는 것은 그 때를 그립고 애절하게 느끼도록 만들었다.

14. wretched

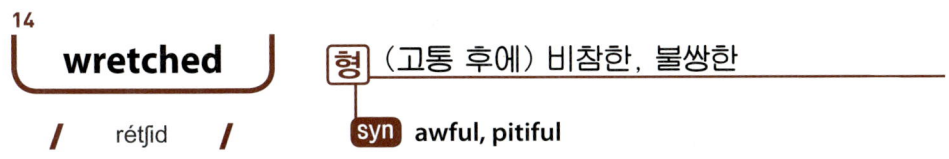

/ rétʃid /

형 (고통 후에) 비참한, 불쌍한

syn awful, pitiful

영영 deeply afflicted, distressed in body or mind

예문 While being hospitalized for concussion suffered by a golf ball, my wife looked so **wretched** in her patient gown.
골프공에 의한 뇌진탕 때문에 병원에 있는 동안 환자복을 입고 있는 나의 아내는 불쌍해 보였다.

15. zeal

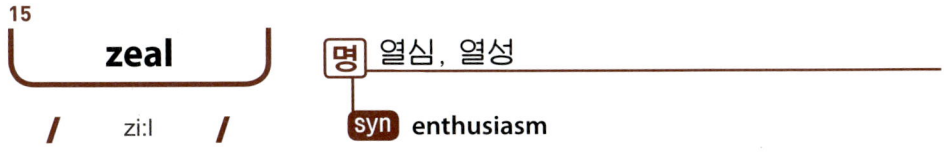

/ ziːl /

명 열심, 열성

syn enthusiasm

영영 a great passion for work, religion and politics

예문 Though he taught students with **zeal** and no complaints, the principal thought less of him.
비록 그는 열정을 가지고 불평 없이 학생들을 가르쳤지만 교장은 그를 높이 사지 않았다.

연습문제

I

1. In many parts of the world, talismans are used to _____ evil.
2. He's sick in bed, feeling very _____ .
3. The wolf is a _____ animal, its hunger never satisfied.
4. After _____ from his old job, he has at last found peace in his life.
5. _____ forms of life differ greatly from those that occupy modern day earth.

/ sequester / transcend / voracious / primeval / wretch /

II

1. rigor, harshness, plainness = _____
2. an insignificant matter = _____
3. free will = _____
4. threatening, evil, menacing = _____
5. enthusiasm, passion, zest = _____

/ sinister / severity / volition / zeal / trifle /

Day 10

01 abrasive
/ əbréisiv /

형 마모시키는, 짜증나게 하는

syn irritating, annoying, rough

영영 applying something on a surface by rubbing

예문 The old woman's **abrasive** manner makes it hard for others to like her with sincerity.
그 나이 든 여성의 기분 나쁜 매너는 주변에 있는 사람들이 그녀를 진심으로 좋아하기 어렵게 만든다.

02 abstinent
/ ǽbstənənt /

형 절제하는, 금욕적인

syn abstemious, moderate, temperate

영영 refraining oneself from indulging in any activities that can provide physical pleasures

예문 One common thing about religions is that they require their believers to lead an **abstinent** life.
종교들에 대한 한 가지 공통점은 그들의 신도들이 금욕적인 삶을 사는 것을 요구하는 것이다.

03 defile
/ difáil /

동 더럽히다, 오염시키다

syn pollute, profane, corrupt

영영 make something filthy, corrupt or violate

예문 Some internet users were charged for **defiling** a movie actor's reputation.
몇몇 인터넷 사용자들은 어떤 영화배우의 명성을 더럽혀서 고발당했다.

04 delude
/ dilú:d /

동 속이다, 기만하다

syn deceive, mislead

영영 deceive or mislead the person on purpose

예문 The escaped convicts **deluded** the pursuers in making them believe that they are headed for a nearby motel.
탈옥한 죄수들은 추격대가 자신들은 인접한 모텔로 향하고 있다고 믿게 만들었다.

05 empower
/ impáuər /

동 ~에게 권한을 부여하다

syn authorize, allow, commission

영영 give the person the qualities or abilities to do something

예문 Modern science **empowers** men to control natural forces.
현대 과학은 인간에게 자연의 힘을 조절할 능력을 부여한다.

06 fleeting
/ flí:tiŋ /

형 어느덧 지나가는, 무상한

syn momentary, passing, brief

영영 describing a feeling or moment that stays only for little time

예문 For a **fleeting** moment, John thought about filing a petition to the ministry of education for unfair treatment.
잠시 동안 John은 불공평한 대우에 대해 교육청에 탄원서를 제출하는 것에 대해 생각해 보았다.

07 grudge
/ grʌdʒ /

명 원한

syn resentment, bitterness, grievance

영영 unpleasant feeling for others because of their action

예문 Don't hold any **grudge** against me. I am just doing what I am told to do.
나에게 원망하지 마. 난 그냥 내가 명령 받은 것을 하고 있을 뿐이야.

106 SAving Time SAT Vocabulary

08 impede
/ impíːd /

동 방해하다, 저지하다

syn hinder, hamper

영영 stop a progress or a movement from proceeding any further

예문 Severe snowstorm **impeded** the rescue work for the mountain climbers who had been trapped in the cabin for several days.
심각한 눈 폭풍은 며칠 동안 통나무집에 갇힌 등산가들을 구조하는 작업을 방해했다.

09 impetus
/ ímpətəs /

명 원동력

syn motivation

영영 a driving force behind certain work which makes it progress more quickly

예문 The recent cloning of an extinct wolf species may provide an **impetus** for medical advances.
최근 멸종한 늑대의 복제는 의학 발전에 원동력을 제공할지도 모른다.

10 lament
/ ləmént /

동 슬퍼하다, 비탄하다

syn complaint, moan, wailing

영영 express great sadness, regret or great disappointment

예문 People of Congo **lamented** the death of a volunteer worker from Korea, because he helped the people with all his heart.
콩고 국민들은 진심으로 자신들을 도왔던 한국 자원봉사자의 죽음을 슬퍼했다.

11 mesmerize
/ mézməràiz /

동 ~에게 최면술을 걸다, 홀리게 하다

syn captivate

영영 make someone so interested in what you do that the person can not turn himself away from it

예문 I swore to myself that I would **mesmerize** every student with my astonishing lecture skills someday.
나는 언젠가 놀라운 강의 실력으로 모든 학생의 마음을 사로잡을 것이라고 스스로 다짐했다.

12 meticulous

/ mətíkjuləs /

형 꼼꼼한, 소심한

syn fastidious, thorough

영영 very careful about doing work

예문 The scientists recently succeeded in mapping Korean human genes after many years of *meticulous* studies.
한국 과학자들은 수년간에 걸친 꼼꼼한 연구 끝에 한국인 유전자 지도를 완성하는데 성공했다.

13 nonchalant

/ nànʃəláːnt /

형 무관심한, 냉담한

syn casual, calm

영영 not bothered by something

예문 Mike didn't have many friends as he was regarded as a *nonchalant* fellow.
마이크는 무편무당의 사람으로 여겨져 그다지 친구가 없었다.

14 obstinate

/ ábstənət /

형 완고한, 고집 센

syn obdurate, stubborn

영영 being very stubborn and not breaking down easily

예문 My father was not liked by many because he was a very *obstinate* and had to have everything done in his way.
나의 아버지는 고집이 셌고 모든 것을 자기 방식대로 해야 했기 때문에 좋아하는 이가 별로 없었다.

15 paradigm

/ pǽrədaim /

명 이론적 틀, 준거

syn model, example, pattern, ideal

영영 a model for something which explains it or shows how it can be produced

예문 Steve Jobs has provided a new *paradigm* for this generation with his I-Phone.
스티브 잡스는 아이폰으로 이 세대에 새로운 패러다임을 제시했다.

연습문제

I

1. The state government _____ him to negotiate the contract.
2. When you _____ someone, you deceive the person on purpose.
3. Accounting is a very _____ profession; there is no room for error.
4. I don't _____ her good fortune, but she should share it with others.
5. We tried to persuade him to give up smoking, but he was _____ and refused to change.

/ delude / grudge / empower / meticulous / obstinate /

II

1. casual, careless = _____
2. hinder, hamper = _____
3. momentary, passing, brief = _____
4. abstemious, moderate, temperate = _____
5. irritating, annoying, rough = _____

/ fleeting / abstinent / abrasive / impede / nonchalant /

Day 11

01
abide

/ əbáid /

동 준수하다, (약속을) 지키다

syn tolerate, suffer, accept, remain

영영 observe and follow certain rules or remain in one place

예문 The crime rate in Japan is much lower than that of western countries as the people ***abide*** by the rules.
일본 사람들은 규칙을 잘 준수하기 때문에 범죄율이 서구보다 낮다.

02
abject

/ æbdʒekt /

형 절망적인, 비참한, 비굴한

syn hopeless, miserable, pitiful

영영 very low in spirit or hope

예문 The life under Japanese occupation was an ***abject*** one as they deprived us of food and freedom.
일본 점령 하의 생활은 식량과 자유를 빼앗기는 실정이어서 절망적이었다.

03
abridge

/ əbrídʒ /

동 요약하다, 단축하다, 줄이다

syn reduce, decrease, simplify

영영 shorten or cut down the content and make it brief

예문 If I have students read my thesis for the term paper, I will need to ***abridge*** it.
만약에 학기말 리포트를 위해 학생들이 나의 논문을 읽게끔 한다면 내용을 단축할 필요가 있을 것이다.

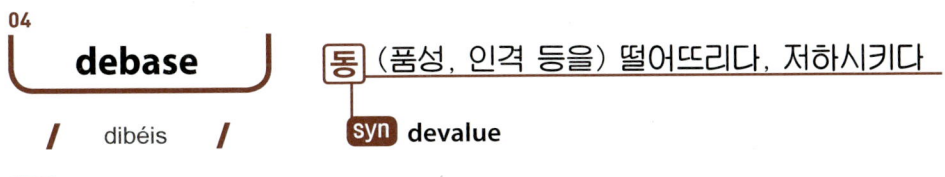

04 debase
/ dibéis /
동 (품성, 인격 등을) 떨어뜨리다, 저하시키다
syn devalue

영영 lower the quality of certain products or value

예문 Many politicians have **debased** themselves by showing unruly behaviors in the assembly hall.
많은 정치가들은 국회 안에서 제멋대로의 행동을 보여줌으로써 자신들의 품위를 떨어뜨렸다.

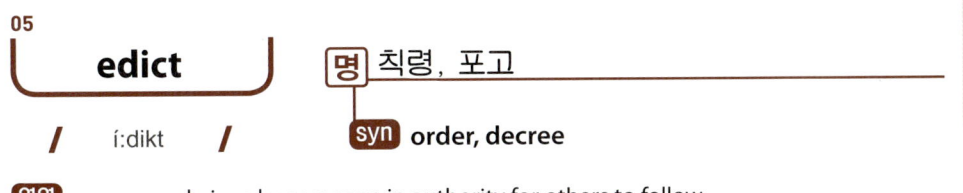

05 edict
/ í:dikt /
명 칙령, 포고
syn order, decree

영영 a command given by someone in authority for others to follow

예문 The emperor of Rome, Augustus, issued an **edict** that officially permitted "Christians" to practice their religion.
로마의 황제 아우구스투스는 기독교인들이 그들의 종교를 섬길 수 있도록 공식적으로 허락하는 칙령을 발표했다.

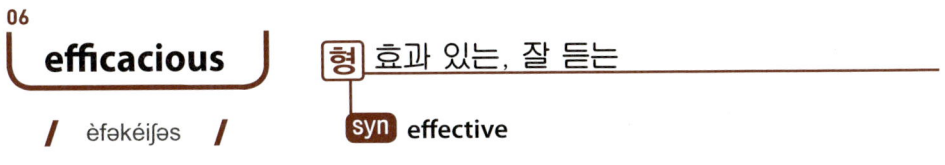

06 efficacious
/ èfəkéiʃəs /
형 효과 있는, 잘 듣는
syn effective

영영 producing positive results and working well

예문 I always go to Cho's otolaryngology as the medicine prescribed there is quite **efficacious** on my son.
조 이비인후과에서 처방된 약이 내 아들에게 꽤 효과가 있어서 나는 항상 그곳으로 간다.

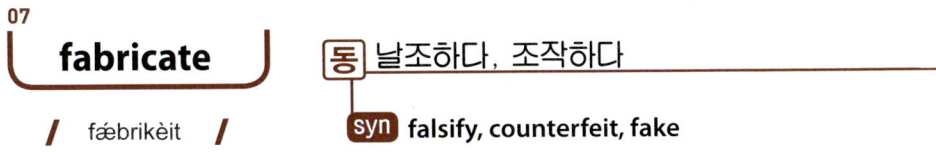

07 fabricate
/ fǽbrikèit /
동 날조하다, 조작하다
syn falsify, counterfeit, fake

영영 come up with a made-up story about something so that you can deceive others

예문 The prosecuting attorney believes that the defendant **fabricated** the evidence so that she will not be charged.
검사는 변호인이 기소를 당하지 않도록 증거를 만들어 냈다고 믿는다.

day by day I 111

08 fallacious

/ fəléiʃəs /

형 논리적 오류가 있는, 불합리한

syn misleading

영영 being incorrect

예문 Many religious people do not realize that they are clinging to a **fallacious** belief.
많은 종교인들은 그들이 잘못된 믿음에 매달리고 있다는 것을 깨닫지 못한다.

09 gluttony

/ glʌ́təni /

명 식탐, 탐욕

syn overindulgence, greed

영영 excessive desire to eat or be rich

예문 For centuries, many scientists have believed that **gluttony** is the prime factor in gaining weight.
수세기 동안 많은 과학자들은 살이 찌는데 있어 식탐이 주된 원인이라고 생각해왔다.

10 goad

/ góud /

동 자극하다, 격려하다

syn spur, impel, incite

영영 constantly bother or persuade the person to do something

예문 I was **goaded** by my friends to drink the beer at the party.
나는 파티에서 맥주를 마시도록 친구들에게 강요받았다.

11 hallowed

/ hǽloud /

형 신성한, 존경받는

syn revered, consecrated

영영 divine and holy

예문 Native American burial grounds were regarded **hallowed** and trespasses were not tolerated.
미국 원주민들의 매장지들은 신성하게 여겨져서 무단 침입은 용인되지 않았다.

12 haughty
/hɔ́ːti/

형 거만한, 오만한

syn arrogant, conceited, proud

영영 acting as if he or she is better than others

예문 The Chinese government appears to act **haughty** when it comes to the dealings with Korean government.
중국 정부는 한국 정부를 다루는데 있어 거만하게 행동하는 것처럼 보인다.

13 idiosyncratic
/ìdiousiŋkrǽtik/

형 특유한, 색다른

syn peculiar, unique

영영 different from the rest or particular to one person

예문 Chan-Wook Park, a famous movie director from Korea, has also gained a cult following in US owing to his **idiosyncratic** style of film making.
한국의 유명한 영화감독인 박찬욱은 그의 독특한 영화 제작 스타일 때문에 미국에서도 열광적인 팬들을 얻었다.

14 impassive
/impǽsiv/

형 무표정의, 감정이 없는

syn emotionless

영영 not expressing any emotion on the face

예문 The witness testified that a young Pakistani male, who appeared to be in his early 20's and carrying an **impassive** look on his face, tried to blow himself up.
그 목격자는 젊은 20대 초반의 무표정한 얼굴을 가진 파키스탄인 남성이 자폭을 시도했다고 진술했다.

15 laceration
/læ̀səréiʃən/

명 (찢긴) 상처, 열상

syn ripping

영영 a cut wound to the skin

예문 Trying to fend off a knife wielding attacker, the young woman received multiple **lacerations** to her right arm.
칼을 휘두르는 공격자를 물리치려고 하다가 젊은 여성은 오른팔에 다수의 열상을 입었다.

연습문제

I

1. This new diet pill that I am taking is so _____ that I lost 10 pounds in 3 days.
2. Some people believe that pornography _____ the morals of a society.
3. The engineers had to _____ a temporary emergency bridge over the river.
4. He says harsh things with _____ face, and that hurts more.
5. Germany and Russia agreed informally to _____ by the agreement.

/ fabricate / efficacious / abide / debase / impassive /

II

1. peculiar, distinctive = _____
2. spur, impel, incite = _____
3. hopeless, miserable, pitiful = _____
4. overindulgence, greed = _____
5. an order, decree = _____

/ abject / idiosyncratic / gluttony / goad / edict /

Day 12

01

abdicate
/ǽbdəkèit /

동 (직위나 왕권에서) 물러나다, 사임하다

syn resign

영영 give up or retire from a position that is of leader's role

예문 Tsar of Russia was forced to **abdicate** from throne and got murdered by the Bolsheviks eventually.
러시아 황제는 왕좌에서 물러나 결국 볼셰비키 당원들에 의해 죽임을 당했다.

02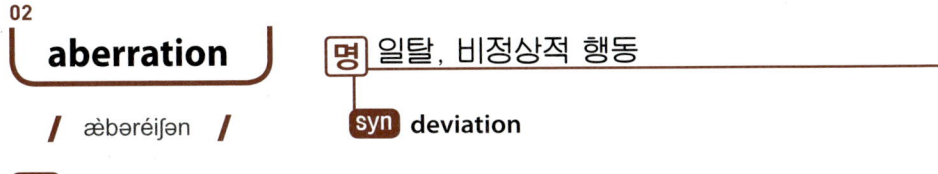

aberration
/ æ̀bəréiʃən /

명 일탈, 비정상적 행동

syn deviation

영영 a behavior or a situation that is not typical

예문 Many people in other countries still think that the advance to semi-final rounds by South Korea in 2002 Korea-Japan Worldcup was an **aberration**.
많은 다른 나라 사람들은 여전히 2002년 한일 월드컵에서 한국이 4강에 진출한 것이 기현상이었다고 보고 있다.

03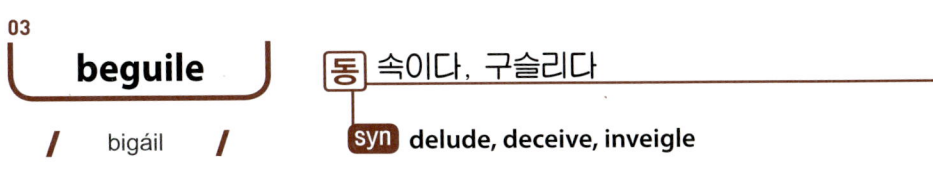

beguile
/ bigáil /

동 속이다, 구슬리다

syn delude, deceive, inveigle

영영 trick or deceive someone

예문 My father was **beguiled** into investing money in a hospital construction project in Malaysia 5 years ago.
5년 전 말레이시아에서 나의 아버지는 병원 건축 프로젝트에 돈을 투자하도록 구슬려졌다.

day by day I 115

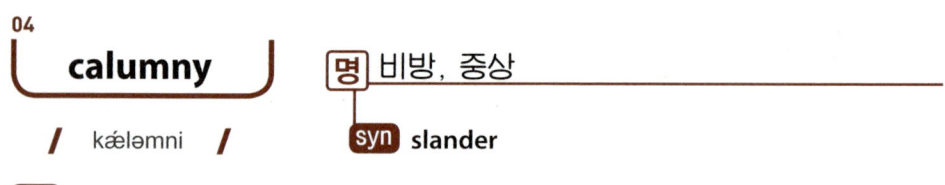

04 calumny / kǽləmni /   명 비방, 중상   syn slander

영영 an act to reduce someone's reputation by making untrue statement

예문 The candidate running for governor's office in Mississippi denounced rumors of bribery as mere *calumny*.
미시피주의 주지사에 출마한 후보는 뇌물 추문을 단순한 비방이라며 비난했다.

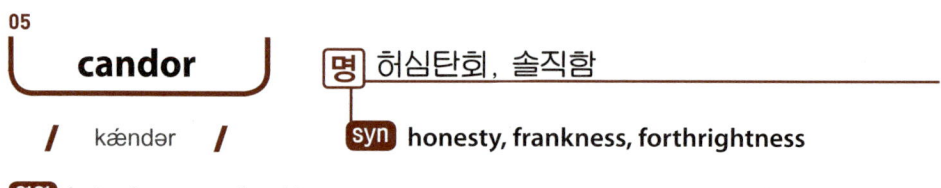

05 candor / kǽndər /   명 허심탄회, 솔직함   syn honesty, frankness, forthrightness

영영 being honest and making true statements

예문 As usual, Eric and I spoke with absolute *candor* about each other's shortcomings.
여느 때처럼 에릭과 나는 서로의 단점에 대해 허심탄회하게 이야기했다.

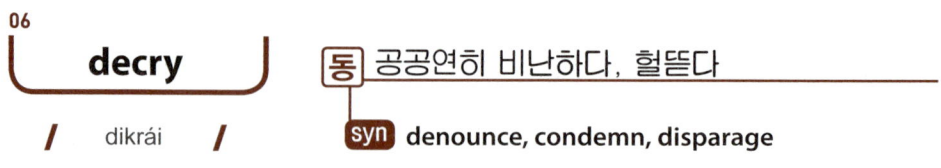

06 decry / dikrái /   동 공공연히 비난하다, 헐뜯다   syn denounce, condemn, disparage

영영 strongly criticize someone for something you have done

예문 Greek government is being *decried* for the decision they made to accept the terms of IMF and European Union in giving them the financial aid.
그리스 정부는 재정 지원을 받는 데 있어 IMF 와 유럽 연합의 조건을 받아들이기로 한 결정 때문에 강한 비난을 사고 있다.

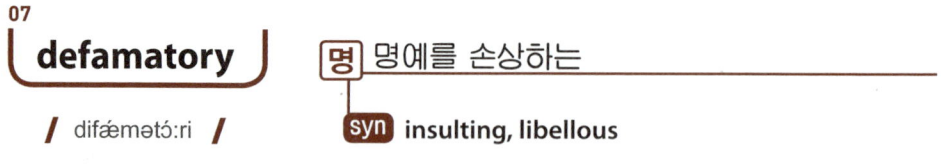

07 defamatory / difǽmətɔ́:ri /   명 명예를 손상하는   syn insulting, libellous

영영 describing a statement or an action that can harm others' honor

예문 A North Korean news broadcast has put out *defamatory* remarks on South Korean President.
북한 뉴스 방송은 남한 대통령의 명예를 손상하는 말들을 쏟아내었다.

08 fastidious
/ fæstídiəs /
형 세심한, 꼼꼼한, 까다로운
syn meticulous, demanding

영영 very careful about details or very hard to please

예문 I regard Mike's attention to detail is often **fastidious** and a waste of time.
나는 마이크의 세부적인 것에 대한 관심은 종종 까다롭고 시간 낭비라고 생각한다.

09 gourmand
/ guərmá:nd /
명 대식가, 식도락가
syn glutton

영영 a person who is really fond of eating and drinking in large amounts

예문 When I was in the states, I would see a lot of **gourmands** eating large quantity of food in pizza parlours, family diners or fast food restaurants.
내가 미국에 있었을 때 피자점이나 패밀리 레스토랑 그리고 패스트 푸드점에서 많은 양의 음식을 먹는 대식가들을 목격하곤 했다.

10 grandiloquence
/ grændíləkwəns /
명 호언장담, 큰 자랑
syn big talk, boasting

영영 speech or writing that consists of lofty, pompous language

예문 Many women are confused into thinking that men who speak with **grandiloquence** are manly.
많은 여자들은 호언장담을 하는 남자들이 남자답다고 생각하는 실수를 저지른다.

11 grandiose
/ grændiòus /
형 거창한, 웅장한
syn haughty, pompous

영영 bigger or more elaborate than necessary

예문 My friend had a **grandiose** scheme about his future, which also impressed me greatly.
내 친구는 미래에 대한 거창한 계획을 가지고 있었는데 그것은 나에게도 큰 인상을 남겼다.

12 hegemony

/ hidʒéməni /

명 헤게모니, 패권

syn **domination**

영영 a situation where a country or an organization has greater power in politics or business affairs over any other countries or groups

예문 Many third world countries often complain about American **hegemony** in world affairs.
많은 제3세계 국가들은 세계 정세에 미치는 미국의 패권에 대해 종종 불평을 한다.

13 ignominious

/ ìgnəmíniəs /

형 불명예스러운

syn **humiliating, disgraceful**

영영 very embarrassing and detrimental to your reputation

예문 Some people consider it **ignominious** for the captain of a warship to survive after losing his vessel in a combat.
어떤 사람들은 전함의 함장이 전투에서 자신의 함선을 잃고 생환하는 것을 불명예스럽게 여긴다.

14 languid

/ læŋgwid /

형 나른한, 활기 없는

syn **sluggish, lethargic**

영영 being very sluggish in movements or reaction and showing little interests in doing something

예문 Our son gets **languid** every summer, so we get some packs of restorative herb medicine prescribed for him in such situations.
우리 아들은 매 여름마다 활기가 없어지기 때문에 그런 상황에서는 보약을 지어 먹인다.

15 malevolent

/ məlévələnt /

형 악의 있는, 심술궂은

syn **malicious, wicked**

영영 deliberately try to hurt or harm others with malicious intent

예문 They finally realized the landlord's **malevolent** purpose when he started to evict poor old tenants from his apartments.
집주인이 그의 아파트 건물에서 가난하고 나이 많은 입주자들을 내쫓기 시작 했을 때 그들은 그의 악의적인 의도를 마침내 깨닫게 되었다.

연습문제

I

1. In Shakespeare's Othello, Iago represents a totally _____ force.
2. Better to die in the attempt than seek an _____ safety.
3. If you are stuck in the same routine every day and you are bored of it, you could dream of an _____ .
4. Refusing the suggestion of a morganatic marriage, the king _____ from the throne when he could not marry the woman he loved.
5. Though he didn't intend to _____ anyone, his message was very confusing.

/ aberration / ignominious / abdicate / beguile / malevolent /

II

1. honesty, frankness, forthrightness= _____
2. meticulous, demanding = _____
3. denounce, condemn, disparage = _____
4. delude, deceive, inveigle = _____
5. sluggish, lethargic = _____

/ languid / fastidious / candor / beguile / decry /

Day 13

01

defer

/ difə́:r /

동 미루다, 연기하다, 존중하다

syn postpone, delay, put off

영영 If you defer, you arrange it to happen later, yield to the opinion or wishes of another

예문 I would like to ask you to **defer** my payment of apartment rent until next week.
제가 아파트 월세 지불하는 것을 다음 주까지 연기해줄 것을 부탁드립니다.

02

elude

/ ilú:d /

동 교묘히 피하다, 회피하다

syn evade, escape

영영 try to escape the notice of others and avoid being caught

예문 Some parents of students I had taught before **eluded** my telephone calls or visits for settling overdue tuition fees.
내가 전에 가르쳤던 학생들의 몇몇 부모는 연체된 회비를 정산하기 위한 전화 연락이나 방문들을 회피했다.

03

fathom

/ fǽðəm /

동 (말의 의미 또는 상황을) 헤아리다

syn comprehend, understand

영영 understand the situation of things or others' statements

예문 Many foreigners cannot **fathom** how competitive and cold-hearted Korean society can be.
많은 외국인들은 한국사회가 얼마나 경쟁적이고 매정한지 이해하지 못할 때가 있다.

04 hardy
/ háːrdi /
형 강인한, 튼튼한
syn robust, tough, strong

영영 strong and surviving in harsh conditions

예문 The first settlers in Newfoundland were a group of **hardy** people who had to survive the harsh living conditions.
뉴펀들랜드의 초기 정착민들은 혹독한 생활 여건들을 이겨내야 했던 강인한 무리였다.

05 hierarchy
/ háiəràːrki /
명 (사회나 조직의) 계급, 계층
syn grading, ranking, social order

영영 a system that carries ranked groups, usually according to social, economic or professional class

예문 If you are to make your advance in the social **hierarchy**, you have to succeed in your profession or become rich.
만약에 당신이 사회 계급의 신분의 상승을 이루고 싶다면 자신의 업종에서 성공하거나 부자가 되어야 한다.

06 hypocrisy
/ hipákrəsi /
명 위선
syn insincerity, pretence, deception

영영 pretension to have qualities, beliefs, or feelings that they do not really have

예문 Despite some great achievements, his **hypocrisy** in the public diminished his reputation.
여러 굉장한 성공에도 불구하고 대중 앞에서의 위선은 그의 명성을 훼손시켰다.

07 impeccable
/ impékəbl /
형 결점 없는, 나무랄 데 없는
syn exemplary, flawless

영영 having no faults or flaws

예문 Although he displays poor judgements at times, his success rate is **impeccable**.
가끔씩 그는 부실한 판단을 내리기도 하지만 그의 성공률은 흠잡을 데가 없다.

08 impecunious

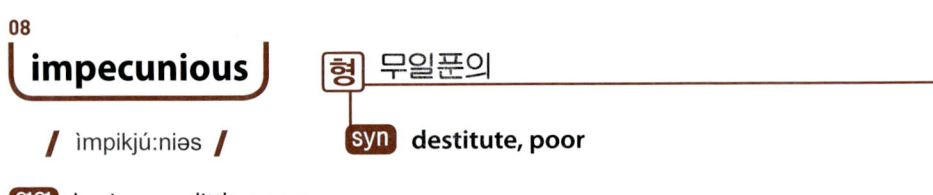

/ ìmpikjúːniəs /

형 무일푼의

syn destitute, poor

영영 having very little money

예문 There are many **impecunious** people living in the outskirt of Manila, the Philippines.
필리핀 마닐라의 외곽에는 많은 가난한 사람들이 살고 있다.

09 keen

/ kíːn /

형 간절한, 열망하는, 예리한

syn eager, intense, enthusiastic

영영 liking something very much or very passionate about doing it

예문 John was very **keen** on publishing his work through a famous publisher.
존은 그의 작품을 유명한 출판사를 통해 출간하는 것에 매우 관심 있었다.

10 libertarian

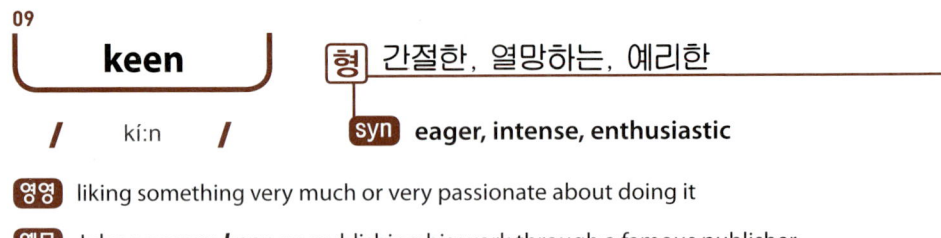

/ lìbərtέəriən /

명 자유의지론자

syn indeterminist

영영 someone who strongly advocates the principles of liberty and free will

예문 My high school teacher who taught Economics didn't mind being labeled as a **libertarian** as he always emphasized the liberty and free will.
경제학을 가르쳤던 나의 고등학교 선생님은 그가 항상 자유와 자유의지를 강조했기 때문에 자유의지론자라고 일컬어지는 것을 꺼리지 않았다.

11 maxim

/ mǽksim /

명 격언, 속담

syn aphorism, epigram, adage

영영 a saying that offers valuable lessons or morals that have been passed down

예문 The **maxim** that says 'A stitch in time saves nine.' is meant to encourage people to do things in timely manner.
'제때의 한 바늘이 아홉 땀의 수고를 덜어준다'라는 격언은 사람들이 일들을 제때 하도록 장려하기 위한 것이다.

12. noisome
/ nɔ́isəm /
형 해로운
syn unpleasant, offensive

영영 unpleasant or harmful to some people

예문 If you don't shower often, especially in the hot summer days, you can produce *noisome* smell.
만약에 당신이 더운 여름날에 자주 샤워를 하지 않는다면 역겨운 냄새를 풍길 수 있다.

13. nourish
/ nə́:riʃ /
동 영양분을 공급하다, (감정, 생각을) 키우다
syn supply, sustain, nurture

영영 provide enough elements or care for plants so that something can grow and sustain itself

예문 Reading bedtime stories can help children *nourish* their minds and develop good personality.
잠잘 때의 동화를 읽어주는 것은 그들의 마음을 발달시키고 좋은 성격을 만들어낼 수 있게 도와준다.

14. obtuse
/ əbtjú:s /
형 둔한, 무딘
syn slow-witted, dull, dense

영영 lacking sensitiveness or intellect in judgement

예문 I couldn't believe how *obtuse* some teachers could be in managing their tasks.
나는 몇몇 교사들이 그들의 업무를 다루는데 있어 어찌나 둔하던지 그것을 믿을 수 없을 정도였다.

15. odious
/ óudiəs /
형 미운, 싫은, 불쾌한
syn horrible, contemptible

영영 being disliked or regarded as an unpleasant presence

예문 Many foreigners in Korea think that eating live octopus is an *odious* experience.
한국에 있는 많은 외국인들은 살아있는 문어를 먹는 것은 불쾌한 경험이라고 생각한다.

연습문제

I

1. As the human body is _____ by food, so is a nation _____ by industry.
2. The caste system categorized Hindus into a social _____ .
3. For once, please try to be in my shoes and _____ what I'm trying to say.
4. Although there are a lot of insects that are _____ , there are some that are actually helpful to mankind.
5. I am very _____ in working with shapes.

/ obtuse / nourish / fathom / hierarchy / noisome /

II

1. insincerity, pretence, deception = _____
2. aphorism, epigram, adage = _____
3. horrible, contemptible = _____
4. postpone, delay, put off = _____
5. destitute, poor = _____

/ defer / hypocrisy / odious / impecunious / maxim /

Day 14

01 caustic
/ kɔ́:stik /

형 신랄한, 부식성의

syn **acrimonious, biting, corrosive**

영영 a person's remark being bitter or criticizing

예문 Most film makers prefer not to receive *caustic* remarks from the critics about their movies.
대부분의 영화 제작자들은 비평가들로부터 그들의 영화에 대한 신랄한 비판을 받는 것을 선호하지 않는다.

02 censure
/ sénʃər /

동 비난하다, 불신임하다

syn **berate, castigate, reproach**

영영 criticize or blame a person

예문 After being *censured* by the President, the prime minister resigned from his office.
대통령에 의해 질책을 받은 후 총리는 그의 직으로부터 사임했다.

03 delegate
/ déligèit /

동 대표를 뽑다, (권한·업무 등을) 위임하다

syn **entrust, transfer**

영영 give a position or an authority to someone

예문 To my surprise, my boss *delegated* the project to me.
놀랍게도 나의 사장은 그 프로젝트를 나에게 위임했다.

04 eminent
/ émənənt /
형 탁월한, 뛰어난
syn distinguished, prominent

영영 well known or famous in one's profession

예문 We are all looking forward to the lecture by an **eminent** scholar from Korea.
우리는 한국에서 온 저명한 학자의 강연을 기대하고 있다.

05 fetid
/ fétid /
형 악취를 내뿜는
syn malodorous

영영 having a foul odor

예문 The place where many people were massacred began to have a **fetid** smell.
많은 사람들이 학살당했던 장소는 악취를 풍기기 시작했다.

06 gregarious
/ grigɛ́əriəs /
형 군거하는, 사교적인
syn outgoing, sociable

영영 seeking and enjoying the company of others

예문 Wolves are **gregarious** creatures that travel in packs.
늑대들은 무리를 지어 돌아다니는 군거성 동물이다.

07 grievous
/ grí:vəs /
형 통탄할, (고통이) 극심한
syn injurious, hurtful

영영 serious or grave in nature

예문 Many political prisoners under past dictatorship were the victims of a **grievous** injustice.
과거 독재정부 하의 많은 정치범들은 통탄할 만한 부당행위의 희생자들이었다.

08 justify

/ dʒʌ́stəfài /

동 정당화하다, 정당성을 부여하다

syn vindicate, support, warrant

영영 show or prove that something is reasonable or really necessary

예문 People do not complain about the high price of Samsung products as the fine quality *justifies* the cost.
사람들은 좋은 품질은 비용을 정당화시킨다고 생각하기 때문에 삼성 제품의 높은 비용에 대해 불평하지 않는다.

09 luminous

/ lúːmənəs /

형 빛을 내는

syn radiating

영영 reflecting light or brightly shining

예문 This is a great opportunity that we can observe such *luminous* stars.
지금은 그와 같은 빛나는 별들을 관측할 수 있는 굉장한 기회입니다.

10 meager

/ míːgər /

동 빈약한, 불충분한, 풍부하지 못한

syn poor, scanty

영영 small in quantity and poor in quality

예문 The young couple can barely live on their *meager* income.
그 젊은 부부는 빈약한 수입으로 겨우 살아간다.

11 negligent

/ néglidʒənt /

형 소홀한, 부주의한

syn careless

영영 habitually careless or neglectful

예문 Although he was not guilty of murder, his behavior was certainly *negligent*.
비록 그는 살인에 대해 무죄였지만 그의 행동은 확실히 부주의한 것이었다.

12 negotiate

/ nigóuʃièit /   syn bargain, deal, discuss

동 협상하다

영영 try to solve a problem in order to make a business arrangement by talking with each other and understanding differences

예문 China wants other countries to **negotiate** with North Korea in solving the nuclear weapon issue.
중국은 핵무기 문제를 해결하는데 있어 다른 나라들이 북한과 협상하기를 원한다.

13 pallid

/ pǽlid /   syn insipid, pale

형 창백한, (눈이) 흐릿한

영영 lacking color, especially on the skin or the eyes, looking unattractive and unnatural

예문 After a week long schedule of writing a book and teaching lessons, John's face looked drawn and **pallid**.
장장 일주일간 책 한 권을 쓰고 수업을 가르친 후에, 존의 얼굴은 핼쑥하고 창백해 보였다.

14 panacea

/ pæ̀nəsíːə /   syn cure-all

명 만병통치약

영영 some medicine that can cure all kinds of illness and problems

예문 Although the drug appeared to work wonders on cancer patients, doctors warned that it was not a **panacea**.
비록 그 약은 암 환자들에게 기적을 낳는 것처럼 보였지만 의사들은 그것이 만병통치약은 아니라고 경고했다.

15 debauch

/ dibɔ́ːtʃ /   syn seduce

동 타락시키다, 더럽히다

영영 corrupt oneself or others by means of sensual pleasures

예문 We should not **debauch** the children with worldly concerns.
우리는 아이들의 마음을 세속적인 문제로 더럽히지 않아야 한다.

연습문제

I

1. You must not _____ him until you know the whole story about his mistakes.
2. A group of the most _____ British scientists put their heads together and made some experiments.
3. After he was promoted to vice president of the company, he became _____ of his former friends.
4. He is very much of a _____ person; he can't stay alone for more than an hour!
5. She says that to generate the right rapport with her predominantly male staff, sometimes she _____ authority to a man.

/ negligent / censure / eminent / delegate / gregarious /

II

1. outgoing, sociable = _____
2. acrimonious, biting, corrosive = _____
3. cure-all = _____
4. radiating = _____
5. malodorous = _____

/ fetid / caustic / luminous / panacea / gregarious /

Day 15

01 denounce
/ dináuns /
동 공공연히 비난하다
syn accuse, blame, censure, condemn

영영 point out as deserving blame or punishment

예문 The opposition party **denounced** members of the government for corruption.
야당은 부패에 연루된 정부 인사를 비난했다.

02 enervate
/ énərvèit /
동 기력을 빼앗다
syn debilitate, devitalize, exhaust

영영 lessen the strength

예문 Years of work in the desert dangerously **enervated** his strength.
사막에서의 수년간의 작업은 위험할 정도로 그의 힘을 소진시켰다.

03 fidelity
/ fidéləti /
명 충실, 충성
syn allegiance, devotion, faithfulness

영영 the trait of being faithful

예문 A medieval knight was required to pledge **fidelity** to his lord.
중세의 기사들은 그들의 주인에게 충성을 맹세해야 했다.

04 grievous
/ gríːvəs /

형 슬픈, 통탄할, 비통한

syn critical, grave, serious, agonizing

영영 causing grief, pain, or anguish

예문 Death would not be **grievous** to me, if I could only see my enemy die before me.
내가 죽기 전에 나의 적이 먼저 죽는 것을 볼 수 있다면 내 죽음이 슬프지 않을 것이다.

05 hereditary
/ hirédətèri /

형 세습의, 부모한테 물려받은

syn ancestral, bequeathed, handed-down

영영 passed down from an older to a younger

예문 Do you think we are influenced more by environment or **heredity**?
너는 우리가 환경과 유전 중 어떤 것에 의해 더 영향을 받는다고 생각하느냐?

06 hefty
/ héfti /

형 무거운, 중량 있는

syn beefy, burly, heavy

영영 of considerable weight

예문 Our president promised **hefty** increase in salary to us.
우리 사장님은 우리에게 확실한 승급을 약속했다.

07 implacable
/ implǽkəbl /

형 달래기 어려운, 화해할 수 없는

syn inexorable, intractable, uncompromising

영영 incapable of being placated or pacified

예문 He was as famous for his **implacable** attitude as for these skills.
그는 이 기술만큼이나 타협하지 않는 태도로도 유명했다.

08 implicit
/ implísit /
형 은연 중의, 함축적인
syn unquestionable, implied, tacit

영영 implied or understood though not directly expressed

예문 In the morning conference, his **implicit** remark was equal to an insult.
아침 회의에서의 그의 암시적인 언행은 모욕에 가까운 것이었다.

09 jeopardy
/ dʒépərdi /
명 위험
syn danger, hazard, menace, peril, risk

영영 risk of loss or injury

예문 Many people regard drugs as a **jeopardy** to society.
많은 사람들은 약물을 사회의 위험인자로 간주한다.

10 kindle
/ kíndl /
동 불을 붙이다, 빛나게 하다
syn burn, fire, ignite, light

영영 set fire

예문 The poor policy for the disabled **kindled** them to revolt.
형편없는 장애자 정책이 그들로 하여금 폭동을 일으키도록 유발하였다.

11 mandate
/ mǽndeit /
동 위임하다, 명령하다
syn command, authorize, empower

영영 assign a colony or territory to a specified nation under a mandate

예문 Optimal regulation will never **mandate** 100 percent deregulation.
규제를 적절하기만 하면 꼭 100% 규제 해제가 필요한 것도 아니다.

12. manifest
/ mǽnəfèst /

형 명백한, 분명한

syn apparent, evident

영영 showing or demonstrating plainly

예문 Their solution to the problem was **manifest** to all.
문제 해결 방법은 누가 봐도 명백했다.

13. nurture
/ nə́:rtʃər /

동 양육하다

syn care for, nourish, parent, rear

영영 help grow or develop

예문 The book told him how to **nurture** the puppy.
그 책은 그에게 강아지 기르는 법을 가르쳐 주었다.

14. obdurate
/ ábdjurət /

형 억지 센, 완고한

syn intractable, recalcitrant, stubborn

영영 not giving in to persuasion

예문 He was **obdurate** in his refusal to listen to our complaints.
그는 우리의 불만을 수렴하는 것에 완강히 반대했다.

15. partisan
/ pá:rtizən /

형 당파심이 강한

syn biased, partial, adherent

영영 strongly supporting a particular person or cause, often without thinking carefully about the matter

예문 The election is 14 months away and politicians are in for interesting times with their regrouping attempts across **partisan** borders.
선거는 14개월이 남아있으며 정치인들은 당파의 기존 경계를 해체하는 새로운 편 가르기를 시도하고 있다.

연습문제

I

1. The opposition _____ members of the government for corruption.
2. They had the _____ agreement that they would help each other.
3. Racial integration of schools was eventually _____ by the government.
4. The blue eyes I have are _____ – my mother has them too.
5. When errors occur in DNA reproductions, they can _____ themselves as mutations.

/ mandate / implicit / denounce / hereditary / manifest /

II

1. incapable of being pacified = _____
2. danger, hazard, menace, peril, risk = _____
3. care for, nourish, parent, rear = _____
4. debilitate, devitalize, exhaust = _____
5. biased, partial, adherent, supporter = _____

/ enervate / implacable / nurture / jeopardy / partisan /

Day 16

01 diminutive
/ dimínjutiv /

형 소형의, 자그마한

syn diminutive, miniature, small, tiny

영영 extremely small in size

예문 Jockeys must be of **diminutive** size for their horses to compete.
말이 달릴 수 있게 하려면 기수들은 체격이 작아야 한다.

02 empirical
/ impírikəl /

형 경험의, 경험적인

syn experimental, observed, practical

영영 relying on or derived from observation or experiment

예문 We should trust **empirical** evidence more than speculation.
우리는 추측보다는 경험적 증거를 믿어야 한다.

03 forge
/ fɔ́:rdʒ /

동 단조하다, 날조하다

syn cast, mold, construct

영영 put a lot of effort into making something

예문 He's getting good at forging his mother's signature.
그는 어머니의 서명을 위조하는 데 능숙해지고 있었다.

04 guise

/ gáiz /

명 외관, 외양, 겉치레

syn appearance, mode

영영 outward appearance or aspect

예문 It is hard to comprehend how ordinary people can be induced to these acts of murder under the **guise** of religion.
어떻게 해서 평범한 사람들이 종교라는 미명 하에 이러한 살인행위들을 저지르도록 이끌려지는지 이해하기 힘들다.

05 haphazard

/ hæphǽzərd /

형 우연한

syn aimless, arbitrary

영영 dependent upon or characterized by mere chance

예문 Are you sure you aren't being too **haphazard** in your search?
대충 찾지 않는 것이 아니냐?

06 harness

/ háːrnis /

동 (바람 등의 자연력을) 동력으로 이용하다

syn exploit

영영 control so as to employ the energy or potential power

예문 Scientists are finding better ways to **harness** the limitless energy of the sun.
과학자들은 태양의 무제한의 에너지를 이용하기 위한 더 나은 방법을 찾고 있다.

07 impudent

/ ímpjudnt /

형 뻔뻔스러운, 건방진

syn audacious, brazen, insolent, impertinent

영영 characterized by offensive boldness

예문 She was **impudent** enough to make faces at his father.
그녀는 건방지게도 아버지에게 찌푸린 얼굴을 했다.

08 impute
/ impjú:t /
동 (불명예 따위를) 돌리다, 탓으로 하다
syn associate, attribute, credit

영영 attribute a fault or responsibility

예문 He *imputed* his failure in his business to his co-workers.
그는 사업 실패를 동료들의 탓으로 돌렸다.

09 modulate
/ mádʒulèit /
동 조정하다, 조절하다
syn adjust, moderate, regulate

영영 adjust or adapt to a certain proportion

예문 The singer's voice coach advised him to *modulate* his voice more when singing.
그 가수의 조언자는 그에게 노래를 할 때 자신의 목소리를 더 조율하라고 충고했다.

10 mollify
/ máləfài /
동 누그러지게 하다, 완화하다
syn assuage, pacify, placate

영영 calm in temper or feeling

예문 Nothing I said could *mollify* the anger of the boss.
내가 한 말은 사장님의 화를 누그러뜨릴 수 없었다.

11 nuance
/ njú:ɑ:ns /
명 뉘앙스
syn hint, shade, trace

영영 a very slight difference in meaning, sound, color

예문 The ability to sniff out such *nuances* quickly is another important quality for job hunters.
그러한 미묘한 차이를 재빨리 알아채는 능력은 구직자들에게 또 다른 중요한 자질이다.

12. null /nʌl/
형 효력이 없는, 영(0)의
syn invalid, void, immaterial
영영 having the value zero
예문 I would like to consider your contract **null** and void.
당신의 계약은 없었던 걸로 하면 좋겠습니다.

13. obsolete /àbsəlíːt/
형 쓸모없이 된, 시대에 뒤진, 진부한
syn antiquated, outdated, outmoded
영영 no longer in use and outmoded in design and style
예문 Although the punched card is now becoming **obsolete**, it was a milestone in the development of the computer.
천공기는 지금 거의 사라져가고 있지만 컴퓨터의 발달사에서 한 중요한 이정표였다.

14. procure /proukjúər/
동 획득하다, (필수품을) 조달하다
syn acquire, gain, secure
영영 get by special effort
예문 Could you **procure** me specimens of the document?
그 문서의 견본을 구해줄 수 있겠는가?

15. quarantine /kwɔ́ːrəntìːn/
명 (전염병 예방을 위한) 격리, 교통 차단
syn isolate, segregate
영영 kept separate from others for a set period of time, usually because they have a disease
예문 The dog was kept in **quarantine** for six months.
그 개는 6개월 동안 격리되어 있었다.

연습문제

I

1. He _____ my decision to his incorrect assumptions about my motives.
2. We tried to _____ the hysterical child by promising her many gifts.
3. The factory needs to change _____ equipment.
4. She might be of a _____ size, but she has big hearts.
5. _____ the instrument, and it will present you with a brand new sound.

/ obsolete / mollify / impute / diminutive / modulate /

II

1. experimental, observed, practical = _____
2. aimless, arbitrary = _____
3. arrogant, audacious, brazen = _____
4. hint, trace, shade = _____
5. isolate, segregate = _____

/ impudent / empirical / quarantine / haphazard / nuance /

Day 17

01
exhort
/ igzɔ́:rt /

동 열심히 타이르다
syn admonish, counsel, entreat

영영 urge, advise, or warn earnestly

예문 My father **exhorted** me to prepare for the final exam.
아버지는 나더러 기말고사 준비를 하라고 설득했다.

02
extol
/ ikstóul /

동 칭찬하다
syn celebrate, glorify, hail

영영 praise highly

예문 Most people at the conference **extolled** his contribution.
회의 참석한 대부분의 사람들이 그의 공헌에 찬사를 보냈다.

03
foil
/ fɔ́il /

명 얇은 박(箔)
syn film, flake

영영 metal made into very thin sheets that is used for covering or wrapping things, especially food

예문 Remove the **foil** you used in the last step.
마지막 단계에서 당신이 사용한 포일을 제거하십시오.

04 gaudy
/ góːdi /

형 번쩍번쩍 빛나는, 번지르르한

syn **flashy, garish, ostentatious**

영영 too brightly colored in a way that lacks taste

예문 These pieces were painted in **gaudy** colors.
이 조각들은 번지르르한 색상으로 채색되었다.

05 generic
/ dʒənérik /

형 일반적인, 상표 등록이 되어 있지 않은

syn **common, general, standard**

영영 applicable or referring to a whole class or group

예문 **Generic** brands of some products are cheaper and at least equal in quality.
상표등록이 안 된 일부 제품들은 더 싸고 그러면서도 최소한 동등한 품질을 가지고 있다.

06 herald
/ hérəld /

동 알리다, 포고하다

syn **broadcast, proclaim**

영영 announce publicly

예문 The president's speech **heralded** a change of policy.
대통령의 연설은 정책의 변화를 예고했다.

07 incessant
/ insésnt /

형 끊임없는, 그칠 새 없는

syn **ceaseless, constant, continuous, interminable**

영영 continuing without interruption

예문 His **incessant** complaining is tiresome to everyone.
그의 끊임없는 불평이 모두를 피곤하게 한다.

08 lavish

/ lǽviʃ /

형 아낌없는, 사치스러운

syn luxuriant, munificent, exhaust, squander

영영 very elaborate and impressive, costing a lot of money

예문 She was not used to their **lavish** mode of living.
그녀는 그들의 사치스러운 생활방식에 익숙하지 않았다.

09 lax

/ lǽks /

형 느슨한, 해이한

syn derelict, negligent, remiss

영영 lacking in rigor, strictness, or firmness

예문 The knots we used to tie him up were so **lax** that he escaped easily.
우리가 그를 묶는 데 사용했던 매듭이 너무 느슨해 그가 쉽게 빠져나갔다.

10 munificent

/ mjuːnífəsnt /

형 인색하지 않은

syn beneficent, generous, magnanimous

영영 showing great generosity

예문 We were astonished by the **munificent** gifts he showered us with.
우리는 그가 우리에게 주었던 아낌없는 선물들에 놀랐다.

11 onslaught

/ ánslɔ̀ːt /

명 돌격, 맹공격

syn assault, attack

영영 a violent attack

예문 We suffered many casualties by the unexpected **onslaught** of the enemy troops.
우리는 예상치 못했던 적군의 맹공격으로 많은 사상자가 발생했다.

12. pathos
/ péiθɑs /

명 비애, 정념

syn commiseration, feeling, pity, sympathy

영영 a quality that arouses feelings of pity, sympathy, tenderness, or sorrow

예문 In the Greek definition of tragedy this suffering would serve as **pathos**.
비극의 그리스적 정의에 의하면 이러한 고통은 정념으로 작용할 것이다.

13. raze
/ réiz /

동 지우다, 무너뜨리다

syn demolish, flatten, level

영영 scrape or shave off

예문 The earthquake **razed** my house to the ground.
지진은 나의 집을 완전히 무너뜨렸다.

14. amiable
/ éimiəbl /

형 붙임성 있는, 사귀기 쉬운

syn cordial, affable

영영 friendly and easy to like

예문 We have come along with each other since some **amiable** gatherings.
몇 번의 스스럼없는 모임을 가진 이후 우리는 줄곧 잘 지내왔다.

15. salutation
/ sæljutéiʃən /

명 인사(모자를 벗고 머리를 숙이는)

syn accolade, applause, honor, recognition

영영 a polite expression of greeting or goodwill

예문 The guards at the university raise their hat in **salutation** to the professors.
대학의 경비들은 교수들에게 인사하기 위해 그들의 모자를 올린다.

연습문제

I

1. The late Shah of Iran angered his people with his pompous and _____ characters.
2. Try not to tie it too _____ . It might fall down.
3. The paint was starting to fall off so I _____ the whole thing.
4. His jokes are so _____ , I've heard of them like a thousand times.
5. A phrase serving as the prefatory greeting in a letter, such as Dear Sir, is called a _____ .

/ lavish / raze / lax / salutation / generic /

II

1. ceaseless, constant, continuous, interminable = _____
2. cordial, affable, friendly = _____
3. commiseration, feeling, pity, sympathy = _____
4. admonish, counsel, entreat = _____
5. celebrate, glorify, hail = _____

/ amiable / pathos / exhort / extol / incessant /

Day 18

01 forbearance
/ fɔːrbέərəns /

명 인내, 자제심

syn patience, abstinence, moderation

영영 tolerance and restraint in the face of provocation

예문 We must have **forbearance** in dealing with him because he is still weak from his illness.
그가 질병으로 인해 여전히 약하기 때문에 우리는 그를 대하는 데 인내심을 가져야 한다.

02 foretell
/ fɔːrtél /

동 예언하다

syn divine, foresee, prophesy

영영 predict or indicate beforehand

예문 He **foretold** that an accident would happen.
어떤 사고가 일어날 것이라고 예언했다.

03 genesis
/ dʒénəsis /

명 발생, 기원

syn commencement, dawn, origin

영영 the coming into being of something

예문 Joseph Campbell studied the **genesis** of the world's creation myths.
조셉 캠벨은 세계의 창조 신화들의 기원에 대하여 연구했다.

04 inclination

/ ìnklənéiʃən /

명 기울기, 경향

syn tendency

영영 The act of inclining or the state of being inclined

예문 It was his **inclination** to give money at Christmas.
그에게는 크리스마스 때 돈을 주는 관행이 있었다.

05 incontrovertible

/ ìnkantrəvə́:rtəbl /

형 논쟁의 여지가 없는, 부정할 수 없는

syn incontestable, indisputable, irrefutable

영영 incapable of being contradicted or disputed

예문 It admits of no further response in sound, either in the way of certification or of contrast, but is **incontrovertible** in its prevailing finality.
검증으로든 대조의 방식으로든 더 이상의 대응을 허용하지 않지만, 그 지배적 결말 앞에서는 어떤 논쟁의 여지도 없다.

06 legitimate

/ lidʒítəmət /

형 합법의, 합리적인

syn authentic, genuine, verifiable, logical, reasonable

영영 being in compliance with the law

예문 The lawyer double-checked to see if it was **legitimate**.
합법성 여부를 알아보기 위해 변호사는 그것을 재확인했다.

07 lenient

/ líːniənt /

형 관대한, 인정 많은, 자비로운

syn permissive, merciful, mild, sympathetic

영영 inclined not to be harsh or strict

예문 The students were admitted to breaking the rules but asked that they be **lenient**.
학생들은 규칙을 어겨도 괜찮다는 허락은 받았지만 좀 더 관대하도록 요청 받았다.

08 mutate
/ mjúːteit /

동 변화하다, 돌연변이하다

syn alter, convert, transfigure, transform

영영 develop different characteristics as the result of a change

예문 The discoveries fanned fears that avian flu could infect the European Union's estimated $27billion egg-and-poultry industry, or **mutate** into a strain more dangerous to humans.
그 발견은 조류독감이 유럽연합의 270억 불 상당으로 추산되는 가금류 산업에 영향 미칠 수 있고 인간에게는 더 위험한 변종으로 돌연변이될 수 있다는 공포를 부채질했다.

09 multilateral
/ mʌ̀ltilǽtərəl /

형 다변의, 3개국 이상이 관계하고 있는

syn many-sided, polygonal

영영 having many sides, involving more than two nations or parties

예문 He was upbeat on the prospects for future **multilateral** nuclear talks.
그는 향후 다자간 핵 회담의 전망에 낙관적이었다.

10 multiplicity
/ mʌ̀ltəplísəti /

명 다수, 중복

syn variety, diversity

영영 the state of being various or manifold

예문 This book covers a wide **multiplicity** of topics.
이 책은 널리 여러 가지 화제들을 다루고 있다.

11 reclusive
/ riklúːsiv /

형 은둔한, 쓸쓸한, 적막한

syn unsocial, seclusive

영영 seeking or preferring seclusion or isolation

예문 His characters are often **reclusive**, and he sticks to these desolate places.
그의 성격은 종종 은둔적이며 이런 황량한 장소에 집착한다.

12 reconcile

/ rékənsàil /

동 화해시키다, 스스로 단념하게 하다

syn appease, conciliate, propitiate, reunite

영영 reestablish a close relationship

예문 She was bound to *reconcile* herself to accepting the post.
그녀는 그 직책을 받아들이지 않으면 안 되었다.

13 rectitude

/ réktətjùːd /

명 정직, 청렴

syn decency, honesty

영영 the quality or condition of being correct in judgment

예문 Although the allegations seemed to be doubtful to other people, I never really doubted his *rectitude*.
그의 주장이 다른 사람들에게 의심스럽게 보였어도 나는 결코 그의 청렴함을 의심하지 않는다.

14 tedious

/ tíːdiəs /

형 지루한, 싫증 나는

syn dull, monotonous, prosaic, unimaginative

영영 tiresome by reason of length, slowness, or dullness

예문 The arguments were *tedious* and complicated.
그 논쟁은 장황하고 복잡했다.

15 temperance

/ témpərəns /

명 절제, 자제

syn moderation, prudence, restraint

영영 self-restraint, as in behavior or expression

예문 Use *temperance* in giving advice to friends.
친구들에게 충고할 때는 절제해서 해라.

연습문제

I

1. I was always curious about _____ and unforced connections among the disparate details.
2. After a bloody and bitter war, the two enemies were finally _____ .
3. The Greeks' "golden mean" preached balance and _____ in all things.
4. No insurance company has ever been bankrupt because the insurance company _____ the future for millions.
5. He was so disappointed with the world that he shut himself and became _____ .

/ temperance / legitimate / foretell / reclusive / reconcile /

II

1. tolerance, restraint = _____
2. commencement, dawn, origin = _____
3. tiresome, slowness, dullness = _____
4. incapable of being disputed = _____
5. permissive, merciful, mild = _____

/ tedious / genesis / incontrovertible / forbearance / lenient /

Day 19

01 grave / gréiv /
형 근엄한, 중대한
syn **consequential, important, momentous**
영영 requiring serious thought
예문 The situation poses a **grave** threat to peace.
그 정세는 평화에 중대한 위협으로 작용한다.

02 hail / héil /
동 큰 소리로 부르다, 환호하여 맞이하다
syn **greet, salute, signal, welcome**
영영 greet or acclaim enthusiastically
예문 Doctors **hailed** the recent advances in medicine.
의사들은 의학에 있어서의 최근의 진보를 높이 평가했다.

03 hale / héil /
형 꿋꿋한, 정정한
syn **hardy, healthy, robust**
영영 strong and healthy
예문 My grandmother still remains **hale** and hearty.
나의 할머니는 아직도 정정하시다

04 hallmark
/ hɔ́:lmà:rk /

명 품질증명, 검증서, 증명

syn certificate, verification

영영 a feature or quality that is typical of something

예문 The preliminary work is part of the **hallmark** process.
예비 작업은 품질증명 과정의 일부이다.

05 implement
/ ímpləmənt /

동 이행하다, (조건 등을) 충족하다

syn achieve, effect, execute, fulfill, realize

영영 to make something that has been officially decided

예문 It was agreed with the Israeli side to **implement** economic reform in the city.
그 도시에 경제 개혁을 수행하기로 이스라엘 측과 합의했다.

06 implication
/ ìmplikéiʃən /

명 (뜻의) 내포, 함축, 연루

syn connotation, effect, insinuation, association

영영 something that is suggested or indirectly stated

예문 Their **implication** of her in the murder was obvious.
그들이 살인에 그녀를 연루시킨 것임이 명백했다.

07 implore
/ implɔ́:r /

동 애원하다, 탄원하다

syn appeal, beg, beseech, entreat

영영 beg for urgently

예문 The students **implored** the teachers to make the examination easier.
그 학생은 선생님들께 시험을 일찍 볼 수 있도록 요청했다.

08 journeyman
/ dʒə́:rnimən /
명 (수습 기간을 마친) 제 구실 하는 직공
syn experienced worker

영영 a person who has training and experience in a job but who is only average at it

예문 If you want to be a **journeyman** electrician, attend a four or five year apprenticeship program.
만약 당신이 쓸 만한 전기기술자가 되길 원한다면, 4~5년 과정의 견습 프로그램을 수료해야 한다.

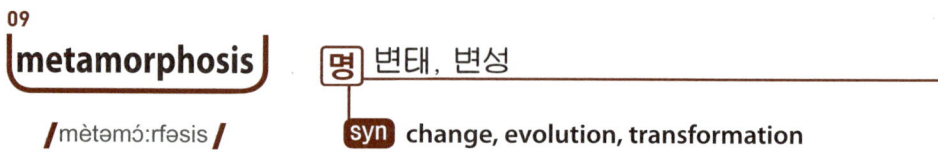

09 metamorphosis
/ mètəmɔ́:rfəsis /
명 변태, 변성
syn change, evolution, transformation

영영 a change in the structure of a particular body tissue

예문 The **metamorphosis** from an agricultural society to today's complex industrial world was accompanied by war.
농업사회에서 오늘날의 복잡다단한 공업세계로의 변화에는 전쟁이 수반되었다.

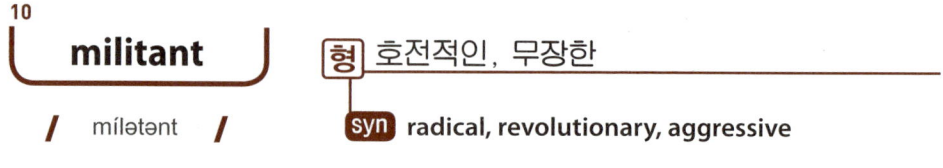

10 militant
/ mílətənt /
형 호전적인, 무장한
syn radical, revolutionary, aggressive

영영 using, or willing to use, force or strong pressure to achieve your aims, especially to achieve social or political change

예문 Galvanized by a deadly bomb blast in Bali, Indonesia is set to question a **militant** Muslim cleric in it.
발리에서의 치명적인 폭탄 폭발에 자극받은 인도네시아는 자국 내 무장한 무슬림 성직자들에 대해 의심을 품기 시작했다.

11 nauseate
/ nɔ́:zieit /
동 욕지기나다, 메스껍게 하다
syn disgust, repulse, revolt

영영 To feel or cause to feel loathing or disgust

예문 Horror movies used to be the movies that would scare you, not **nauseate** you.
옛날 공포 영화는 공포를 주지 메스껍게 하는 것은 결코 아니었다.

12. imperturbable

/ impərtə́:rbəbl /

형 냉정한, 침착한

syn calm, self-possessed, tranquil

영영 not easily upset or worried by a difficult situation

예문 He performed his role with **imperturbable** composure.
그는 침착하게 자기 역할을 수행했다.

13. penitent

/ pénətənt /

형 죄를 뉘우치는, 참회하는

syn contrite, humbled, repentant

영영 feeling or expressing remorse for one's misdeeds or sins

예문 **Penitent** pilgrims flock to that famous shrine every year.
회개하는 청교도들은 그 유명한 성당으로 매년 모인다.

14. perfidious

/ pərfídiəs /

형 불신의, 불성실한

syn deceitful, disloyal, faithless

영영 tending to betray

예문 King Richard was in the power of the **perfidious** and cruel Duke of Austria.
리처드 왕은 교활하고 잔인한 오스트리아 공작의 손아귀에 있었다.

15. quietude

/ kwáiətjù:d /

명 안식, 평온

syn serenity, stillness

영영 a state of stillness

예문 A naturalist is fond of the **quietude** and beauty of unadulterated wilderness.
자연주의자는 때 묻지 않은 야생의 평온함과 아름다움을 좋아한다.

day by day I 153

연습문제

I

1. She smiled, but the _____ was that she didn't believe me.
2. Many employers prefer to hire people who are _____ and hearty over those who seem sickly and lethargic.
3. We all went to the president's office and _____ for a raise in income.
4. The _____ from a pupa to a butterfly still fascinates me.
5. I am unwilling to _____ this plan until I have assurance that it has the full approval of your officials.

/ hale / implication / metamorphosis / implement / implore /

II

1. activist, radical, revolutionary, terrorist, aggressive = _____
2. certificate, verification = _____
3. calm, self-possessed, tranquil = _____
4. greet or acclaim enthusiastically = _____
5. contrite, humbled, repentant = _____

/ hallmark / militant / hail / penitent / imperturbable /

Day 20

01 abrasion
/ əbréiʒən /

명 (피부 등의) 벗겨짐, 마멸

syn scratch, brush burn, excoriation

영영 the process of wearing down or rubbing away by means of friction

예문 Dusts and mists frequently cause **abrasion** and binding, with consequent generation of high temperature surfaces or flames in mechanical equipment, which can, in turn, ignite the dispersion.
분진과 미립자는 종종 마손과 결착을 야기하며 표면에서의 고열발생 혹은 기계장치에서의 화염을 동반하여, 그로 인해 이어서 확산점화를 일으킨다.

02 abstain
/ əbstéin /

동 그만두다, 끊다, 삼가다

syn withhold, keep back

영영 refrain from something by one's own choice

예문 He **abstained** from eating for six days.
그는 6일간 단식을 했다.

03 accentuate
/ ækséntʃuèit /

동 강조하다, 두드러지게 하다

syn emphasize, highlight, punctuate, stress, underscore

영영 stress, single out as important

예문 He **accentuated** his remarks with gestures.
그는 도중에 제스처를 쓰며 자신의 말을 강조했다.

04 certitude
/ sə́:rtətjùːd /

명 확신

syn certainty, assurance, certitude, confidence

영영 the state of being certain

예문 We have no **certitude** that he will come.
그가 온다는 보장은 없다.

05 deciduous
/ disídʒuəs /

형 탈락의, 낙엽성의

syn nonpermanent

영영 falling off or shed at a specific season or stage of growth

예문 The oak is a **deciduous** tree.
오크는 낙엽성 나무이다.

06 deduce
/ didjúːs /

동 연역하다, 추론하다

syn conclude, gather, infer, presume

영영 infer from a general principle

예문 From this we **deduce** a method for the construction.
이것으로부터 그 건설 공법을 추론해 낸다.

07 dejected
/ didʒéktid /

형 기운 없는, 낙담한

syn depressed, despondent, discouraged, disheartened

영영 affected or marked by low spirits

예문 She looked so **dejected** when she lost the game.
그녀는 게임에 졌을 때, 많이 낙담해 보였다.

08 formulate
/ fɔ́:rmjulèit /

동 만들어 내다, 공식화하다

syn devise, design

영영 come up with a plan or scheme after a long period of careful study

예문 People say I have a lot of good ideas, but I have some difficulties in **formulating** them.
사람들은 내가 좋은 아이디어가 많다고 하지만 나는 그것들을 표현해 내는 데 어려움이 있다.

09 egomania
/ ì:gouméiniə /

명 (병리적) 자기중심성향

syn egotism

영영 obsessive preoccupation with the self

예문 I find myself moving in the direction of **egomania**, but not just any kind of egomania, "spiritual" egomania.
내 자신이 자기중심적으로 되어가고 있다는 것을 알지만 그냥 그런 자기중심적이 아닌 영적인 자기중심이다.

10 embed
/ imbéd /

동 (물건을) 끼워 넣다, 묻다

syn deposit, implant, inlay

영영 fix firmly in a surrounding mass

예문 The crystals are **embedded** in the tire tread, and the signals they emit are picked up.
이 수정이 타이어의 접지 면에 삽입되면 이 수정에서 발하는 신호가 포착되는 것이다.

11 fictitious
/ fiktíʃəs /

형 허위의, 가짜의

syn fanciful, fictional, imaginary

영영 formed or conceived by the fancy or imagination

예문 The unicorn was a **fictitious** creature with wondrous magical powers.
유니콘은 불가사의한 마법을 가진 허구의 창조물이었다.

12 gist
/ dʒíst /

명 (논문·일 따위의) 요점, 요지

syn crux, kernel, point

영영 main idea

예문 She was asked to give the *gist* of the essay in two sentences.
그녀는 그 에세이를 두 문장으로 요약할 것을 요청 받았다.

13 imminent
/ ímənənt /

형 절박한, 급박한

syn approaching, impending, looming, near, pending

영영 about to occur

예문 Most seismologists predict that a big earthquake is *imminent* in China.
대부분의 지진학자들은 큰 지진이 중국에 임박했다는 것을 예측했다.

14 imperceptible
/ ìmpərséptəbl /

형 감지할 수 없는, 미세한

syn minimal, slight, subtle, unapparent, undetectable

영영 impossible or difficult to perceive by the mind or senses

예문 Atoms were once thought to be the *imperceptible* units that compose all matter.
원자는 한때 모든 물질을 구성하는 감지할 수 없는 단위로 여겨졌다.

15 miscellaneous
/ mìsəléiniəs /

형 잡다한, 이종 혼합의

syn assorted, mixed, sundry

영영 made up of a variety of parts or ingredients

예문 It took weeks to assort the *miscellaneous* items she had collected on her trip.
그녀가 여행 중에 수집했던 잡동사니들을 분류하는 데 수 주가 걸렸다.

연습문제

I

1. Anything we could not clearly classify belonged to a _____ group.
2. The teacher _____ the importance of the final exam.
3. _____ is a condition describing psychologically abnormal egotism.
4. I can't understand a thing you are saying. What is the _____ of your speech?
5. He looked very _____ when he heard that he didn't pass the exam.

/ gist / miscellaneous / deject / accentuate / egomania /

II

1. refrain from something by one's own choice = _____
2. conceived by the fancy or imagination = _____
3. the process of wearing down by friction = _____
4. infer from a general principle = _____
5. impossible or difficult to perceive = _____

/ deduce / fictitious / abrasion / imperceptible / abstain /

Day 21

01 absolve
/ æbzálv /
동 용서하다, 면제하다
syn acquit, clear, exonerate, vindicate

영영 pronounce clear of guilt or blame

예문 The captain is **absolved** from all blame and responsibility for the shipwreck.
그 선장은 배의 난파에 대한 모든 비난과 책임을 면제 받았다.

02 abstract
/ æbstrǽkt /
형 추상적인, 관념상의
syn conceptual, intangible, pure, theoretical

영영 considered apart from concrete existence

예문 She has no idea of poverty but in the **abstract**.
그녀는 관념적으로밖에 가난을 모른다.

03 accede
/ æksíːd /
동 (요구 등에) 동의하다
syn acquiesce, concede, submit

영영 give one's consent, often at the insistence of another

예문 After months of refusing to help him, she finally **acceded** to his request.
몇 달 동안 그를 돕기를 거절한 후, 그녀는 결국 그의 요청을 받아들였다.

04 accolade
/ ǽkəlèid /

명 칭찬, 영예, 표창

syn commendation, honor, laurel, tribute

영영 an expression of approval

예문 Luckily, because of some good shots of the Vietnam War, the man received the **accolade** after the war.
운 좋게도 몇 장의 베트남전 사진 덕분에 그 사람은 전쟁 후에 기사 작위를 받았다.

05 capsize
/ kǽpsaiź /

동 (배가) 뒤집히다, 전복시키다

syn invert, keel, overturn, tip over

영영 overturn or cause to overturn

예문 In his maladroit way, he managed to **capsize** the cart and spill the food.
서툴게도 그는 카트를 뒤엎었고 음식을 쏟았다.

06 decease
/ disíːs /

동 사망(하다)

syn die, expire

영영 pass from physical life and lose all bodily attributes and functions necessary to sustain life

예문 Now that his siblings are all **deceased** he feels completely alone.
그의 형제가 모두 죽었기 때문에 그는 엄청난 외로움을 느꼈다.

07 deceptive
/ diséptiv /

형 (사람을) 현혹시키는, 거짓의

syn deceitful, false, fraudulent, illusive

영영 causing one to believe what is not true or fail to believe what is true

예문 Appearances can be **deceptive**.
사물(사람)은 겉보기와는 다를 수 있다.

day 21

day by day I 161

08 default
/ difɔ́:lt /
명 불이행, 초기 설정
syn delinquency, dereliction, negligence
영영 failure to do something required by duty or law
예문 Close the property pages before changing the **default** setting.
초기 설정에서 변경하기 전에 그 속성 페이지들을 닫으십시오.

09 defiant
/ difáiənt /
형 도전적인, 반항적인
syn bold, insolent, insubordinate, rebellious
영영 openly and fearlessly refusing to obey
예문 That **defiant** child needs discipline.
저 무례한 아이는 벌을 받아야 되겠다.

10 embody
/ imbádi /
동 구체화하다, 유형화하다
syn illustrate, incarnate, personify, represent
영영 incarnate, to express in definite form
예문 The book **embodies** all the rules.
그 책에는 모든 규칙이 수록되어 있다.

11 falter
/ fɔ́:ltər /
동 비틀거리다, 발에 걸려 넘어지다, 주저하다
syn hesitate, quaver, vacillate, waver
영영 move unsteadily, hesitate in purpose or action
예문 Never **falter** in doing good.
선을 행하는 데 주저하지 말라.

12 fable
/féibl/

명 우화, 교훈적 이야기

syn allegory, folk tale, legend, parable

영영 a short narrative making an cautionary point and employing as characters animals that act like humans

예문 He regarded it as a mere **fable**.
그는 그것을 단지 꾸며낸 이야기쯤으로 생각했다.

13 homogeneous
/hòumədʒíːniəs/

형 동종의

syn alike, consistent, identical, similar

영영 of the same or similar nature or kind

예문 It was a **homogeneous** crowd of teenage girls, all wearing jeans and sweaters.
모인 인파는 모두가 일관되게 청바지와 스웨터를 입고 있는 십대 소녀들이었다.

14 horde
/hɔ́ːrd/

명 유목민의 무리, 대집단, 군중

syn crowd, host, multitude, swarm, throng

영영 a large group or crowd

예문 The streets were filled with **hordes** of people.
거리는 군중들로 혼잡했다.

15 imperil
/impérəl/

동 위태롭게 하다, 위험하게 하다

syn endanger, hazard, jeopardize, risk

영영 pose a threat, present a danger

예문 Smoking is known to **imperil** the smoker's health and also those around him.
흡연은 흡연자와 그 주변에 있는 사람들의 건강을 해치는 것으로 알려져 있다.

day by day Ⅰ

연습문제

I

1. We _____ at the precise moment our contribution was required.
2. The arguments of contemporary science are so _____ that they are no longer intelligible.
3. There were many _____ on his computer after the power went out.
4. People praised the medalist as _____ the ideal of the Olympic spirit.
5. She asked them to _____ her of the guilt she felt about her failure.

/ abstract / falter / embody / absolve / default /

II

1. commendation, honor, laurel, tribute = _____
2. hesitate, quaver, vacillate, waver = _____
3. bold, insolent, insubordinate, rebellious = _____
4. of the same or similar nature or kind = _____
5. pose a threat to; present a danger = _____

/ homogeneous / accolade / defiant / imperil / falter /

Day 22

01 commensurate
/ kəménsərət /

형 같은 양의, 비례하는
syn commensurable

영영 equal in measure or extent

예문 We want to keep our expenditures **commensurate** with our income.
우리는 수입에 맞게 지출을 유지하기 원한다.

02 commemorate
/ kəménsərət /

동 (축사·의식 등으로) 기념하다
syn exalt, glorify, revere, venerate, acclaim

영영 call or recall to mind

예문 We gathered on the anniversary of the disaster to **commemorate** the victims.
우리는 재난의 희생자들을 기리기 위해 기념일에 모였다.

03 decentralize
/ di:séntrəlàiz /

동 (권한을) 분산시키다, 집중을 배제하다
syn disperse, breakup

영영 move from central to smaller areas

예문 The purchasing departments have attempted to **decentralize** their purchasing functions over the last five years.
구매부서는 지난 5년간 구매기능의 분산을 시도해왔다.

04 degrade

/ digréid /

동 지위를 낮추다, 격하하다

syn debase, demean, disgrace, humiliate, lower

영영 lower in rank or status, demote

예문 She wouldn't **degrade** herself by cheating.
그녀는 부정행위로 자신의 명예를 실추시키려 하지는 않는다.

05 elevate

/ élәvèit /

동 (들어)올리다, 높이다

syn heave, hoist, levitate, lift

영영 move something to a higher place or position from a lower one

예문 The Bell company **elevated** him to the section chief.
벨 회사는 그를 과장으로 승진시켰다.

06 endeavor

/ indévәr /

동 노력하다, 애쓰다

syn aspire, assay, attempt, strive

영영 make an effort

예문 The boy made an honest **endeavor** to do the work right.
소년은 그 일을 제대로 하기 위해 노력했다.

07 endow

/ indáu /

동 (능력·자질 등을) 주다, 부여하다

syn bequeath, bestow, confer, grant

영영 furnish with something freely or naturally

예문 At birth the human infant is **endowed** with a large number of possible abilities.
태어날 때 유아는 많은 자질들을 부여받는다.

08 fervid

/ fə́:rvid /

형 뜨거운, 열정적인, 열렬한

syn ardent, impassioned, inflamed

영영 eager, showing a passionate feeling

예문 Her novels are well-known for the **fervid** emotions of their characters.
그녀의 소설들은 등장 인물들이 보이는 열정적인 감정으로 정평 났다.

09 gerrymander

/ dʒérimæ̀ndər /

동 선거구를 유리하게 고치다

syn manipulate the boundaries

영영 divide a geographic area into voting districts so as to give unfair advantage to one party in elections

예문 The State Legislature **gerrymandered** this area in order to favor the majority party.
주 의회는 여당에 유리하도록 이 지역의 선거구를 변경했다.

10 heyday

/ héidèi /

명 전성기

syn prime, bloom

영영 the period of greatest popularity, success, or power

예문 That pitcher's **heyday** is over.
저 투수의 전성기는 지났다

11 illegitimate

/ ìlidʒítəmət /

형 불법의, 위법의

syn illegal, illicit, unacceptable, unlawful

영영 against the law

예문 He did many **illegitimate** things.
그는 많은 불법적인 일들을 자행했다.

12. levy
/ lévi /
동 징수하다, 징발하다
syn charge, exact

영영 impose or collect

예문 The president cannot **levy** taxes; that is the prerogative of the legislative branch of government.
대통령은 세금을 거둘 수 없다; 그것은 의회의 특권이다.

13. mar
/ máːr /
동 손상시키다, 훼손하다
syn blemish, impair, sully, taint

영영 inflict damage or disfigure

예문 The new power station **mars** the beauty of the countryside.
새 발전소가 들어서서 그 전원 풍경을 망치고 있다.

14. partiality
/ pàːrʃiǽləti /
명 편파, 불공평, 치우침
syn prejudice, fondness

영영 the state of being partial

예문 He has a **partiality** for sweets.
그는 단것을 좋아한다.

15. ratify
/ rǽtəfài /
동 비준하다, 실증하다
syn confirm, endorse

영영 approve and give formal sanction

예문 Congress will often not **ratify** bills proposed by the President.
의회는 대통령이 제안한 법안을 종종 비준하지 않는다.

연습문제

I

1. The American Constitution says that all men are _____ with certain rights.
2. She was _____ and became the vice president.
3. The Army captain was _____ for a recent violation of military law.
4. A concert will be held to _____ the opening of the civic center.
5. Dividing a region into voting districts in a certain way is called _____ .

/ commemorate / gerrymandering / elevate / endow / degrade /

II

1. move from central to smaller areas = _____
2. charge, exact, impose = _____
3. ardent, impassioned, inflamed = _____
4. make an effort = _____
5. approve and give formal sanction to = _____

/ ratify / decentralize / endeavor / levy / fervid /

Day 23

01 acquit
/ əkwít /

동 무죄로 하다, 석방하다

syn clear, free, release

영영 declare someone not to have committed a crime

예문 People couldn't believe that the jury **acquitted** O.J. Simpson of murdering his wife.
사람들은 O.J. Simpson의 아내 살해 사건에 대해 배심원들이 그를 무죄 선언한 것을 믿을 수 없었다.

02 adhere
/ ædhíər /

동 부착하다, 집착하다

syn cling, stick, abide

영영 give support or maintain loyalty

예문 When you are in another country, you must **adhere** to their rules.
당신이 다른 나라에 있을 때 그들의 법규에 따라야 한다.

03 admonish
/ ædmániʃ /

동 책망하다, 권고하다

syn caution, criticize, reprove

영영 scold very seriously about something done wrong

예문 She was **admonished** for talking loudly with another student.
그녀는 다른 학생과 시끄럽게 이야기 하는 것 때문에 꾸지람을 들었다.

04 bestow
/ bistóu /

동 선물 주다, (존경의 뜻으로) 수여하다

syn present, award, confer

영영 give a present to someone

예문 The Queen **bestowed** a knight title to the man who saved a child.
여왕은 한 아이를 구한 남자에게 기사 작위를 수여했다.

05 blunder
/ blʌ́ndər /

명 실수

syn mistake, slip, fault

영영 a stupid mistake

예문 The greatest **blunder** in his life was divorcing his ex-wife.
그의 인생에서의 가장 큰 실수는 전 부인과 이혼한 것이었다.

06 bureaucratic
/ bjùərəkrǽtik /

형 관료주의적인

syn complicated, delaying

영영 involving complicated rules or procedures at public institutions that causes constant delays

예문 People would be scared of the **bureaucratic** omnipotents.
사람들은 관료주의적인 무소불위를 두려워할 것이다.

07 captivate
/ kǽptəvèit /

동 마음을 사로잡다

syn charm, fascinate

영영 attract and get hold of one's attention

예문 The fireworks **captivated** the young children who had never seen such things before.
그 폭죽놀이는 그같은 것을 본 적이 없는 어린 아이들을 매료시켰다.

08 chronicle
/ kránikl /

명 연대기

syn annals, chronology, record

영영 an account or record of a series of events

예문 Many scholars often regard the bible as a **chronicle** that recorded ancient history.
많은 학자들은 종종 성서를 과거의 역사를 기록한 하나의 연대기로 간주한다.

09 deplore
/ diplɔ́:r /

동 한탄한다, 탄식하다

syn condemn, denounce

영영 feel or express sorrow and disapproval for something

예문 My friend **deplored** the lack of compassion for the homeless people in our society.
나의 친구는 우리 사회에서 노숙자들에 대한 동정심 부족을 한탄했다.

10 entail
/ intéil /

동 수반하다, 일으키다

syn require, produce

영영 involve or cause as a necessary accompaniment

예문 History has taught us the lesson that liberty **entails** responsibility.
역사는 우리에게 자유에는 책임이 따른다는 교훈을 가르쳐 주었다.

11 fortitude
/ fɔ́:rtətjùːd /

명 불굴의 정신

syn strength, guts

영영 being brave especially in the face of adversity

예문 Becoming a Buddhist monk requires a great deal of zeal and **fortitude**.
불교 승려가 되는 것은 상당한 열의와 불굴의 정신을 필요로 한다.

12. genuine
/ dʒénjuin /

형 진짜의, 순종의

syn authentic, original

영영 being true and not fake

예문 The teacher felt that **genuine** paternal guidance was lacking in the child.
그 선생님은 그 아이가 진정한 부모의 지도를 받지 못하고 있다고 느꼈다.

13. increment
/ ínkrəmənt /

명 인상, (수 또는 양의) 증가

syn increase, growth

영영 the increase in the value of an object or the amount of asset

예문 According to your work performances, you will receive annual salary **increments** at the resigning of your contract.
당신의 근무실적에 따라 재계약시에 연봉 인상을 받을 수 있다.

14. indigenous
/ indídʒənəs /

형 토착의, 원산의

syn native, local

영영 originating in a region and not found anywhere else

예문 The **indigenous** peoples of America and Australia have been persecuted or killed by European settlers.
미국과 호주의 원주민들은 유럽 이주민들에 의해 박해받거나 죽임을 당했다.

15. indigent
/ índidʒənt /

형 가난한, 곤궁한

syn needy, impoverished

영영 very poor

예문 **Indigent** people often depend on the charity of others to get by.
가난한 사람들은 살아가기 위해 종종 다른 사람들의 자선에 의지한다.

연습문제

I

1. A historian often relies on ancient _____ to reconstruct history.
2. He was awarded the medal for his _____ in the battle.
3. Friendship must be based on _____ respect for the other.
4. I have a habit of _____ to not stepping on lines as I walk.
5. Divorce appears to bring with it a sudden _____ in mortality rates.

/ genuine / fortitude / chronicle / adhere / increment /

II

1. to give someone something or give a present to the person = _____
2. mistake, slip, fault = _____
3. involve, require, produce = _____
4. charm, attract, fascinate = _____
5. clear, free, release = _____

/ blunder / bestow / entail / acquit / captivate /

Day 24

01 bizarre
/ bizá:r /

형 기괴한, 이상한

syn grotesque, extraordinary

영영 very weird and strange

예문 The teacher used to tell his students some **bizarre** stories which made his class a little bit more interesting.
그 선생님은 수업을 좀 더 흥미 있게 만들려고 그의 학생들에게 괴담들을 들려주곤 했다.

02 boisterous
/ bɔ́istərəs /

형 거친, 떠들썩한, 활기찬

syn rough, noisy, lively

영영 loud and full of energy

예문 Although my wife is good-natured, she sometimes gets a bit **boisterous** and bossy to her juniors.
나의 아내는 좋은 성격의 소유자지만 후배들에게는 다소 거칠고 윗사람 행세를 한다.

03 clandestine
/ klændéstin /

형 비밀스럽게 하는

syn secret

영영 doing something with secrecy

예문 My friend and his fiancee had a **clandestine** marriage because their parents didn't consent their marriage.
나의 친구와 그의 약혼녀는 양가 부모님들이 결혼을 반대했기 때문에 비밀 결혼식을 올렸다.

04 ephemeral
/ ifémərəl /

형 하루밖에 안가는, 단명의

syn fleeting, short-lived

영영 lasting for a very short time

예문 People make new year's resolution, but it is sometimes **ephemeral**.
사람들은 새해의 결심을 세우지만 그것은 대개 얼마 가지 못한다.

05 fluctuate
/ flʌ́ktʃuèit /

동 변동하다

syn vacillate, swing

영영 move up and down or back and forth like a wave

예문 The currency value of Korean Won has **fluctuated** widely all year around.
원화 가치가 연중 내내 변동했다.

06 forlorn
/ fərlɔ́:rn /

형 버려진, 쓸쓸해 보이는

syn abandoned, hopeless

영영 lonely or alone

예문 Despite being surrounded by good people and supportive family, John felt **forlorn** and helpless.
좋은 사람들과 협조적인 가족이 곁에 있었지만, John은 외롭고 무기력했다.

07 effuse
/ ifjú:z /

동 (액체 · 빛 · 향기 따위를) 발산시키다, 방출하다

syn dispense, emit, gush

영영 pour or flow out

예문 Water was **effused** from this hole in the ground.
물이 지하의 구멍으로부터 방출되었다.

08 forum
/ fɔ́:rəm /

명 토론장, 토론회

syn debate

영영 exchange ideas and discuss on something that is a very important public issue

예문 In ancient Rome, a **forum** could be held by anyone in any place where public matters are concerned.
고대 로마에서 포럼은 중요한 사회적 문제가 있는 어느 곳 어떤 누구에 의해서라도 개최될 수 있었다.

09 indomitable
/ indάmətəbl /

형 굴복하지 않는, 불굴의

syn dauntless, iron-willed

영영 not capable of being conquered

예문 In order to succeed, one has to develop an **indomitable** spirit.
사람은 성공하기 위해서 불굴의 정신을 가져야 한다.

10 notorious
/ noutɔ́:riəs /

형 악명 높은

syn infamous, disreputable, opprobrious

영영 unfavorably known for a reason

예문 South Africa is getting a **notorious** reputation as a country of violence and lawlessness instead of one that hosted the World Cup matches.
남아공화국은 월드컵 경기를 주최한 나라가 아니라 폭력과 무법천지의 나라로서의 악명을 얻고 있다.

11 penchant
/ péntʃənt /

명 애호, 선호

syn partiality, preference, fondness

영영 having a special liking for something or a tendency to do it

예문 The principal has a **penchant** of being rude to the teachers whom he dislikes.
교장 선생님은 자기가 싫어하는 교사들에게 무례하게 행동하는 경향이 있다.

12. penetrate
/ pénətrèit /

동 관통하다, 침투하다

syn pierce, enter

영영 get into something or pass through it

예문 It is very hard for Korean products to **penetrate** Japanese market because of the prejudice.
한국 제품은 편견 때문에 일본 시장을 뚫는 것이 매우 어렵다.

13. repentant
/ ripéntənt /

형 뉘우치는, 회개하는

syn contrite, remorseful

영영 being sorry for something wrong that has been done

예문 Christians are taught to forgive sinners who are **repentant**.
기독교인들은 회개하는 사람들을 용서하도록 가르침 받는다.

14. reprehensible
/ rèprihénsəbl /

형 비난할 만한

syn despicable, deplorable

영영 very bad and morally wrong

예문 Her conduct was **reprehensible** but her heart was pure.
그녀의 행동은 비난 받아 마땅했지만 마음만큼은 순수했다.

15. serene
/ sərí:n /

형 고요한, 평화로운

syn tranquil, halcyon

영영 all quiet and calm

예문 The expression on the dead soldier's face looked surprisingly **serene**.
그 죽은 병사의 얼굴 표정은 놀라울 만큼 평온해 보였다.

연습문제

I

1. The fame that models and actresses have are oftentimes _____ .
2. He's _____ for his violent behavior.
3. She had a naturally cheerful and _____ expression.
4. After getting divorced, he really looks _____ .
5. He told me the most _____ story I had ever heard.

/ bizarre / ephemeral / notorious / forlorn / serene /

II

1. loud and full of energy = _____
2. dauntless, iron willed = _____
3. secret = _____
4. to moves up and down or back and forth like a wave = _____
5. dispense, emit, gush = _____

/ fluctuate / boisterous / clandestine / indomitable / effuse /

Day 25

01 codify / kάdəfài /
동 체계적으로 정리하다, 성문화하다
syn arrange, assort
영영 define a set of rules or present them in a clear way
예문 After a fatal car accident, the government **codified** a rule that prohibits the use of fluorescent head lights.
치명적인 자동차 사고 후 정부는 형광 헤드램프의 사용을 금지하는 법을 제정했다.

02 coerce / kouə́:rs /
동 강제하다, 위압하다
syn force, compel
영영 make somebody do something or obedient by force
예문 The defendant claims that he was being **coerced** to confess to something which he did not commit.
피고는 자신이 저지르지 않은 일을 자백하도록 강요 받았다고 주장한다.

03 deprecate / déprikèit /
동 불찬성하다, 비난하다
syn belittle, depreciate
영영 express earnest disapproval of something and criticize it
예문 Although the Korean composer has been **deprecated** recently, his works still remain influential in the music circle.
비록 그 한국인 작곡가는 최근에 비난을 받았지만 그의 작품들은 아직도 음악계에서 영향력 있다.

04 ineffable
/ inéfəbl /

형 말로 표현할 수 없는

syn unutterable

영영 so great that it can not be expressed in words

예문 The joy that Koreans felt during 2002 world cup was **ineffable**.
2002년 월드컵에서 한국인들이 느꼈던 기쁨은 말로 표현할 수 없었다.

05 inequitable
/ inékwətəbl /

형 불공평한, 불공정한

syn partial, biased

영영 unfair or unjust

예문 The main reason why communism was so wide spread in the third world nations was the **inequitable** distribution of wealth.
제3세계에서 공산주의가 만연했던 주된 이유는 불공평한 재산의 분배 때문이었다.

06 infamy
/ ínfəmi /

명 오명, 불명예

syn dishonor, notoriety

영영 being in disgrace

예문 America still regards the Japanese attack on Pearl Harbor in Hawaii as an **infamy**.
미국인들은 아직도 일본의 진주만 공격을 오명으로 여긴다.

07 laborious
/ ləbɔ́:riəs /

형 (많은 노력이 들어) 힘든

syn onerous, taxing, arduous

영영 investing a lot of time and effort because it is not easy

예문 Writing a book takes **laborious** effort and zeal.
한 권의 책을 쓰는 것은 고된 노력과 열정을 요구한다.

day 25

08 perplex
/ pərpléks /

동 당혹케 하다

syn delinquency, dereliction, negligence

영영 confuse and worry someone causing difficulty

예문 The unsolved case of five missing boys who went out to catch frogs still **perplexes** the police.
개구리를 잡으러 간 다섯 명의 실종된 아이들의 미해결 사건은 아직도 경찰을 당혹하게 하고 있다.

09 persevere
/ pə́:rsəvíər /

동 인내하다, 견디다

syn endure, bear

영영 not give up and be patient although it can get difficult at times

예문 I keep telling my students to **persevere** even if they find studying English difficult.
나는 학생들에게 영어 공부하는 것이 어렵더라도 인내하도록 말해 준다.

10 rationalize
/ rǽʃənəlàiz /

동 합리화하다, 이론적으로 설명하다

syn justify

영영 justify actions that others have problems agreeing with

예문 People try to **rationalize** their misconduct because they feel guilty.
사람들은 죄책감을 느끼기 때문에 자신들의 잘못된 행동을 정당화하려 한다.

11 repulse
/ ripʌ́ls /

동 구역질나게 하다, (공격을) 물리치다

syn repel, reject, thwart

영영 cause to feel intense distaste

예문 I was **repulsed** by sight and smell of the spoiled food in the pot.
나는 냄비 안의 상한 음식의 모양새와 냄새에 구역질이 났다.

12. solicitous
/səlísətəs/ — 형 걱정하는, 열심인
syn concerned, attentive

영영 concerned and anxious over something

예문 The students seemed extremely **solicitous** over their grades.
학생들은 그들의 성적에 대해 매우 신경 쓰는 것처럼 보였다.

13. solidarity
/sàlədǽrəti/ — 명 결속, 연대
syn unity, unification, accord

영영 a strong support for one another that helps people to achieve their goal

예문 The **solidarity** of Korean people that they showed at the time of financial crisis can not be found in Greece which is experiencing the same crisis.
금융 위기에서 보여준 한국인들의 결속을 같은 양상의 위기를 겪고 있는 그리스에서는 발견할 수 없다.

14. transgress
/trænsgrés/ — 동 (도덕적으로) 벗어나다
syn violate

영영 conduct or deed gets out of line and become morally unacceptable

예문 It is the parents' duty to mind their children's conduct not to **transgress** the bounds of decency.
아이들의 행동이 무례함의 경계를 넘어서지 않도록 돌보는 것은 부모들의 의무이다.

15. transient
/trǽnʃənt/ — 형 일시적인, 순간적인
syn fleeting, temporary

영영 lasting only for a short time and passing through

예문 Buddhist monks teach people not to concern themselves over worldly affairs as the life itself is **transient**.
불교 승려들은 사람들에게 삶 자체가 일시적이기 때문에 세속적인 문제에 신경 쓰지 않도록 가르친다.

연습문제

I

1. People seem to think that they can easily _____ celebrities and say bad things about them.
2. It requires measuring a _____ event occurring in a few milliseconds.
3. A new law was _____ to prevent domestic violence.
4. The union leaders appealed for workers' _____.
5. I was very _____ when I heard that you were leaving town.

/ solidarity / deprecate / codify / perplex / transient /

II

1. too great to be expressed in words = _____
2. concerned, attentive = _____
3. unfair, unjust = _____
4. force, compel = _____
5. onerous, taxing, arduous = _____

/ solicitous / inequitable / ineffable / laborious / coerce /

Day 26

01 aggrieved
/ əgríːvd /
형 분개한, 억울해 하는
syn distressed, wronged, injured

영영 upset about being mistreated

예문 The decision by Japanese government to refuse the war compensation request has made many people feel **aggrieved**.
일본 정부가 전쟁 보상 요청을 거절한 결정은 많은 사람들을 분개하게 만들었다.

02 agnostic
/ ægnástik /
명 회의론자, 불가지론자
syn skeptic, atheist

영영 someone that is suspicious about a theory

예문 I grew up in an **agnostic** household, which didn't help me bring myself to believe in God.
나는 무신론자 집안에서 자랐고 신을 믿을 수 있는 기회가 없었다.

03 colloquial
/ kəlóukwiəl /
형 일상적인 대화체의
syn informal

영영 used in familiar and informal conversation

예문 The **colloquial** and slang expressions of Australia are unique.
호주의 구어체 표현과 속어는 독특하다.

04 combustion

/ kəmbʌ́stʃən /

명 연소, 격동

syn burning

영영 the act or process of burning

예문 A cigarette butt initiated the **combustion** of volatile substance near the gas station.
담배꽁초가 주유소 가까이 있는 휘발성 물질에 불을 지폈다.

05 deter

/ ditə́:r /

동 제지하다, 만류하다, 단념시키다

syn discourage, inhibit

영영 discourage or stop in carrying out an action

예문 We must do everything in our power to **deter** North Korea from committing another terror.
우리는 북한이 다른 테러를 저지르는 것을 막기 위해 우리가 할 수 있는 모든 것을 해야 한다.

06 deteriorate

/ ditíəriərèit /

동 악화되다, 저하되다

syn decline, worsen, degenerate

영영 become progressively worse

예문 The relationship between Korea and Japan **deteriorated** when some Japanese politicians claimed an ownership on an island that every Korean calls Dokdo.
한일 관계는 몇몇 일본 정치가들이 모든 한국인이 독도라고 부르는 한 섬에 대한 영유권을 주장했을 때 악화되었다.

07 inhibit

/ inhíbit /

동 금지하다, 억제하다

syn hinder, constrain, frustrate

영영 prevent or restrain something from happening

예문 There is some fear that the environmental controls will **inhibit** industrial progress.
자연환경 통제가 산업의 발달을 막을 것이라는 두려움이 조금 있다.

08 initiate
/ iníʃièit /

동 시작하다, 가입하다

syn begin, start, open

영영 let something happen or accept someone into a group

예문 The Thai government **initiated** several steps to put an end to the civil unrest in Bangkok.
태국 정부는 방콕에서의 사회불안을 해소하기 위해 몇 가지 조치를 취하기 시작했다.

09 ostensible
/ ɑsténsəbl /

형 외면의, 표면의

syn apparent, seemingly

영영 describing an outwardly appearance

예문 In the beginning of westward movement in America, the **ostensible** purpose for giving lands to the settlers was to develop, which proved to be false.
미국에서 서부 개척시대에 정착민들에게 땅을 나눠준 외견상 목적은 땅을 개발하는 것이었지만 그것은 명목에 불과했다.

10 pertinacious
/ pə́ːrtənéiʃəs /

형 굽히지 않는, 완고한

syn stubborn, persistent

영영 not giving up one's work and continuing to do it

예문 People elected him as their new president because they believed his **pertinacious** attitude will help to get rid of the corruption in their country.
그의 소신 있는 태도가 나라의 부패 척결에 도움이 되리라 여겨져 사람들은 그를 새 대통령으로 선출했다.

11 perverse
/ pərvə́ːrs /

형 (사고방식이) 비뚤어진, 괴팍한

syn stubborn, obstinate, dogged

영영 insisting on doing things in irrational way that can bring negative results

예문 He has a **perverse** way of thinking that causes conflicts with the people around him.
그는 자신 주변에 있는 사람들과 충돌을 일으키는 비뚤어진 사고방식을 가지고 있다.

12 perfunctory

/ pərfʌ́ŋktəri /

형 형식적인, 마지못한

syn cursory

영영 showing only a little enthusiasm in relationship with other people

예문 His attitude toward others seems **perfunctory** and mechanical.
다른 사람을 향한 그의 태도는 형식적이고 기계적으로 보인다.

13 permeate

/ pə́:rmièit /

동 스며들다, 침투하다, 퍼지다

syn infiltrate, permeate

영영 spread throughout something

예문 If a sense of shame **permeates** into the mind of a student, he or she is likely to fail the study.
학생의 마음에 자괴감이 생기면 그 학생은 공부를 실패할 가능성이 있다.

14 revoke

/ rivóuk /

동 취소하다, 철회하다

syn cancel, withdraw

영영 cancel or take back the right of a project

예문 The franchise **revoked** the license of a franchisee due to its poor performance.
그 프랜차이즈는 한 가맹점의 부진한 매출 때문에 면허를 박탈했다.

15 rendition

/ rendíʃən /

명 연출, 연주, 번역

syn performance, interpretation

영영 a play or a performance of music

예문 The audience praised the beautiful **rendition** of orchestra that played Verdi's 'Aida.'
관객은 베르디의 아이다를 연출한 그 오케스트라의 아름다운 연주를 칭찬했다.

연습문제

I

1. I tried to _____ him from committing a suicide but he didn't listen to me.
2. The society _____ a powerful anti-cancer campaign.
3. The government has _____ its permission for them to enter the country.
4. Although every other member of her family was an _____, she grew a devout faith in religion.
5. The car rolled off the edge of the highway, turned over, and then burst into _____ .

/ initiated / revoked / agnostic / combustion / deter /

II

1. decline, worsen, degenerate = _____
2. try to prevent something from happening = _____
3. stubborn, obstinate, dogged = _____
4. apparent, seemingly = _____
5. involving or using conversation = _____

/ ostensible / inhibit / pertinacious / colloquial / deteriorate /

Day 27

01 enthrall
/ inθrɔ́ːl /

동 매료시키다, 사로잡다

syn capture, enslave

영영 charm or hold someone spellbound

예문 It is every teacher's wish to **enthrall** a large group of students and leave a lasting impression.
많은 학생들을 매료시키고 오래 남는 인상을 주는 것은 모든 교사의 바램이다.

02 entice
/ intáis /

동 유인하다, 유혹하다

syn lure, attract, tempt

영영 persuade someone with an offer of pleasure or reward

예문 The picture of delicious looking noodle on the restaurant entrance **enticed** many passers-by.
식당 출입구의 맛있어 보이는 국수의 사진은 많은 행인들을 유혹했다.

03 innate
/ inéit /

형 타고난, 선천적인

syn inborn, inherent

영영 natural and not taught but be born with

예문 Some birds have an **innate** tendency to mate for life.
어떤 새들은 평생 동안 짝짓기하는 습성이 있다.

04 lethal
/ líːθəl /

형 치사의, 치명적인

syn fatal, deadly, terminal

영영 quite deadly or negative

예문 A person trained in Taekwondo can deliver **lethal** kicks with their feet.
태권도를 훈련 받은 사람은 소위 치명적 발차기를 할 수 있다.

05 pertain
/ pərtéin /

동 속하다, 적용하다

syn belong, apply

영영 belong to something

예문 His long discourse did not **pertain** to the reason for our meeting.
그의 긴 담화는 우리 회의의 논지에 해당되지 않는 것이었다.

06 scrupulous
/ skrúːpjuləs /

형 세심한, 꼼꼼한

syn meticulous, careful

영영 painstakingly going through all the necessary steps without errors

예문 His **scrupulous** attention to detail and subtlety makes him an excellent artist.
세부적인 것과 섬세함에 대한 그의 세심한 관심은 그를 아주 훌륭한 화가로 만든다.

07 tenacious
/ tənéiʃəs /

형 집요한, 완강한

syn stubborn, persistent

영영 insistent on doing something and not accepting others' suggestion

예문 The national soccer team of Korea is known to be **tenacious** and unrelenting, and such characteristics make other countries to hold them in high regards.
한국 축구 대표팀은 집요하고 멈추지 않은 것으로 알려져 있고 그와 같은 특징들은 다른 나라들의 존경을 산다.

08 tenure
/ténjər/

명 보유(기간, 조건), 소유, 유지

syn maintain

영영 an official term one can hold for a duration of time

예문 Unlike those in Korea, American university professors must earn their **tenure** through thesis and pursuing projects.
한국과는 달리 미국 대학 교수들은 논문과 프로젝트에 참여하는 것을 통해 재신임을 얻어야 한다.

09 ventilate
/véntəlèit/

동 통풍하다, 환기시키다

syn air

영영 allow the free expression of all sides, let fresh air in

예문 It is a must that a laboratory should be **ventilated** after an experiment.
실험 후 실험실을 환기시키는 것은 필수다.

10 veracity
/vəræsəti/

명 진실, 정직, 진상

syn truthfulness, truth

영영 a quality that carries truth only

예문 The **veracity** of a witness is what the prosecuting office demands.
검찰이 원하는 것은 증인의 진실이다.

11 verbose
/vəːrbóus/

형 말 많은, 수다스런

syn wordy, talkative

영영 speaking more than what one is supposed to speak

예문 When angry, my teacher has the weird tendency of being **verbose**, instead of harsh yelling or criticism.
화가 날 때 나의 선생님은 심한 고함이나 비난을 하는 것이 아니라 말이 많아지는 이상한 경향이 있다.

12. wrongful
/ ˈrɔːŋfəl /

형 부당한, 불법의

syn unjust, unlawful

영영 unjust and morally wrong which can not be justified

예문 Confronted with undeniable evidence, the suspect in the murder case confessed to the **wrongful** act of killing his wife.
부인할 수 없는 증거를 맞닥뜨리자 그 살인 용의자는 아내를 죽인 도덕적으로 부당한 행위를 자백했다.

13. xenophobia
/ ˌzènəfóubiə /

명 (외국(인)에 대한) 혐오

syn racism

영영 It is an irrational hatred or fear of strangers or foreigners

예문 Almost everyone I met in Russia seems to carry some degree of **xenophobia**.
내가 러시아에서 만난 대부분의 사람은 어느 정도 외국인 혐오증을 가지고 있는 것처럼 보였다.

14. yearn
/ jə́ːrn /

동 열망하다

syn long, desire

영영 want something desperately and long persistently

예문 Throughout my years in overseas, I **yearned** for the day when I would go home and be with my friends and family.
해외에 있는 동안 나는 집에 가서 친구와 가족들과 함께 할 날을 간절히 원했다.

15. zealot
/ zélət /

명 열중하는 사람, 광신자

syn fanatic

영영 a person who displays a fanatical devotion for someone or a belief

예문 In order to be a successful teacher online, you have to have some **zealots** who follow you and tell good things about you.
온라인에서 성공적인 선생님이 되기 위해서 당신은 당신을 따라다니며 좋은 이야기를 하는 열성팬들을 가져야 한다.

연습문제

I

1. He cleans the house in a very _____ way, following every step and not leaving any dust behind.
2. I _____ for the day that I can actually be in space.
3. A person trained in martial arts can deliver _____ blows by hand.
4. Her natural beauty is an _____ weapon of hers.
5. This room stinks. Let's _____ this place.

/ yearn / innate / ventilate / lethal / scrupulous /

II

1. charm or hold someone spellbound = _____
2. an irrational hatred or fear of strangers = _____
3. unjust and morally wrong = _____
4. lure, attract, tempt = _____
5. fanatic, radical = _____

/ zealot / wrongful / enthrall / xenophobia / entice /

Day 28

01 absurd
/ æbsə́:rd /

형 어리석은, 불합리한, 우스꽝스런

syn foolish, ridiculous, unreasonable

영영 looking silly, stupid and crazy

예문 It is **absurd** that I bend over backward and do everything for them.
내가 그들을 위해 시키는 대로 다하고 그들을 위해 모든 것을 다하는 것은 어리석다.

02 accomplice
/ əkámplis /

명 공범, 연루자

syn accessory, conspirator

영영 someone who helps another person commit a crime

예문 Police apprehended an **accomplice** to the robbery who was waiting in a parked car outside the bank.
경찰은 은행 바깥에 주차한 차안에서 기다리고 있던 강도 공범을 체포했다.

03 accumulate
/ əkjú:mjulèit /

동 모으다, 축적하다

syn build up, increase, store

영영 save constantly to make asset become greater in quantity

예문 For the past one year, I have **accumulated** enough information to write a book.
지난 일 년간 나는 책을 쓰기 위해 충분한 정보를 축적했다.

04 anguish
/ ǽŋgwiʃ /

명 격통, 고뇌, 고민

syn agony, suffering, distress

영영 an extreme sadness that one goes through when faced with great hardships

예문 The families of victims in the air crash were in great **anguish**.
비행기 사고의 유족들은 큰 슬픔에 빠져 있었다.

05 beckon
/ békən /

동 고개를 끄덕이다, 신호하다

syn gesture, sign, wave

영영 give the signal for someone to follow or do something

예문 I **beckoned** my son to follow me when I saw him falling behind.
나는 아들이 뒤처지는 것을 봤을 때 나를 따라오도록 손짓했다.

06 benevolence
/ bənévələns /

명 자비심, 박애, 선행

syn mercy, philanthropy

영영 a showing of kindness to give and help others

예문 Had it not been for the **benevolence** of my teacher, I would not have been able to graduate from high school.
나의 선생님의 자비심이 아니었더라면 나는 고등학교에서 졸업하지 못했을 것이다.

07 decree
/ dikríː /

동 포고하다, 판결하다

syn order, rule, command

영영 issue a legally binding command that everyone must respect

예문 What the emperor **decrees** is a rule that everyone must obey.
황제가 포고하는 것은 모든 사람이 복종해야하는 법령이다.

08 discomfit

/ diskʌ́mfit /

동 좌절시키다, 당황케 하다

syn thwart, baffle, disconcert

영영 make someone get confused

예문 The hostility and friendship gesture that North Korea displays toward South Korea *discomfits* many.
북한이 남한에게 보여주는 적대감과 그에 상반된 우호적 제스처가 많은 사람들을 당황하게 만든다.

09 discrete

/ diskríːt /

형 따로따로의, 별개의

syn separate

영영 different from others

예문 These days, the grammarians avoid testing *discrete* points only, but prefer context.
요즘의 문법학자들은 낱낱의 부분들만 다루는 것을 피하고 맥락을 중요시한다.

10 forebode

/ fɔːrbóud /

동 예감하다, ~의 전조가 되다

syn forecast, portend

영영 sense the outcome of the work, or show a sign of what is to come

예문 The oracles at delphi *foreboded* the ill fortune of Spartan King, Leonidas.
그 델파이 사원의 사제들은 스파르타의 왕 레오니다스의 암울한 미래를 예언했다.

11 forego

/ fɔːrgóu /

동 멀리하다, 삼가다

syn forgo

영영 do without

예문 I really like the dog but I must *forego* the woman.
나는 그 개를 좋아하지만 여자는 별로야.

12. inauspicious

/ ìnɔːspíʃəs /

형 불길한, 불운한

syn ill-omened

영영 a sign of something that could be unfortunate

예문 In some cultures, it is **inauspicious** to see one's dead relatives or parents in his or her dream.
어떤 문화에서는 자신의 죽은 친척이나 부모들을 보는 것은 불길한 징조이다.

13. perturb

/ pərtə́ːrb /

동 교란하다, 동요하게 하다

syn agitate, alarm

영영 make someone get worried a lot

예문 During my lesson, I got quite **perturbed** at a sleeping student.
나는 수업 도중에 자고 있는 학생에게 매우 화가 났다.

14. philanthropic

/ fìlənθrápik /

형 인정 많은, 인자한

syn charitable, giving

영영 very compassionate and caring for others

예문 The music concert which was aired on a TV channel yesterday was for a **philanthropic** purpose.
어제 TV에 방영된 음악 콘서트는 자선이 그 목적이었다.

15. ravage

/ rǽvidʒ /

동 황폐화시키다, 파괴하다

syn damage, despoil, ruin

영영 destroy something completely and make it irreparable

예문 Despite the public education and campaign, the rain forests of the world are being **ravaged**.
대중 교육과 캠페인에도 불구하고 세계의 열대우림 숲들은 황폐화되고 있다.

연습문제

I

1. It's _____ to believe the earth is flat.
2. The mother waited in _____ for news of her missing child.
3. He _____ me to come play with him.
4. The _____ of Mother Theresa is known all over the world.
5. Tom experienced a state of _____ after being hounded by a pack of extremely meddlesome reporters.

/ benevolence / beckon / absurd / discomfit / anguish /

II

1. separate, detached = _____
2. charitable, giving = _____
3. agitate, alarm = _____
4. mercy, philanthropy = _____
5. accessory, conspirator = _____

/ accomplice / discrete / perturb / philanthropic / benevolence /

Day 29

01
adroit / ədrɔ́it /
형 능숙한, 노련한
syn **deft, skillful**

영영 being skillful in handling affairs or management of a relationship

예문 His **adroit** use of computer programs helped to get the attention from a company and get scouted.
컴퓨터 프로그램의 능숙한 사용이 한 회사의 관심을 사 그는 스카우트되었다.

02
adulterate / ədʌ́ltərèit /
동 품질을 떨어뜨리다, 섞음질을 하다
syn **degrade, lower, debase, corrupt**

영영 get something mixed with an original content and drop its quality

예문 I didn't realize that the milk I put outside of the fridge was **adulterated** due to the heat.
나는 냉장고 밖에 놓아둔 우유가 더위 때문에 상한 것을 몰랐다.

03
advent / ǽdvent, -vənt /
명 (중요한 인물·사건 등의) 도래, 출현
syn **arrival, appearance**

영영 an important event or invention coming into existence

예문 Long before, scientists predicted the **advent** of wireless phone which is now called a cell phone.
오래 전부터 전문가들은 오늘날의 핸드폰이라 불리는 무선 전화기의 출현을 예고했다.

04 bias
/ báiəs /

형 선입견, 편견

syn prejudice, leaning, tendency

영영 tendency to prefer one thing or a person over the other and discriminating as such

예문 I treat students without **bias** against their personal attributes.
나는 각자의 개인 자질에 대한 편견이 없이 학생들을 다룬다.

05 clarify
/ klǽrəfài /

동 분명하게 하다

syn define, elucidate

영영 make something very clear or explain oneself for others

예문 We will give you one more chance to **clarify** yourself.
우리는 당신에게 스스로를 해명하기 위한 기회를 한 번 더 줄 것이다.

06 encompass
/ inkʌ́mpəs /

동 둘러싸다, 포위하다

syn surround, include, hold

영영 encircle, envelop and contain other things

예문 The new housing project is going to **encompass** the entire neighbourhood in the area.
새로운 주택 프로젝트는 그 구역 전체를 포함할 것이다.

07 endowment
/ indáumənt /

명 기증, 기부, 재능

syn talent, charity

영영 money usually given to charities by an organization or rich individuals

예문 Until now, the orphanage has depended on the generous **endowment** from its supporters.
지금까지 그 고아원은 후원자들로부터의 후한 기부금에 의존해 왔다.

08 ghastly
/ gǽstli /

형 무서운, 유령의, 희미한

syn horrible, shocking, terrible

영영 so scary and horrible

예문 Police found the murder scene so **ghastly** that they couldn't stop talking about it afterwards.
경찰은 그 살인 현장이 너무 끔찍해서 나중에도 그것이 회자되었다.

09 hallucination
/ həlù:sənéiʃən /

명 환각

syn illusion

영영 an experience of seeing something that is not real

예문 Sometimes the patients experience **hallucination** when they take pain killers.
가끔씩 환자들이 진통제를 먹으면 환각 증세를 경험한다.

10 hasten
/ héisn /

동 서두르게 하다, 재촉하다

syn hurry, rush

영영 make someone hurry with work

예문 The principal **hastened** her teachers to complete the compiling process of student records.
그 교장은 교사들이 학생 기록 정리 작업을 빨리 마치도록 재촉했다.

11 hemisphere
/ hémisfiər /

명 (지구의) 반구

syn half

영영 the upper part or lower part of the globe

예문 The rich countries are all located in the northern **hemisphere**.
잘사는 나라들은 대부분 북반구에 위치해 있다.

12. impose

/ impóuz /

동 부과하다, 과하다

syn levy, charge

영영 force something unwelcome

예문 The government *imposes* tax on all sold goods in its country.
정부는 나라 안에서 팔리는 모든 물건들에 세금을 부과한다.

13. imprint

/ ímprint /

동 찍다, 각인하다

syn engrave, print

영영 leave a lasting impression

예문 It is important not to show horrible things to the children as such images will be *imprinted* on their memory.
아이들에게 있어 끔찍한 것은 기억에 새겨지기 때문에 그런 것들을 보여주지 않는 것이 중요하다.

14. inclusive

/ inklú:siv /

형 포함하여, 모든 것을 포함한

syn comprising, comprehensive

영영 being included in a process

예문 The cost of the school excursion is *inclusive* of motel, meals, and transportation costs.
학교 수학여행의 비용은 모텔, 식사, 교통비를 포함한다.

15. lukewarm

/ lú:kwɔ́:rm /

형 미지근한

syn tepid

영영 slightly warm

예문 You have to make sure that the water your child bathe is *lukewarm*.
당신은 당신의 아이가 목욕하는 물이 살짝 따뜻하도록 해야 한다.

연습문제

I

1. Am I looking at a _____ or have you really come back from the dead?
2. It is a quite well-known fact that _____ foods like kimchi are good for preventing cancer.
3. Only if I had been given one more chance to _____ myself, I wouldn't be hated by everyone else by now.
4. I was _____ myself not to be late.
5. The cost of the hotel is _____ of service fees and VAT.

/ hasten / hallucination / clarify / inclusive / adulterate /

II

1. make something very clear = _____
2. prejudice for or against something = _____
3. skillful, deft = _____
4. levy, charge = _____
5. surround, include, hold = _____

/ adroit / clarify / impose / bias / encompass /

Day 30

01 condone
/ kəndóun /
동 용서하다, 너그럽게 보아주다
syn excuse, forgive, pardon

영영 overlook or forgive one's faults by being understanding

예문 Now that sometime has passed, I can **condone** my brother's double sideness, for which I hated him.
이제 시간이 좀 흘렀으므로 나는 내 동생의 가증스러웠던 양면성을 용서해 줄 수 있다.

02 confine
/ kənfáin /
동 제한하다, 가둬넣다
syn enclose, isolate, jail

영영 keep or hold, restrict something within limits

예문 Please **confine** the subject of your talk to the topic.
제발 당신이야기의 주제를 이야기의 주제에 한정시키십시오.

03 dawdle
/ dɔ́:dl /
동 빈둥거리다, 시간을 헛되이 보내다
syn waste time, loiter

영영 spend time wastefully or stay idly

예문 I always **dawdle** around a TV when it is time to go and miss my bus.
나는 가야 할 시간에 항상 TV 앞에서 시간을 보내고 버스를 놓친다.

04 decisive
/ disáisiv /

형 결정적인

syn crucial, critical

영영 very important for the final result of a particular situation

예문 Domination over the sky of Korean peninsular was the **decisive** factor in deterring North Korean advance.
한반도 영공의 장악은 북한의 진격을 막는 데 결정적인 요소였다.

05 defy
/ difái /

동 도전하다, 문제 삼지 않다

syn confront, resist, oppose

영영 show no fear or respect

예문 Many parents do not expect the day when their children would **defy** them.
많은 부모들은 자녀들이 자기네에게 감히 도전할 날이 오는 것을 기대하지 않는다.

06 detest
/ ditést /

동 싫어하다, 혐오하다

syn loathe

영영 dislike someone or something so much

예문 I **detest** a person who does not put in his or her best but idles around.
나는 자기의 최선을 다하지 않고 빈둥거리는 사람을 싫어한다.

07 ensue
/ insú: /

동 후에 결과로서 일어나다

syn befall, follow, result

영영 happen as a result right afterwards an incident

예문 My only problem is that I speak my mind whatever it is and not care what might **ensue** afterwards.
나의 유일한 문제는 어떤 일이 결과로 일어나든 상관하지 않고 내 마음속에 있는 것을 무엇이든지 말한다는 것이다.

08 feasibility
/ fíːzəbíliti /

명 실행가능성

syn possibility, viability

영영 the ability to succeed in an operation

예문 The **feasibility** of project to relocate a government office to a local province is not yet certain due to many oppositions.
정부 청사를 지방으로 이전하는 계획의 실현은 많은 반대 때문에 아직 확실하지 않다.

09 ferocious
/ fəróuʃəs /

형 사나운, 모진, 지독한

syn fierce, savage, violent

영영 very violent and fierce, quite often dangerous

예문 Many people don't know that badgers are one of the most **ferocious** animals on earth, as they are unrelenting and courageous.
포기할 줄 모르는 용맹한 성격 때문에 오소리가 세상에서 가장 사나운 동물들 중의 하나라는 사실은 많은 사람들이 모른다.

10 formidable
/ fɔ́ːrmidəbl /

형 무서운, 무시무시한

syn menacing, threatening

영영 imposing serious difficulties so that one has hard time going against it

예문 The national soccer team of Argentina looks very **formidable** compared to other teams of the group.
아르헨티나 축구 국가대표팀은 그 조의 다른 팀과 비교해서 매우 강력해 보인다.

11 hoist
/ hɔ́ist /

동 (기 등을) 올리다, 감아올리다

syn raise

영영 raise or lift (a flag)

예문 To celebrate the independence day, practically all the people **hoisted** the national flags outside in their lawns.
독립기념일을 축하하기 위하여 거의 모든 사람이 그들의 마당에 국기를 올렸다.

day by day I 207

12 impair

/ impέər /

동 해치다, 손상시키다

syn damage, worsen

영영 inflict a damage

예문 His hearing was **impaired** when he got over the age of 70.
그가 70세를 넘어서면서 청각이 손상되었다.

13 indicative

/ indíkətiv /

형 표시하는, 나타내는

syn expressing, displaying

영영 giving a look at the possible outcome

예문 Cloudy night sky is an **indicative** sign of rainy weather.
구름이 낀 밤하늘은 비가 온다는 징조이다.

14 industrious

/ indʌ́striəs /

형 근면한, 부지런한

syn assiduous, hard-working

영영 working really hard

예문 The main reason Korea could rise from the ashes of war was the **industrious** nature of its people.
전쟁의 잿더미 속에서 한국이 일어날 수 있었던 주된 이유는 근면한 국민성 때문이었다.

15 infinity

/ infínəti /

명 무한

syn endlessness, infinitude

영영 having no end in value and boundaries

예문 The ancients believed that sky was stretched to **infinity** but we know it is not true.
고대인들은 하늘이 무한대까지 뻗어 있다고 믿었지만 우리는 이것이 사실이 아닌 것을 안다.

연습문제

I

1. One could _____ his mistake but not his arrogance.
2. Many Korean people _____ chess simply because they don't understand the rules of the game.
3. If I had known what would _____ afterwards, I wouldn't have said that.
4. A little _____ is enough to challenge myself.
5. Your problems seem less _____ and easier to solve.

/ feasibility / condone / formidable / ensue / detest /

II

1. fierce, savage, violent = _____
2. assiduous, hard-working = _____
3. enclose, isolate, jail = _____
4. damage, worsen = _____
5. waste time, loiter = _____

/ dawdle / industrious / ferocious / impair / confine /

SAving Time
SAT Vocabulary

day by day II

Day 1

01 albeit
/ ɔːlbíːit /

접 비록 ~일지라도

syn though

영영 to introduce a fact or comment which reduces the force of what you have just said

예문 ***Albeit*** slowly, he recovered from his illness.
비록 느리지만 그는 질병으로부터 회복했다.

02 macabre
/ məkáːbrə /

형 섬뜩한, 으스스한

syn frightening, terrifying, gruesome

영영 strange and horrible or upsetting, usually because it involves death or injury

예문 Tom has a knack for telling stories of ***macabre*** in nature.
톰은 섬뜩한 이야기를 말하는 재주가 있다.

03 bail
/ béil /

명 동 보석(금), 보석으로 풀어주다

syn security, bond, guarantee

영영 a sum of money that an arrested person puts forward as a guarantee

예문 The man who was accused of murdering his ex-wife was released on ***bail*** despite many protests from the prosecution.
전처를 살해한 의심을 받고 있는 그 남자는 검사측의 반대에도 불구하고 보석금으로 풀려났다.

04 natal
/ néitl /

형 출생의 (명사 앞에서만 씀)

syn of birth

영영 of or relating to birth

예문 The police claimed that the woman who murdered her baby was suffering from the post-***natal*** depression.
경찰은 아기를 죽인 여자가 산후 우울증을 겪고 있었다고 주장했다.

05 calamity
/ kəlǽməti /

명 재앙, 재난

syn disaster, misery, misfortune

영영 an event that causes a great deal of damage or personal distress

예문 The earthquake that hit Chile was recorded as the worst ***calamity*** in the 21st century.
칠레를 강타한 지진은 21세기 최악의 자연 재난으로 기록되었다.

06 cadre
/ kǽdri /

명 간부단, 핵심그룹

syn main, vital, the core

영영 a small group of people who have been specially organized for a particular purpose

예문 ***Cadres*** from naval academy came to our college to gather new recruits.
해군사관학교의 핵심 간부단 일원들이 새로운 모집인원을 충당하기 위해 우리학교로 왔다.

07 objurgate
/ ábdʒərgèit /

타 비난하다, 책망하다

syn criticize, rebuke, reprimand

영영 scold or tell off

예문 The CEO of the company ***objurgated*** his subordinates for the task entrusted upon them not being managed in satisfactory manner.
그 회사의 최고 경영자는 부하직원들에게 맡긴 일이 잘 관리되지 않은 것에 대해 그들을 꾸짖었다.

08 dainty

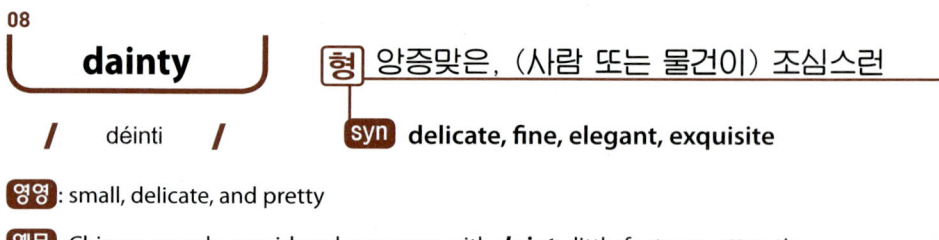

/ déinti / **syn** delicate, fine, elegant, exquisite

영영: small, delicate, and pretty

예문 Chinese people considered a woman with **dainty** little feet very attractive.
중국 사람들은 조그맣고 섬세한 발을 가진 여성을 매력적으로 여겼다.

09 daub

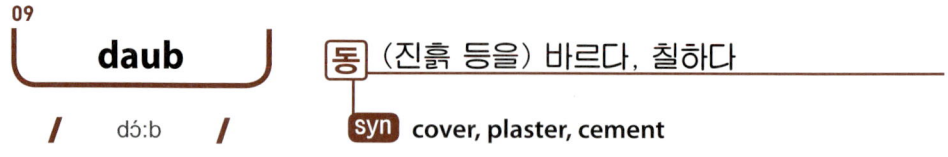

/ dɔ́:b / **syn** cover, plaster, cement

영영 you spread a substance on something in a rough or careless way

예문 The walls of the old temples in Greece might have been **daubed** with rhyme stone powders.
그리스에 있는 고대 신전들의 벽들은 석회석 가루로 발라졌을 것이다.

10 ebb

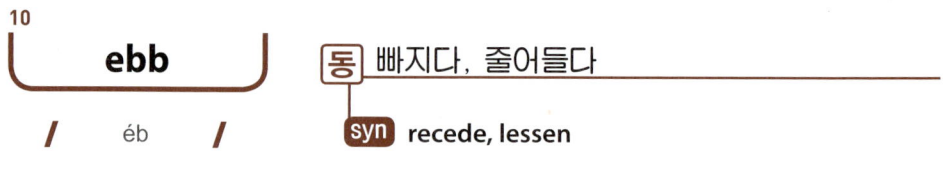

/ éb / **syn** recede, lessen

영영 something's level gradually falls

예문 Her memory of the past began to **ebb** away as Parkinson's disease slowly took its hold on her.
파킨슨병 증세가 심해지면서 그녀의 과거 기억은 사라지기 시작했다.

11 ebullient

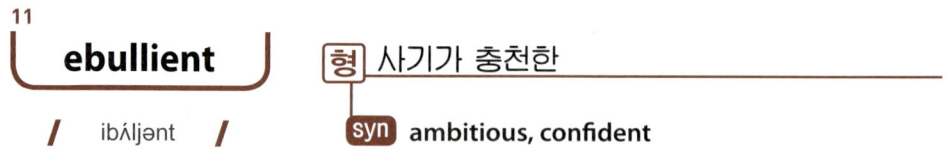

/ ibʌ́ljənt / **syn** ambitious, confident

영영 being lively and full of enthusiasm or excitement

예문 The classroom was filled with **ebullient** mood as they were told to leave early.
그 교실은 일찍 귀가 조치가 내려지자 신나는 분위기가 되었다.

12 galore

/ gəlóːr /

형 풍부한, 많은 (명사 뒤에서)

syn abundant, plenty, ample

영영 something you like existing in very large quantities

예문 Come spring, there will be tourists **galore** from Japan, who are intent on purchasing many souvenirs.
봄이 오면 많은 기념품을 사려고 많은 일본인 관광객들이 올 것이다.

13 haggle

/ hǽgl /

동 흥정하다

syn negotiate, bargain with

영영 argue about something before reaching an agreement

예문 Much noise was coming from a shop where there were a bunch of people **haggling** over the price of some goods.
물건 가격을 두고 흥정하고 있는 사람들이 있어서 가게가 시끌벅적했다.

14 hauteur

/ houtə́ːr /

명 거만한 태도

syn arrogance

영영 behavior which is proud and arrogant

예문 People were put off by the **hauteur** of the movie star.
사람들은 그 영화배우의 거만한 태도에 실망했다.

15 idiosyncrasy

/ ìdiəsíŋkrəsi /

명 특이한 성격

syn eccentricity

영영 rather unusual habits or characteristics

예문 Van Gough's painting works reveal his **idiosyncrasy** and talent.
반 고흐의 그림 작품들은 그의 특이한 성격과 재능을 보여준다.

Day 2

01 **maelstrom**
/ méilstrəm /

명 대혼란, 소용돌이

syn mayhem, pandemonium, snafu

영영 being very confused or violent

예문 We are living in a political **maelstrom**.
우리는 정치적인 대혼란 속에서 살고 있습니다.

02 **nadir**
/ néidər /

명 최하점, 최저점

syn the worst

영영 the lowest or most unsuccessful point in a situation

예문 When he failed to get the promotion, he felt it was the **nadir** of his career.
그가 승진을 받지 못했을 때 그는 그의 이력에 있어 최악의 슬럼프라고 느꼈다.

03 **nefarious**
/ nifέəriəs /

형 범죄의, 악한

syn immoral, amoral

영영 wicked and criminal

예문 Korean government is trying to curb the **nefarious** dealings of organized crime syndicates.
한국 정부는 범죄 조직 단체의 불법적 거래를 억제하기 위해 노력하고 있다.

04 obfuscate
/ ábfəskèit /   syn confuse, stir

동 애매하게 만들다, 혼란스럽게 만들다

영영 deliberately make something seem confusing and difficult to understand

예문 You are trying to **obfuscate** others by dragging in irrelevant facts.
너는 타당하지 않은 사실을 끌어들여서 다른 사람들을 혼란스럽게 만들고 있다.

05 palliate
/ pǽlièit /   syn alleviate, mitigate

동 임시로 통증을 완화시키다

영영 lessen the severity of pain without curing or removing

예문 Terminally ill patients are given dosages of drug to **palliate** excruciating pain.
말기 환자들에게 극심한 고통을 일시적으로나마 완화시키기 위해 마약들이 투여된다.

06 quandary
/ kwándəri /   syn predicament

명 진퇴양난, 곤경

영영 a state of perplexity or uncertainty

예문 Alex appears to be in a **quandary** about what to do with his asset management.
알렉스는 그의 자산운용을 어떻게 해야 할지 갈피를 못 잡는 것처럼 보인다.

07 quibble
/ kwíbl /   syn grouse

명 동 사소한 불만, 옥신각신하다

영영 petty and small complaints over nothing

예문 It doesn't help a politician to get too concerned over minor **quibbles** from people if he is to see carry out his policies.
정치인이 그의 정책들을 관철되게 함에 있어 사람들의 사소한 불만에 너무 신경을 쓰는 것은 도움이 되지 않는다.

08 rabid

/ ræbid /

형 맹렬한, 과격한, 열광적인

syn crazed

영영 having very strong and unreasonable opinions or beliefs about a subject

예문 Palestinians carry the **rabid** hatred of Jews for their deed during the occupation.
팔레스타인 사람들은 유태인들이 점령 기간 동안 자행한 일들로 인해 그들에 대한 증오가 극심하다.

09 rancid

/ rǽnsid /

형 썩은 냄새가 나는

syn fetid

영영 generating bad odor, smell of spoiled matter

예문 When I came home from work, I smelled something **rancid** from the kitchen.
내가 집으로 돌아왔을 때 부엌에서 썩는 듯한 냄새를 맡았다.

10 tangent

/ tǽndʒənt /

형 본래의 목적에서 벗어나는

syn peripheral, digressing

영영 not related to the issue or subject

예문 Our boss sometimes went off at a **tangent** when he was criticising us.
우리의 사장은 우리를 비판할 때 가끔씩 주제에서 벗어나는 이야기를 했다.

11 upbraid

/ ʌpbréid /

동 꾸짖다, 비난하다

syn scold, reproach

영영 criticise for something wrong

예문 The principal called the teacher to **upbraid** him for not making his students behave in the classroom.
교장은 그 선생님을 불러 그의 학생들이 교실에서 품행이 바르지 않았던 것에 대해 꾸짖었다.

12. unkempt
/ ʌnkémpt /
형 단정치 못한
syn dishevelled

영영 not looking neat or clean

예문 My wife who has been hospitalized for the past week due to a car accident appeared to be somewhat **unkempt**.
교통사고 때문에 지난 1주일간 병원에 있었던 나의 아내는 다소 흐트러져 있었다.

13. vacillate
/ vǽsəlèit /
동 흔들거리다, 망설이다
syn waver

영영 keep changing one's mind

예문 The exchange rates of Korean currency for the past year have **vacillated**, which added to the uncertainty of economy.
지난 1년간의 한국 환율은 계속 요동치며 경제의 전망을 불투명하게 했다.

14. vagrant
/ véigrənt /
형 방랑하는, 헤매는
syn wandering, roaming

영영 keeping moving around from a place to place

예문 The **vagrant** tribes of the desert without a settled home were called the nomads.
정착지 없이 사막을 떠도는 부족들은 유목민이라고 불려졌다.

15. yoke
/ jóuk /
명 멍에, 예속, 굴레
syn subordination, subjugation

영영 being hindered and facing restrictions

예문 More than ever, Korean economy is getting **yoked** to Chinese economy.
점점 더 한국 경제는 중국경제에 예속되어 가고 있다.

Day 3

01 baleful / béilfəl /
형 악의적인, 해로운
syn evil, harmful

영영 harmful, or expressing harmful intention

예문 It is said that Medusa's **baleful** look would turn men into stone.
메두사의 악의에 찬 눈빛은 사람들을 돌로 바꿀 수 있다고 전해진다.

02 banal / bənǽl /
형 지극히 평범한, 따분한, 시시한
syn rite, cliche

영영 so ordinary that it is not at all effective or interesting

예문 Many poems are not popular in modern times since they are regarded '**banal**'.
오늘날 많은 시들은 따분한 것으로 여겨지기 때문에 별로 인기가 없다.

03 cadence / kéidns /
명 (말소리의) 억양
syn rhythm

영영 the way one's voice gets higher and lower while speaking

예문 It is imperative that everyone who wants to be a news anchor try to carry pleasing **cadence**.
뉴스 앵커가 되려는 사람이라면 듣기 좋은 억양을 지니려 애쓰는 것이 필요하다.

220 SAving Time SAT Vocabulary

04

cajole
/ kədʒóul /

동 꼬드기다, 회유하다
syn coax

영영 persuade one to do something with sweet-talk

예문 I **cajoled** my friend into skipping school with me.
친구를 꼬드겨 같이 학교를 빼먹었다.

05

debunk
/ di:bʌ́ŋk /

동 (생각이) 틀렸음을 밝히다
syn reveal, expose

영영 show that a widely held belief is false

예문 Opponents of President Lee vowed to **debunk** the claim that the river projects would be beneficial for the environment.
이 대통령의 반대 세력들은 하천 사업이 환경에 유익할 것이라는 주장이 틀렸음을 밝힐 것을 천명했다.

06

eclectic
/ ikléktik /

형 절충적인, 다방면에 걸친
syn compromising

영영 wide-ranging and coming from many different sources

예문 The famous Broadway critic was **eclectic** in her own response to the plays she reviewed.
그 유명한 브로드웨이 비평가는 자신이 본 연극에 대한 소감에서 절충적 입장을 피력했다.

07

ecumenical
/ i:kju:ménikl /

형 전 기독교적인, 세계교회주의의
syn all-embracing

영영 movements that try to unite different Christian Churches

예문 The family of victim in recent car crash said that they will hold an **ecumenical** funeral tomorrow afternoon.
최근 자동차 사고 희생자의 가족은 내일 오후 기독교식으로 장례를 치를 것이라 말했다.

12
illation
/ iléiʃən /

명 추리, 추론

syn theory, conclusion

영영 a rare word for inference

예문 The investigators searching for the cause of airplane crash have not yet come up with an *illation* as to what caused it.
비행기 추락 사고의 원인을 조사하고 있는 조사단은 무엇이 그 사건을 유발했는지 아직 결론을 내리지 못하고 있다.

13
jabber
/ dʒǽbər /

동 (알아듣기 힘들게 흥분해서) 지껄이다

syn gabble

영영 talk very quickly and excitedly

예문 The principal, being angered by his teachers' mistake in their duties, began *jabbering* away in loud voice.
선생님들의 업무 실수에 화가 난 교장은 큰 목소리로 지껄이기 시작했다.

14
jargon
/ dʒá:rgən /

명 (특정 분야의) 전문용어

syn dialect, parlance, idiom

영영 words that are used in special ways by particular groups of people

예문 We should not make excessive use of *jargon* in front of young students as they might have hard time understanding our lecture.
우리는 어린 학생들이 우리의 수업을 못 알아들을까 봐 전문 용어의 과다한 사용을 자제해야 한다.

15
knack
/ næk /

명 (타고난) 재주, (경험에 의한) 요령

syn skill, ability

영영 a particularly skilful way of doing something difficult

예문 She has a *knack* for playing the violin.
그녀는 바이올린을 연주하는 데 재능이 있다.

Day 4

01 lacerate
/ læsərèit /
동 (피부 등을 예리하게) 찢다
syn cut, slash

영영 make a serious cut or wound

예문 The young girl's left arm was so badly **lacerated** in the accident that she may need plastic surgery after recovery.
어린 소녀의 팔은 심하게 베여져서 회복 후 성형수술이 필요할 수 있다.

02 machiavellian
/ mækiəvéliən /
형 권모술수적인
syn cunning, unscrupulous

영영 clever and good at making secret plans to achieve one's aim by every means

예문 Many dictators use **machiavellian** method of controlling people.
많은 독재자들은 사람들을 다루는데 있어 권모술수적인 방법을 쓴다.

03 magisterial
/ mædʒəstíəriəl /
형 위엄 있는, 권위 있는
syn authoritative

영영 showing great authority

예문 My father used to talk with the **magisterial** authority as the head of the family.
나의 아버지는 가장으로서의 권위를 가지고 말씀하곤 하셨다.

04 oblong

/ ábló:ŋ /

형 직사각형의, 길쭉한

syn rectangle

영영 of a shape with two long sides and two short sides

예문 We need to use an **oblong** serving tray to arrange cookies on it.
우리는 과자들을 나열하기 위해 직사각형의 쟁반이 필요하다.

05 obsecration

/ àbsəkréiʃən /

명 탄원, 간청

syn appeal, petition

영영 begging for the mercy or pardon

예문 Japanese government sent a letter of **obsecration** to Chinese embassador to ask for the pardon of three Japanese drug traffickers who face the death penalty in China.
일본 정부는 중국 대사에게 중국에서 사형 대기 중인 3명의 일본 마약 사범들의 석방을 요청하는 탄원서를 보냈다.

06 obstreperous

/ əbstrépərəs /

형 정신없이 날뛰는, 시끄러운

syn noisy

영영 too noisy to control

예문 Sometimes, the **obstreperous** committee meeting reminds me of the zoo.
가끔씩 정신없는 위원회 모임은 나에게 동물원을 연상시키곤 한다.

07 pagan

/ péigən /

명 이교도, 토속 신앙인

syn heathen, infidel

영영 those who don't believe in Christianity or Catholicism

예문 The **pagan** belief in Korea is not known to many.
한국의 토속 신앙은 많은 사람들에게 알려져 있지는 않다.

08 palatable
/ pǽlətəbl /

형 맛있는, 맛좋은

syn delicious, tasty, wonderful

영영 very delicious

예문 I seldom find Korean seafood very **palatable**.
나는 한국 해산물 음식이 맛있다고 느끼지 않는다.

09 quizzical
/ kwízikəl /

형 약간 놀란 듯한, 재미있는

syn confused, surprised

영영 indicating mild or amused puzzlement

예문 When asked by a reporter, Bill Gates had that **quizzical** look on his face and didn't answer for a while.
기자에 의해 질문 받았을 때 빌 게이츠는 말없이 특유의 놀란 듯한 표정을 지었다.

10 quixotic
/ kwiksátik /

형 돈키호테 같은, 비현실적인

syn impractical, unrealistic

영영 someone who is too daring or ignorant just like Don Quixote

예문 A recent comic strip on New York Times satirized the **quixotic** motivations of the president regarding the health care issue.
뉴욕 타임즈 시사만화는 건강보험에 관한 대통령의 비현실적 동기에 대해 풍자했다.

11 ramify
/ rǽməfài /

동 가지를 내다, 분기하다

syn divide

영영 divide a network into small sub branches

예문 The subway railroads are **ramified** all over in London.
런던에 있는 지하철은 전역에 걸쳐 퍼져 있다.

12. rampant
/ rǽmpənt /

형 (나쁜 것이) 걷잡을 수 없는, 만연한

syn widespread, prevalent

영영 spread and can not be controlled

예문 Some say that bribery and distortion are still **rampant** in Russia.
몇몇 사람들은 뇌물수수와 왜곡이 아직도 러시아에 만연해 있다고 말한다.

13. rapacious
/ rəpéiʃəs /

형 탐욕스러운

syn grasping, greedy

영영 being greedy and not satisfied

예문 The Roman empire's **rapacious** appetites helped destroy Rome.
로마 제국의 탐욕은 로마를 멸망하게 했다.

14. sacrosanct
/ sǽkrousæŋkt /

형 신성불가침의, 신성한

syn sacred

영영 special and hard to criticise

예문 People flocked to temples to escape the dangers of war as they believed no soldiers would use violence on **sacrosanct** ground.
사람들은 어떤 병사도 신성한 땅에서 폭력을 행사하지 않을 것이라고 믿기 때문에 전쟁 시에 사원으로 모여들었다.

15. waive
/ wéiv /

동 취소하다, 철회하다

syn cancel, withdraw

영영 choose not to pursue or possess something, give up

예문 The defendant agreed to the offer to **waive** some of his rights in return for a reduced sentence.
피고는 형량을 줄여주는 대신 다른 권리들은 포기하라는 제안에 동의했다.

Day 5

01 abnegate
/ ǽbnigèit /
동 (쾌락을) 끊다, (신념을) 버리다
syn restrain, quit

영영 abstain from or dessert what one cherishes the most

예문 Although he faced many difficulties, he did not **abnegate** his faith in god.
비록 많은 어려움을 마주하고 있었지만 그는 신에 대한 믿음을 저버리지 않았다.

02 balk
/ bɔ́:k /
동 방해하다, 좌절시키다, 피하다
syn obstruct

영영 hinder or prevent

예문 Though it was my time to pick up the bill for the food, I **balked** at paying the bill due to lack of cash.
비록 내가 계산을 할 차례였지만 현금이 부족해서 계산서 지불을 망설였다.

03 baneful
/ béinfəl /
형 파괴적인, 해로운
syn evil, wicked, malicious

영영 not positive, being negative

예문 The domestic disputes exert a **baneful** influence on children.
부부싸움은 아이들에게 해로운 영향을 끼친다.

04 capitulate
/ kəpítʃulèit /

동 항복하다, 굴복하다

syn yield, surrender, give in

영영 stop resisting or putting up a fight and give in to the demands

예문 The generals of Japanese miliary **capitulated** to the demands of American government for unconditional surrender.
일본 군부의 장군들은 미국 정부의 무조건적 항복 요구에 굴복했다.

05 ebb
/ éb /

동 뒤로 빠지다, 밀리다, 줄어들다

syn decline, diminish, decrease, dwindle, subside

영영 recede or lessen

예문 The UN's role in policing the world has **ebbed**.
세계의 치안을 담당하는 유엔의 역할은 줄어들었다.

06 fain
/ féin /

부 기꺼이 하는, 기꺼이

syn gladly, willingly

영영 aiding someone without hesitation

예문 If you need my help, I would **fain** help you.
만약에 당신이 나의 도움을 필요로 하면 기꺼이 도와주겠습니다.

07 gallant
/ gǽlənt /

형 용감한, 웅장한

syn brave, dauntless, intrepid

영영 behaving bravely or in dangerous situation

예문 The **gallant** act of soldiers in saving their fellow comrades set an example for others to follow.
동료 전우들을 구한 군인들의 용감한 행위는 다른 사람에게 본보기가 되었다.

08 galore

/ gəlɔ́:r /

형 많은, 풍부한

syn abundant, plentiful

영영 being in large quantity, more than enough

예문 There will be music and food **galore** to make it the biggest party ever.
성대한 파티가 되게끔 많은 음식과 음악이 준비될 것이다.

09 gamut

/ gǽmət /

명 (특정 종류의) 범위 전반

syn extent, range, scope

영영 whole range of a subject, including the smallest details

예문 Our internet shopping mall provides whole **gamut** of electrical appliances.
저희의 인터넷 쇼핑몰은 모든 종류의 가전제품들을 제공합니다.

10 harangue

/ hərǽŋ /

동 (장황하게) 연설하다

syn fulminate

영영 persuade others in a forceful manner

예문 We do not **harangue** students into making them sign up for something they do not wish to.
우리는 학생들이 원하지 않는 것들을 하도록 강요하지 않는다.

11 heathen

/ hí:ðən /

명 비종교인, 이교도

syn unbeliever, stranger

영영 those who have no religions, worshippers of other beliefs

예문 In the New Testament, Paul refers to non-Christians as "**heathens**".
신약성서에서 바울은 비기독교도를 이교도로 불렀다.

12 imbrue

/ imbrú: /

타 더럽히다, 물들게 하다

syn corrupt, taint

영영 lead oneself in negative ways, to leave bad reputation

예문 Hitler **imbrued** his hands in blood by making millions of jews die in concentration camps.
히틀러는 수백만의 유태인들이 수용소에서 죽게 만듦으로써 자기 손을 피로 물들였다.

13 immanent

/ ímənənt /

형 내재하는, 내재적인

syn inborn

영영 existing or operating within

예문 In bible, the god is said to be **immanent** everywhere.
성경에서 신은 모든 곳에 내재해 있는 것처럼 일컬어진다.

14 jiffy

/ dʒífi /

명 순간, 잠깐

syn moment, instant

영영 very quickly or soon

예문 I will join you in a **jiffy**.
나는 곧 당신에게 갈 것입니다.

15 jostle

/ dʒásl /

동 밀다, 밀치다

syn push

영영 push others to get past them

예문 In rush hour, passengers on the subway are often **jostled** to and fro.
통근 시간에는 지하철 승객들끼리 서로 밀치고 밀린다.

day by day II 231

Day 6

01 abode / əbóud /

명 주소지, 주소

syn address, residence

영영 the place where one lives

예문 The police had problems catching the prime suspect as he had no fixed **abode**.
경찰은 유력 용의자가 일정한 거주지를 가지고 있지 않아 그를 잡는데 어려움이 있었다.

02 bedeck / bidék /

동 장식하다, 꾸미다

syn adorn, garnish, prettify

영영 decorate certain place or room to make it rook presentable

예문 The streets were **bedecked** with flowers and flags which were meant to commemorate the independence day.
길거리는 독립일을 기념하기 위한 꽃들과 깃발들로 장식되어 있었다.

03 bellicose / bélikòus /

형 호전적인, 투쟁을 좋아하는

syn aggressive, warlike

영영 likely to cause an argument.

예문 Even if one disagrees, he or she should not be **bellicose** about expressing it.
어떤 것에 대해 동의를 하지 않더라도 그것을 표현하는 데 너무 호전적일 필요는 없다.

04 carnal

/ká:rnl/

형 육체의, 세속적인

syn fleshly, sensual, worldly

영영 being sexual or physical without any significance

예문 Some people commit rapes because they are overwhelmed by **carnal** desires.
어떤 사람들은 육욕에 압도되어 강간을 저지르기도 한다.

05 ebullient

/ibʌ́ljənt/

형 열광적인

syn having high morale

영영 lively and full of enthusiasm

예문 Having defeated the archrival, the head coach of Greenbay Packers seemed to be in **ebullient** mood.
숙적 팀을 이긴 것 때문에 그린베이 패커스팀의 감독은 사기가 충천한 것처럼 보였다.

06 egress

/í:gres/

동 밖으로 나가다

syn exit, go out

영영 leave or get out of certain area or property

예문 The professor was startled to see a student **egress** from his lecture room.
그 교수는 한 학생이 강의실에서 뛰어나가는 것을 보고 놀랐다.

07 genial

/dʒí:njəl/

형 온화한, 다정한

syn agreeable, mild, pleasant, affable

영영 being kind and friendly to someone

예문 My mother is always **genial** to my brother but me.
나의 어머니는 나 말고 동생에게만 따뜻하게 대하신다.

08 impalpable

형 실체가 없는

/ impǽlpəbl / syn inessential

영영 having no real physical properties

예문 The ***impalpable*** images from my dream still linger on in my mind.
내 꿈으로부터 나온 그 무형의 이미지는 아직까지 마음속에 남아 있다.

09 jurisdiction

명 사법〔재판〕권, 관할권

/ dʒùərisdíkʃən / syn imperium

영영 an authority that a court of law utilizes to enforce the law

예문 The police could not make an arrest on the suspect as they had no legal ***jurisdiction*** in the area.
경찰은 그 지역에 사법관할권이 없었기 때문에 용의자를 체포할 수 없었다.

10 kernel

명 핵심

/ kə́:rnl / syn essence, core

영영 the most important thing of all

예문 I want you to cut to the ***kernel*** of the problem.
나는 당신이 문제의 핵심을 다루기를 원합니다.

11 perforate

동 ~에 구멍을 내다

/ pə́:rfərèit / syn punch, pierce

영영 make a hole or holes in something

예문 The bullets ***perforated*** the doors of the car.
탄환들은 차의 문들에 구멍을 내었다.

12 peripheral

/ pərífərəl /

형 주위의, 주변의

syn inessential, minor, marginal

영영 not really important compared with other things, being on the edge away from center

예문 I spent substantial amount of money on buying **peripheral** device for my home entertainment system.
나는 홈 엔터테인먼트 시스템을 위한 주변기기를 사느라 상당히 많은 돈을 썼다.

13 rapprochement

/ ræ̀prouʃmá:ŋ /

명 화해, 관계회복

syn reconciliation, making up

영영 repaired relationship

예문 North Korea's **rapprochement** to the United States is being regarded as a plot to exclude South Korea in the nuclear missile issue.
북한의 미국에 대한 화해 조치는 핵미사일 문제와 관련해 한국을 소외시키려는 계획으로 여겨진다.

14 sedulous

/ séd3uləs /

형 공들인, 꼼꼼한

syn diligent, elaborate, meticulous

영영 with all one's heart and putting in the best effort

예문 The company gives out a commendation to an employee who has been **sedulous** in his or her work.
회사는 자기 일에 근면한 직원에게 표창을 수여한다.

15 temerarious

/ tèmərɛ́əriəs /

형 무모한, 경솔한

syn rash, reckless

영영 not caring about the outcome or effect of a particular behavior

예문 I was **temerarious** to blame my wife for the theft of our family vehicle.
내가 우리 가족의 차 도난에 대해 아내를 비난한 것은 경솔했다.

Day 7

01

bode
/ bóud / 　動 ~의 전조가 되다, 예언하다
　syn **foreshow, foretell, predict**

영영 talk about or guess what will happen

예문 The recent economic signals do not **bode** well as to how it will recover.
최근의 경제 신호는 경제가 어떻게 회복될 것인지를 잘 보여주지 않는다.

02

celibate
/ séləbət / 　名 독신
　syn **single, unmarried**

영영 not marrying for one's religious belief

예문 Catholic priests and nuns vow to remain **celibate** throughout their lives.
천주교 신부들과 수녀들은 평생 독신으로 살기로 맹세한다.

03

cessation
/ seséiʃən / 　名 중단, 정전, 단절
　syn **ceasing, suspension, severance**

영영 an act to stop certain process or relationship

예문 The first step in bringing peace to the Korean peninsular is to have **cessation** of hostilities between two Korean states.
한반도에 평화를 가져오는 데 있어서의 첫 단계는 북한과 남한 사이에 적대감을 없애는 것이다.

04 demented
/ diméntid /

형 미친, 제 정신이 아닌, 오류가 있는

syn insane, out of mind, deranged

영영 being strange with thoughts or acting in foolish or uncontrolled ways

예문 The villain broke into **demented** laughter.
그 악당은 미친 듯이 웃었다.

05 fiasco
/ fiǽskou /

명 큰 실수, 대실패

syn flop, failure, disaster, mess

영영 a complete failure

예문 The women's expedition to the Himalayas was a complete **fiasco**.
히말라야 여성 탐험은 완전한 실패였다.

06 gratification
/ grǽtəfikéiʃən /

명 만족감

syn contentment, satisfaction, enjoyment

영영 feeling of satisfaction and happiness which come from accomplishment

예문 Buddist monks hope to find meaning in a non-material world beyond ego-**gratification**.
불교 승려들은 자기 만족을 뛰어넘어 비물질적인 세계에서 의미를 찾기를 원한다.

07 homespun
/ hóumspʌ̀n /

명 소박한, 투박한

syn plain, austere

영영 not special but simple

예문 To maintain a healthy lifestyle, you must have a **homespun** diet.
건강한 생활을 유지하기 위하여 소박한 식습관을 가져야 한다.

08 impetuous

/ impétʃuəs /

형 맹렬한, 성급한, 충동적인

syn rash, impulsive, violent

영영 acting too quickly without giving much thought

예문 She was so **impetuous** in buying the brand new car.
그녀는 새 차를 사는 것에 있어서 너무 성급했다.

09 jitter

/ dʒítər /

명 신경과민, 초조

syn anxiety, nervousness

영영 acting nervous or being overly concerned

예문 I have the **jitters** before going to the dentist.
나는 치과에 가기 전에 초조하다.

10 judicious

/ dʒu:díʃəs /

형 신중한, 판단력이 있는

syn thoughtful, considerate

영영 showing good judgement and sense

예문 We considered the issue carefully before making the **judicious** decision.
우리는 신중한 판단을 내리기 전에 그 문제를 심사숙고했다.

11 mortified

/ mɔ́:rtəfàid /

동 굴욕감을 받다

syn disgraced, humiliated

영영 be embarrassed a lot

예문 I was **mortified** by the behavior of my children in public.
나는 공공장소에서 내 아들의 행동 때문에 창피했다.

12. mundane
/ mʌndéin /

형 재미없는, 일상적인

syn ordinary, routine, commonplace

영영 not so interesting or just being the usual

예문 Spiritual people can help others with the **mundane** problems of life.
영적인 사람들은 다른 사람들의 세속적 문제들을 해결하는데 도움을 줄 수 있다.

13. nescient
/ néʃənt /

형 무지한

syn agnostic, ignorant, atheist

영영 not caring about other facts, not having any belief in a religion

예문 He was a **nescient** person when it came to the issue of god's existence.
그는 신의 존재에 관한 문제에 대해서는 불가지론자였다.

14. opulent
/ ápjulənt /

형 풍부한, 부유한

syn abundant, luxurious, wealthy

영영 extremely rich

예문 In Chosun dynasty, the nobles were able to live an **opulent** lifestyle by having many servants work on their lands.
조선 왕조에서 귀족들은 많은 노비들이 귀족 소유의 땅에서 일하는 것으로 부유한 삶을 살 수 있었다.

15. perpetrate
/ pə́:rpətrèit /

동 (나쁜 일을) 범하다, 저지르다

syn commit

영영 do something bad or harmful to others

예문 During world war II, Japanese military **perpetrated** one of most heinous crimes against humanity in China by massacring countless number of people.
제2차 세계 대전 중 일본 군부는 중국에서 수많은 사람들을 학살하여 인류에 대한 가장 악독한 범죄들 중 하나를 저질렀다.

Day 8

01 cede / síːd /

동 (자발적이지 않게) 양도하다, 이양하다

syn surrender, yield

영영 hand one's power or assets to someone but not voluntarily

예문 Japan **ceded** their five northern islands to Russia when they lost the war.
일본은 전쟁에서 졌을 때 그들의 북방 5도를 러시아에 이양했다.

02 chaste / tʃéist /

형 순결한, 정숙한

syn virtuous, faithful

영영 abstaining from sexual intercourse

예문 In most Asian cultures, young women are expected to be **chaste** until they marry.
대부분의 아시아 국가들에서 어린 여성들은 결혼할 때까지 순결을 지키도록 요구된다.

03 decorum / dikɔ́ːrəm /

명 예의바름, 단정함

syn propriety, seemliness

영영 a correct and polite behavior

예문 Our school expects all the students to conduct themselves with **decorum**.
우리 학교에서는 모든 학생들이 정숙하게 행동할 것을 원합니다.

240 SAving Time SAT Vocabulary

04 embezzle

/ imbézl /

동 유용하다, 횡령하다

syn misuse

영영 take money fraudulently by breach of trust

예문 The banker **embezzled** $150,000 from the bank where he worked and used it for gambling.
그 은행가는 그가 일하던 은행에서 15만 불을 횡령해서 도박하는 데 사용했다.

05 figurative

/ fígjurətiv /

형 수식이 많은, 비유적인

syn metaphorical, symbolic

영영 using words with abstract or imaginative meanings

예문 The guest speaker's use of **figurative** language made his lectures very interesting.
초청 강사의 비유적 언어 사용은 그의 강의를 매우 흥미롭게 만들었다.

06 hoard

/ hɔ́:rd /

동 축적하다, 저장하다

syn accumulate, store

영영 save or store something valuable

예문 He **hoarded** money for many years and eventually became wealthy, but felt miserable because he sacrificed so many things.
그는 수 해 동안 돈을 축적했고 결국 부자가 되었지만 많은 것을 희생했기 때문에 우울해했다.

07 homocentric

/ hòuməséntrik /

형 중심을 공유하는

syn mutual

영영 carrying same attitude, same mentality

예문 In the assembly hall, the **homocentric** sentiment to help America was brewing in the air as politicians were condemning the terrorist attacks in New York.
국회에서는 정치가들이 뉴욕에서 일어난 테러를 비난하는 중에 미국을 돕자는 공감대가 형성되었다.

08 levitate
/ lévətèit /
동 공중에 뜨다
syn float

영영 look as if something is floating in the air without any support

예문 Some Yoga masters in India are believed to possess the skill to **levitate** in the air without any support.
인도의 요가 마스터들은 지탱해주는 것 없이 공중 부양할 수 있는 것으로 믿어진다.

09 licentious
/ laisénʃəs /
형 방탕한, 음탕한
syn promiscuous, debauched

영영 considered sexually immoral

예문 Hanna had a very **licentious** life as she would go out with several men at a time.
한나는 한 번에 여러 남자와 문어발식으로 데이트하는 등 매우 방탕한 생활을 했다.

10 lucent
/ lúːsnt /
형 빛을 내는, 반짝이는
syn shinning, gleaming

영영 being very bright and shiny

예문 After waxing the car, the surface of car was so **lucent** that it caught everyone's eyes.
차를 왁스칠한 후 차의 표면이 너무 반짝거려서 모든 사람의 눈길을 사로잡았다.

11 magniloquent
/ mægnílǝkwənt /
형 과장된, 호언하는
syn exaggerated, inflated, grandiloquent

영영 exaggerating or overestimating something

예문 The **magniloquent** way in explaining the theory on the explosion of a naval vessel has made everyone suspect that truth is not yet revealed.
해군 함정의 폭파에 관한 가설을 설명하는데 있어서의 과장된 방식이 사람들에게 모든 사실은 아직 밝혀지지 않았다고 생각하게 만들었다.

12 nondescript

/ nàndiskrípt /

명 막연한, 특징이 없는

syn dull, uninteresting

영영 looking ordinary, dull and not quite attractive to others

예문 His initial impression was **nondescript**, and many women didn't think of him much.
그의 첫 인상은 너무 무난해서 많은 여자들이 그를 별로 신경 쓰지 않았다.

13 parlous

/ pá:rləs /

형 위험한, 다루기 힘든

syn perilous

영영 being in a dangerous state

예문 The economy of Greece is in a **parlous** state until European Union decides how it will aid the financially strapped country.
그리스의 경제는 유럽연합이 재정적으로 쪼들리는 그리스를 어떻게 도울 것인지 결정하기 전까지 위험한 상황에 처해 있다.

14 prehensile

/ prihénsl /

형 물건 잡기에 적합한, 이해력 있는

syn holding

영영 able to hold on to certain objects

예문 It is amazing how monkeys can use their **prehensile** tails to help them move through trees.
원숭이들이 물건을 잡을 수 있도록 꼬리를 써서 나무 사이로 움직이는 것은 아주 흥미롭다.

15 reciprocate

/ risíprəkèit /

동 보답하다, 보복하다

syn respond, repay

영영 give and receive mutually

예문 Japanese people feel obligated to **reciprocate** any kindness or gifts they receive.
일본 사람들은 그들이 받는 어떤 친절이나 선물들도 보답해줘야 한다는 의무감을 느낀다.

Day 9

01
nexus
/ néksəs /

명 (사람과의) 관계
syn relationship, union

영영 connection to a certain system or a situation

예문 The **nexus** of Taleban and Pakistan government is yet to be proved.
텔레반과 파키스탄 정부의 관계는 아직도 증명될 여지가 있다.

02
nugatory
/ njúːgətɔ́ːri /

형 하찮은, 무가치한
syn inconsequential, insignificant

영영 of little value and insignificant

예문 The value of stock shares for some companies fell to **nugatory** level due to the financial crisis.
몇몇 회사들의 주가는 금융위기 때문에 미미한 수준으로 떨어졌다.

03
oscillate
/ ásəlèit /

동 진동하다; 망설이다
syn swing, fluctuate

영영 keep moving from one position to another repeatedly

예문 The engineers monitoring the control panel knew something wasn't right as the needles on the gauges kept **oscillating** back and forth.
계기판을 감시하던 기술자들은 계기판 바늘이 왔다갔다할 때 뭔가 심상치 않은 일이 벌어지고 있음을 알았다.

04 oust

/ áust /

동 내쫓다

syn eject, drive out, expel

영영 force someone out of position

예문 The opposition party members looked for ways to **oust** their own party leader.
야당 의원들은 그들의 당 지도자를 축출할 방법을 모색했다.

05 preordain

/ prìːrdéin /

타 예정하다

syn predetermine

영영 decide something beforehand

예문 The fatal car accident at the junction last night was **preordained** due to some signal alterations.
어젯밤 교차로에서의 그 치명적 사고는 신호등 변경 때부터 이미 내정된 것이나 다름없었다.

06 presumptuous

/ prizʌ́mptʃuəs /

형 건방진, 뻔뻔한

syn arrogant

영영 failing to observe the limits

예문 It was **presumptuous** of him to make the demand that I give up my running for the student president position.
그가 나로 하여금 전교 회장 후보 자리를 포기하도록 요구한 것은 너무 뻔뻔했다.

07 quell

/ kwél /

동 진압하다, 소멸시키다

syn suppress, extinguish

영영 put an end to a certain behavior or an opposition

예문 According to the record of Chosun dynasty of Korea, quite a few groups of peasants rose up in revolt against the royal authority in late 19th century, but they were **quelled** by an modernized army.
한국의 조선 왕조 기록에 따르면 꽤 많은 무리의 농민들이 왕권에 대항하여 일어섰지만 현대화된 군대에 의해 제압되었다고 한다.

08 querulous

/ kwérjuləs /

형 불평을 하는, 흠잡는

syn complaining, faultfinding, peevish

영영 complaining, not always content

예문 In a court of law, a judge would reprimand any prosecuting or defense lawyers who show **querulous** behavior.
법정에서 재판관은 불평하는 모습을 보이는 어떤 검사들이나 변호사들에게 경고를 할 것이다.

09 relapse

/ rilǽps /

동 되돌아가다, 재발하다

syn recurrence, recur

영영 go back to one's original state

예문 If you pick up smoking again, the tumors will **relapse**.
다시 담배를 핀다면 종양은 다시 자라날 겁니다.

10 remand

/ rimǽnd /

동 송환하다, (추후 재판까지) 방면하다

syn release

영영 order someone to be bailed on bond or kept in jail until the charge is made

예문 The suspect is **remanded** until he is consulted by a psychiatrist.
그 용의자는 정신과 진찰을 받을 때 까지 송환되어 있을 것이다.

11 slumberous

/ slʌ́mbərəs /

형 졸리는, 나태한

syn drowsy, sleepy

영영 being very tired or sleepy

예문 The construction workers resting in the shade looked **slumberous**.
그늘에서 쉬고 있는 그 건설 노동자들은 나태해 보였다.

12 solstice
/ sálstis /

명 극점, 하지/동지

syn zenith

영영 the time when the sun reaches the highest or lowest point

예문 It is known that there is a celebration for the summer **solstice** at the stonehenge site in Scotland.
스코틀랜드에 있는 스톤헨지에서 하지 축제를 여는 것으로 알려져 있다.

13 trudge
/ trʌdʒ /

동 터벅터벅 걷다

syn plod

영영 walk slowly because someone is tired or troubled

예문 When I looked back to see if my son was keeping the pace with me, I saw him **trudging** along looking disgruntled.
아들이 제대로 따라오고 있는지 확인하려고 고개를 돌렸을 때 나는 그 아이가 불만스럽게 터벅터벅 걷고 있는 것을 보았다.

14 vying
/ váiiŋ /

형 겨루는, 경쟁하는

syn struggling

영영 competing with someone to take an honor

예문 Wayne and Didier of English Premier League are **vying** for the top scorer position.
영국 프리미어 리그의 웨인과 디디에는 득점왕의 자리를 차지하기 위해 경쟁하고 있다.

15 wrath
/ræθ/

명 격노, 분노

syn rage, temper, fury

영영 an extreme anger

예문 His extreme **wrath** in that situation surprised everyone as he was considered quiet by others.
그가 조용한 타입으로 여겨졌기에 그의 격렬한 분노는 모든 이를 놀라게 했다.

Day 10

01 abysmal / əbízməl /
형 최악의, 최저의
syn worst, nadir
영영 very bad in quality
예문 He tried to put his business on the right track but the future prospect was looking rather **abysmal**.
그는 사업을 정상 궤도로 올려놓으려고 했으나 미래의 전망은 조금은 절망적으로 보이고 있었다.

02 bemoan / bimóun /
동 슬퍼하다, 탄식하다
syn lament, mourn
영영 show one's great dissatisfaction or sorrow over something
예문 All the people in Poland **bemoaned** the unfortunate passing of their president, Lech Kaczynski.
폴란드의 모든 시민들은 대통령인 레흐 카친스키의 불행한 서거를 슬퍼했다.

03 bereave / birí:v /
동 (생명, 희망 등을) 빼앗다
syn rob, depredate
영영 take most precious thing from someone against his will
예문 The orphans are **bereaved** of their parents' love and affection.
고아들은 부모들의 사랑과 애정을 받지 못한다.

04 bludgeon
/ blʌ́dʒən /

동 (몽둥이로) 때리다, 위협하다

syn beat, bash, club

영영 hit someone with a heavy and dangerous object

예문 New York police department reported after the autopsy that the victim was **bludgeoned** to death with a hammer or something.
뉴욕 경찰서는 부검에서 희생자가 망치나 또는 다른 것으로 죽을 때까지 맞은 것이라고 발표했다.

05 chagrin
/ ʃəgrín /

명 억울함, 원통함

syn vexation, mortification

영영 a feeling of disappointment one has because of not being able to accomplish his goal

예문 Much to the **chagrin** of the players, the team, Manchester United, was unable to win four consecutive championship title thanks to the defeat suffered to Chelsea.
선수들에게는 유감스럽게도 맨유는 첼시에 겪은 패배 때문에 리그 우승 4연패를 달성할 수 없었다.

06 chastise
/ tʃæstáiz /

동 혼내주다, 억제하다

syn punish, beat

영영 scold someone to punish

예문 I had to **chastise** several students for their lack of participation in the class activities.
나는 수업 활동에 참여가 저조한 것 때문에 몇몇 학생들을 꾸짖었다.

07 embroider
/ imbrɔ́idər /

동 수를 놓다, 과장하다

syn embellish, ornament

영영 ornament garment materials with needles

예문 In the past, women of American west **embroidered** their quilts with various patterns so that they can be reminded of their roots and history.
옛날 미국 서부 여자들은 자신의 뿌리와 역사를 기억하기 위해 다양한 문양으로 퀼트에 수놓았다.

08 emulate
/ émjulèit /

동 우열을 다투다, 경쟁하다

syn **imitate, follow, copy**

영영 strive to equal and imitate

예문 He strove to **emulate** the example of his father and honor him.
그는 아버지의 모범을 본받고 그를 공경하려고 노력했다.

09 grim
/ grím /

형 엄격한, 험상스러운

syn **severe, stern, harsh, terrible**

영영 describing strict atmosphere or a feeling that is difficult to accept

예문 You must face the **grim** reality.
당신은 그 냉엄한 현실을 받아들여야 한다.

10 hurtle
/ hə́:rtl /

동 충돌하다, 돌진하다

syn **rush, charge**

영영 When you hurtle at something, you go for it with speed and in rough manner

예문 The stolen car, chased by police cars, **hurtled** toward the people on the pedestrian.
경찰차의 추격을 받은 그 도난 차량은 보행도로의 사람들 쪽으로 돌진 했다.

11 husbandry
/ hʌ́zbəndri /

명 절약, 가정 관리

syn **saving, frugality, conservation**

영영 taking good care of a house, a farm or money

예문 Many Korean women get lessons in good **husbandry** before getting married.
많은 한국 여성들은 결혼하기 전 가정을 잘 꾸리는 것에 대한 교육을 받는다.

12 jocund
/ dʒákənd /

형 명랑한, 즐거운

syn cheerful, merry

영영 filled with happy thoughts and pleasure

예문 The dinner with family was filled with a ***jocund*** atmosphere which made him forget about the stress from work.
가족과 함께한 저녁은 그에게서 직장 스트레스를 잠시 잊게 해줄 만큼 즐거운 분위기로 가득했다.

13 lampoon
/ læmpúːn /

동 풍자하다

syn satire, satirize

영영 strongly criticise a matter in a humorous way

예문 Korean people ***lampoon*** at almost everything they see on the internet or newspapers.
한국 사람들은 그들이 인터넷이나 신문에서 보는 거의 모든 것을 풍자한다.

14 matriculate
/ mətríkjulèit /

동 입학을 허가하다

syn admit, register

영영 formally register as a student after satisfying all the requirements

예문 People who ***matriculate*** into MBA programs have at least 4 or 5 years of working experience.
MBA 프로그램에 입학하는 사람들은 적어도 4년 내지 5년의 직장 경험을 가지고 있다.

15 nocturnal
/ nɑktə́ːrnl /

형 밤의, 야행성의

syn diurnal

영영 very active at night

예문 Many species of monkeys and rodents have been evolved to become ***nocturnal*** beings so that they can escape predators.
많은 종류의 원숭이들과 설치류들은 포식자로부터 피할 수 있도록 야행성 동물로 진화했다.

day by day II 251

Day 11

01
abrogate
/ ǽbrəgèit /
동 폐지하다, 취소하다
syn annul, repeal

영영 put an end or stop a law or practice

예문 Many people think the regulations meant to curb the private education will be **abrogated** after current president's term.
많은 사람들은 사교육을 억제하기 위한 규제들이 현 대통령 임기 후에는 완화될 것으로 본다.

02
bilk
/ bílk /
동 속이다, 사기로 돈을 취하다
syn chat, defraud

영영 cheat or defraud money

예문 There is one student who always **bilks** her friends by saying that she will pay back the money she borrowed.
친구들에게 늘 빌린 돈을 갚겠다고 하며 돈을 취하는 한 학생이 있다.

03
blandish
/ blǽndiʃ /
동 감언으로 설득하다
syn persuade, coax

영영 take someone into doing something with sweet talks

예문 The government, avoiding prolonged public exposure, tried to **blandish** the bereaved families into accepting the compensation.
추가 외부 공개를 기피하면서 정부는 유족들이 보상을 받아들이도록 감언이설로 설득했다.

04 blemish
/ blémiʃ /

명 흠, 오점, 결점

syn imperfection, flaw, shortcoming

영영 a spot on the surface

예문 He has built a long career that is without **blemish**.
그는 오점 없이 오랜 경력을 쌓아 왔다.

05 calibrate
/ kǽləbrèit /

동 (계기의) 눈금을 조정하다

syn standardize

영영 mark with a standard scale of readings

예문 The astronauts failed in **calibrating** Hubble telescope due to certain faulty parts.
우주비행사들은 특정 결함 부품 때문에 허블 망원경의 계기판 조정에 실패했다.

06 camaraderie
/ kà:mərá:dəri /

명 동지애

syn brotherhood

영영 a friendly feeling and goodwill between comrades in hardships

예문 What I regretted the most about the working experience is that the **camaraderie** at work was not shared by many.
내가 직장 경험에서 가장 아쉬웠던 부분은 많은 사람들 사이에서 동지애가 존재하지 않았다는 점이다.

07 dearth
/ dé:rθ /

명 부족, 결핍

syn scarcity, shortage

영영 a lack of something

예문 It is assumed that Korea will experience a **dearth** of fresh water required for farming in 2012.
2012년에 한국은 농업용 담수 부족 사태를 겪을 것이라 예상된다.

08 debacle

/ deibá:kl / 　명 대실패, 도산, 붕괴
　syn disaster, catastrophe, fiasco

영영 a great failure or sudden collapse

예문 In the movie "Black Hawk Down," the plot of movie centers around an attempt to capture a local militia leader that turned into a **debacle**.
영화 '블랙 호크 다운'은 한 현지 민병대 지도자를 잡으려는 작전이 완전히 수포로 돌아가게 된다는 줄거리이다.

09 expunge

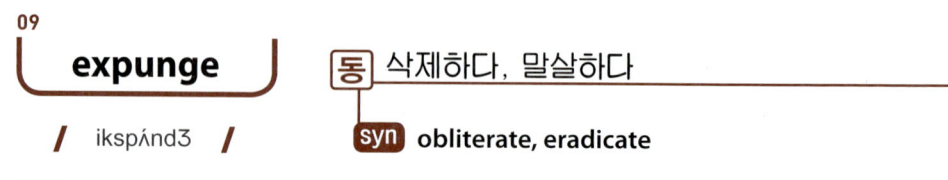

/ ikspʌ́ndʒ /　동 삭제하다, 말살하다
　syn obliterate, eradicate

영영 get rid of something as it may have certain badness in it

예문 The Japanese government is trying to **expunge** all the records pointing out their involvement in war prostitution allegation.
일본 정부는 전쟁 중의 위안부 징집 혐의와 관련된 모든 기록들을 제거하려 하고 있다.

10 garish

/ gɛ́əriʃ /　형 유난히 번쩍거리는, 지나치게 화려한
　syn flamboyant, gaudy

영영 showy in an excessive manner

예문 I didn't like my mom going to the PTA meeting because she would wear **garish** clothes and jewelry which made her stand out in the crowd.
나는 어머니가 눈에 띄는 화려한 옷과 장신구를 걸치기 때문에 학부모회에 가시는 것을 좋아하지 않았다.

11 iconoclast

/ aikánəklæ̀st /　명 인습타파론자
　syn nonconformist

영영 a person who criticizes common beliefs or institutions

예문 Oscar Wilde was known not only as a writer but as an outspoken **iconoclast**.
오스카 와일드는 작가인 것 말고도 입바른 인습타파론자로 유명했다.

12
jumble

/ dʒʌmbl /

동 섞다, 뒤죽박죽 만들다

syn confuse, mess

영영 mix things up in a confused way

예문 Many different kinds of stores are jumbled up close together around ports.
항구 주변에는 많은 상점들이 난립해 있다.

13
juxtaposition

/dʒʌkstəpəzíʃən/

명 병렬, 병치

syn parallel

영영 an act of comparing and contrasting two things in an explicit way

예문 The sculptor put his art works in **juxtaposition** so that they are compared and different messages can be conveyed.
그 조각가는 서로 비교되고 다른 메시지들이 전달될 수 있도록 그의 예술 작품들을 병치시켰다.

14
knell

/ nél /

명 (죽음을 알리는) 종소리, 조종

syn a mourning bell

영영 the sound of a bell that indicates someone's passing

예문 Many scholars implied that slow and tardy recovery of the dictator from his illness could sound the **knell** of the regime.
많은 학자들이 그 독재자의 더딘 회복은 정권의 몰락을 예고하는 것일 수 있다고 암시했다.

15
kudos

/ kjú:dous /

명 칭찬, 영광

syn prestige, praise

영영 a praise one gets from achieving something splendid

예문 The CEO gave **kudos** to executives and staff for their part in achieving record profit.
그 대표이사는 임직원들에게 최고 수익을 달성한 것에 대해 칭찬을 했다.

Day 12

01 bane
/ béin /
명 죽음, 골칫거리
syn trouble, nuisance

영영 a feeling of burden on one's shoulder

예문 Not having completed the book writing was a **bane** for John as he couldn't do anything with his family on the weekends.
존에게 책 집필을 마치지 못한 것은 가족들과 주말을 제대로 보낼 수 없을 만큼 골칫거리로 작용했다.

02 behemoth
/ bihí:məθ /
명 거대 기업 (단체)
syn giant, mammoth

영영 a huge organization

예문 Samsung has become a **behemoth** in an electronics industry, but it is still mistaken as a Japanese company in other countries.
삼성은 전자 업계에서 거대 기업체가 되었지만 다른 나라에서는 일본 기업으로 잘못 알려져 있다.

03 amicable
/ ǽmikəbl /
형 우호적인, 원만한
syn harmonious, peaceful

영영 done or achieved in a polite or friendly way

예문 **Amicable** divorce might be the best solution for us as well as them.
합의 이혼은 그들 뿐 아니라 우리에게도 최선의 해결책이 될 것이다.

04 decorous

/ dékərəs /

형 예의 바른, 품위 있는

syn proper

영영 respectable and socially acceptable

예문 Princess of Denmark who visited Korea on invitation charmed many reporters and politicians with her **decorous** manner.
한국의 초청으로 온 덴마크의 공주는 그녀의 품위 있는 행동으로 많은 기자들과 정치가들을 매료시켰다.

05 effrontery

/ ifrʌ́ntəri /

명 뻔뻔스러움

syn impudence, nerve, insolence

영영 an act that is very rude or disrespectful

예문 When the Prime Minister could no longer tolerate the **effrontery** of a TV reporter, he simply banned him from next press release.
총리가 한 TV 기자의 무례함을 더 이상 용인할 수 없게 되자 그는 그 기자의 다음 회견 출두를 금지시켰다.

06 effulgent

/ ifʌ́ldʒənt /

형 눈부신, 찬란한

syn radiant, splendorous

영영 very shiny and bright

예문 The person who witnessed a UFO hovering over a mountain top said that it seemed to have **effulgent** surface.
UFO가 산 정상위에 떠 있는 것을 목격한 사람은 그것이 빛나는 표면을 가지고 있는 것처럼 보인다고 말했다.

07 dilate

/ dailéit /

동 넓히다, 자세히 설명하다

syn enlarge, expand

영영 make or become wider or more open

예문 The pupils of the eyes **dilate** as darkness increases.
눈의 동공은 어두워질수록 팽창한다.

day 12

day by day II 257

08 felicitous

/ filísətəs /

형 교묘한, 적절한

syn suited, apt

영영 suitably expressed or deemed appropriate

예문 Compared to myself, my brother used to be more **felicitous** and direct in expressing arguments.
나 자신과 비교해서 동생은 말다툼에서 더 적절한 표현을 했고 직설적이었다.

09 hackneyed

/ hǽknid /

형 진부한, 상투적인

syn unoriginal, trite

영영 not being for the first time, therefore being likely to cause no interest

예문 What I heard at the campaign rally for coming election was full of **hackneyed** pledges, which I doubt will be realized.
다가오는 선거 유세에서 내가 들었던 것은 실현이 의심스러운 상투적 공약뿐이었다.

10 idolatrous

/ aidálətrəs /

형 우상 숭배하는, 맹신하는

syn overcredulous

영영 excessively worshipping over a cult image or an object

예문 Many Christians label Catholicism as an **idolatrous** religion due to many saint figures the catholics pray to.
많은 기독교인들은 기도를 하는 대상인 성자의 모형물들 때문에 천주교를 우상 숭배하는 종교로 묘사한다.

11 largess

/ lɑːrdʒés /

명 많은 부조, 아낌없이 금품 주기

syn contribution

영영 the generous giving of lavish gifts or money at social events

예문 My co-teacher demonstrated great **largess** by giving a monetary gift for my wedding.
나의 동료 교사는 내 결혼식에 많은 부조를 냄으로써 후하다는 것을 입증해 보여주었다.

12. latent
/léitnt/
형 숨어있는, 보이지 않는
syn dormant

영영 not obvious and hidden

예문 The best psychiatrist is able to bring out the **latent** feelings of his patients with efficient means.
최고의 정신과 의사는 효과적인 방법으로 환자들의 잠재적 감정을 이끌어 낼 수 있다.

13. malleable
/mǽliəbl/
형 펴 늘일 수 있는
syn ductile

영영 easily shaped or transformed

예문 Copper is a **malleable** reddish metallic chemical element.
구리는 펴 늘일 수 있는 빨간색의 금속성 화학 원소이다.

14. mawkish
/mɔ́:kiʃ/
형 감상적인
syn sentimental

영영 overly sentimental or silly

예문 Not many women realize that a man's wedding propose can be **mawkish**.
한 남성의 결혼 제안이 감상에 그친다는 것을 깨닫는 여성은 많지 않다.

15. nascent
/nǽsnt/
형 초기의
syn initial

영영 beginning to exist

예문 Many astronomers and physicists are trying to find out the **nascent** stages of the universe.
많은 천문학자들과 물리학자들은 우주의 초기 단계들을 알아내려 하고 있다.

Day 13

01 bequeath
/ bikwíːð /

동 유증하다, 유산을 남기다, (후세에) 전하다

syn leave, endow

영영 pass on one's property or legacy to someone after death

예문 My grandfather **bequeathed** me his farm and all its equipment when he died.
나의 할아버지는 그의 농장과 모든 장비들을 돌아가신 후 나에게 남겼다.

02 berate
/ biréit /

동 비난하다, 몹시 꾸짖다

syn reprimand, reproach, chastise

영영 scold or criticise someone with seriousness

예문 We are used to hearing the woman next door **berate** her children frequently.
우리는 이웃집 여자가 자기 아이들을 심하게 나무라는 것을 듣는 것에 익숙하다.

03 canny
/ kǽni /

형 교활한, 간교한, 교묘한

syn deceptive, shrewd

영영 shrewd and careful, quick in response

예문 Other teachers at school think the English teacher is dopey but they don't realize that he is quite **canny**.
학교의 다른 선생님들은 그 영어 교사가 어리숙하다고 생각하고 그가 아주 약삭빠르다는 것을 모른다.

04 carouse

/ kəráuz /

동 술을 마시며 흥청거리다

syn party, celebrate

영영 drink a lot of alcohol and behave noisily

예문 The guests at the wedding reception *caroused* all night even after the bride and groom left for their honeymoon.
결혼 피로연에 온 하객들은 신랑신부가 신혼여행을 떠나고 없는데도 밤새 내내 흥청거렸다.

05 caucus

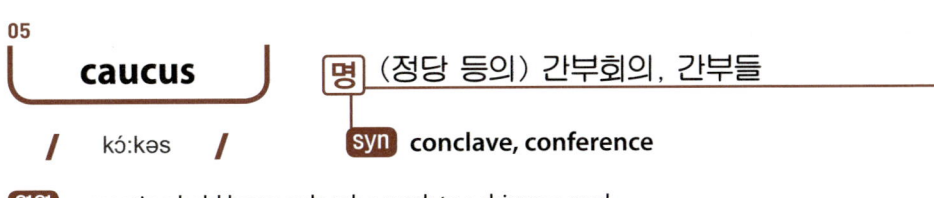

/ kɔ́ːkəs /

명 (정당 등의) 간부회의, 간부들

syn conclave, conference

영영 a meeting held by people who work to achieve a goal

예문 The *caucus* by auto workers' union on staging a strike fell through due to many rejections.
자동차 노조의 파업 관련 간부회의는 많은 반대 때문에 결렬되었다.

06 deferential

/ dèfərénʃəl /

형 경의를 표하는, 공손한

syn respectful

영영 polite and respectful towards others

예문 A manager who doesn't display *deferential* attitude toward his employees is going to lose everything at the end.
자기 직원들을 존중하지 않는 관리자는 결국에 가서 모든 것을 잃을 것이다.

07 deleterious

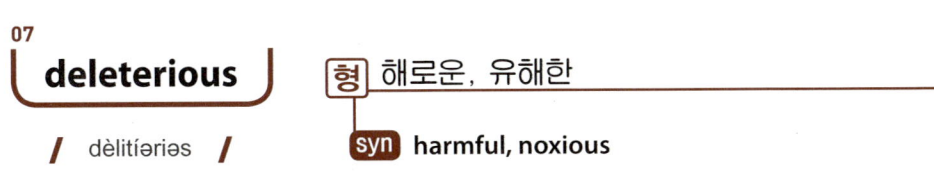

/ dèlitíəriəs /

형 해로운, 유해한

syn harmful, noxious

영영 containing negative elements and being harmful

예문 Many healthcare officials are investigating *deleterious* effects the semi-conductor production plants have on their workers.
많은 보건 의료 관계자들은 반도체 생산 공장들이 직원들에 끼치는 유해한 영향에 대해 조사를 벌이고 있다.

08

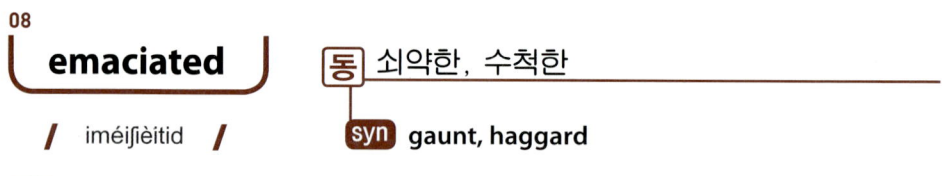

emaciated 동 쇠약한, 수척한

/ iméiʃièitid /   syn **gaunt, haggard**

영영 appearing to be very thin or enfeebled

예문 When the Jews in the concentration camp were freed, they looked dangerously **emaciated**.
강제 수용소에 있는 유태인들이 해방되었을 때 그들은 매우 수척해 보였다.

09

emote 동 감정을 과장되게 드러내다

/ imóut /   syn **exaggeration**

영영 express an emotion in an exaggerated manner

예문 If the President **emotes** his feelings in a public gathering, opposition parties will come out with strong criticisms.
만약에 대통령이 공식 석상에서 자신의 감정을 드러낸다면 야당들은 강한 비난을 할 것이다.

10

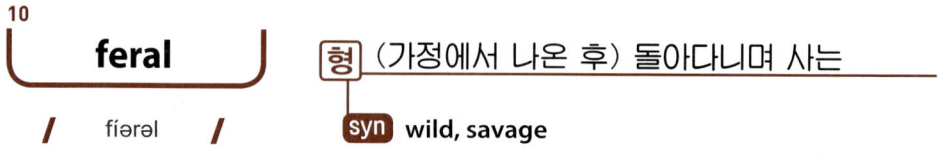

feral 형 (가정에서 나온 후) 돌아다니며 사는

/ fíərəl /   syn **wild, savage**

영영 once domesticated but now living in the wild

예문 On our way to the mountain top, we came across some treks of **feral** cats and goats in the forest trail.
산 정상으로 가는 도중 우리는 야생 고양이와 염소들의 흔적을 숲속 길에서 발견했다.

11

gratuitous 형 불필요한, 쓸데없는

/ grətjúːətəs /   syn **unwarranted, unnecessary**

영영 being meant to be good, but unnecessary or burdensome

예문 When I tried to pay for the drinks, I was told that it was **gratuitous**.
내가 그 음료수들의 값을 지불하려 했을 때 그럴 필요가 없다는 이야기를 들었다.

12 limpid
/ límpid /

형 깨끗한, 투명한
syn lucid, clear

영영 transparent and clear

예문 Fish can not live in **limpid** water as birds can easily pick them.
새들에게 쉽게 잡힐 수 있기 때문에 물고기들은 투명한 물에서 살 수 없다.

13 linchpin
/ líntʃpìn /

명 핵심이 되는 인물 (사물)
syn core, key

영영 very important or vital in a process

예문 The presence of American military in Korean peninsular is the **linchpin** in maintaining peace in Northeast Asia.
한반도의 미군 주둔은 동북아에서 평화를 유지하는 데 중요한 부분이다.

14 maudlin
/ mɔ́:dlin /

형 눈물을 잘 흘리는, 감상적인
syn sentimental

영영 tearfully sentimental

예문 The **maudlin** plots of television soap operas in Korea have made them very popular in various Asian countries.
한국의 TV 드라마는 그 감상적 줄거리 덕분에 여러 아시아 국가들에서 인기를 끌었다.

15 neophyte
/ níːəfàit /

명 초보자, 신참
syn beginner, novice

영영 a person who is new to certain profession

예문 John was a **neophyte** in the literary circle as the last book he published was his first.
존은 지난번 출간한 책이 그의 첫 작품이었던 만큼 문학계에서 초보자였다.

Day 14

01 cavort / kəvɔ́:rt /
동 (신이 나서) 뛰어다니다
syn **gambol, caper**

영영 leap about and behave boisterously with excitement

예문 Someday, I would like to take my son to an island in the mediterranean sea and see him **cavort** on the white sand beach.
언젠가는 나의 아들을 지중해에 있는 한 섬에 데려가 하얀 모래 해변에서 뛰어다니게 하고 싶다.

02 delineate / dilínièit /
동 윤곽을 그리다, 묘사하다
syn **depict, outline**

영영 draw the outline of a subject

예문 An artist has to be good at **delineating** an object he wants to draw.
예술가는 자신이 그리고자 하는 사물의 윤곽을 잘 그릴 수 있어야 한다.

03 elated / iléitid /
형 마냥 행복해하는
syn **overjoyed, thrilled**

영영 filled with excited joy and pride

예문 My son was **elated** when law school accepted his application.
나의 아들은 로스쿨 입학 허가를 받았을 때 마냥 기뻐했다.

04 empathy
/ émpəθi /

명 감정이입, 공감
syn sympathy

영영 an emotional identification shared with another

예문 Many Korean people felt tremendous **empathy** with the families of dead soldiers who died in the sinking of a naval vessel.
많은 한국 사람들은 해군 함정 침몰 유가족들에 대해 상당한 동정을 느꼈다.

05 flair
/ flέər /

명 재주, 재능
syn talent

영영 a natural ability to do certain things

예문 My high school teacher who taught geography had an uncanny **flair** for discovering which students were lying about their homework.
고등학교 때 지리를 가르쳤던 한 선생님은 숙제에 대해 거짓말을 하는 학생들을 용케 잡아내는 비상한 능력을 가지고 계셨다.

06 imperious
/ impíəriəs /

형 고압적인
syn commanding, domineering

영영 being arrogant and haughty

예문 The **imperious** manner of police can make people to dislike them.
경찰의 고압적인 태도는 사람들로 하여금 그들을 싫어하게 만들 수 있다.

07 impervious
/ impə́:rviəs /

형 통과시키지 않는, 휘둘리지 않는
syn impenetrable, unswayed

영영 not easily influenced or affected

예문 In order to be a good teacher, you must be **impervious** to irrational demands.
좋은 선생님이 되기 위해 당신은 불합리한 요구에 휘둘려서는 안 된다.

08 impinge

/ impíndʒ /   동 ~에 나쁜 영향을 주다
syn encroach, infringe

영영 make an impression on someone in a negative way

예문 The noise of construction work **impinged** on us so badly that we couldn't continue our lessons.
건축공사의 소리가 우리에게 너무 커서 우리는 수업을 계속할 수 없었다.

09 lithe

/ láið /   형 유연한, 나긋나긋한
syn graceful, flexible, supple

영영 moving about or bending down with ease

예문 All ballerinas learn to be **lithe** and beautiful on stage.
모든 발레리나들은 무대에서 유연하고 아름답게 되는 것을 배운다.

10 litigation

/ lìtəgéiʃən /   명 소송, 기소
syn lawsuit, case, action

영영 a process of fighting or defending a case in court

예문 Although I knew my neighbours were angry about the noise I make at night, I was surprised that they decided to pursue a **litigation**.
나는 이웃들이 밤에 내가 내는 소리에 대해 화 나있는 것을 알았지만 그들이 소송을 결심한 것이 놀라웠다.

11 mendacious

/ mendéiʃəs /   형 허위의
syn lying

영영 either telling lies or being dishonest

예문 Some people sometimes believe that their government is **mendacious**, and ,therefore, should not be trusted.
어떤 사람들은 가끔씩 그들의 정부가 허위적이므로 신뢰하지 말아야 한다고 생각한다.

12. mercurial
/ mərkjúəriəl /

형 변덕스러운, 활달한

syn capricious, volatile

영영 changing one's opinions or display temperament

예문 Eric quit dating the girl because she had a **mercurial** temperament.
에릭은 그 여자가 변덕스러워서 교제를 그만두었다.

13. onerous
/ ánərəs /

형 아주 힘든, 부담되는

syn burdensome

영영 experiencing difficulties because the task is too much to bear

예문 The job he is doing is **onerous** because it involves teaching students with mental handicaps.
그의 일은 정신박약아들을 가르치는 일이어서 힘들다.

14. oration
/ ɔːréiʃən /

명 공식 연설

syn speech, address

영영 a speech given in a formal occasion

예문 The president gave an **oration** at the opening session of the National Assembly.
대통령은 국회 개원 연설을 했다.

15. ornate
/ ɔːrnéit /

형 잘 꾸민, 화려하게 장식한

syn elaborate, decorative

영영 highly elaborate or excessively decorated

예문 My friends thought my suit looked too **ornate** for such a simple occasion.
친구들은 나의 정장이 그런 단출한 행사에는 너무 화려해 보인다고 생각했다.

day 14

Day 15

01 demarcation
/ dìːmaːrkéiʃən /
명 경계, 분계
syn boundary
영영 a conceptual separation
예문 After the war, both sides wanted a clear **demarcation** of their national borders.
전쟁 이후, 양측은 그들의 분계선에 대해 명확히 하기를 원했다.

02 demure
/ dimjúər /
형 점잔 빼는, 진지한
syn bashful, modest, reserved
영영 always behaving well
예문 His greetings were cordial but still slightly **demure**.
그의 인사는 따뜻했지만 여전히 경직되어 있었다.

03 effervescent
/ èfərvésnt /
형 거품이 있는, 활기 있는
syn animated, gay, hilarious
영영 giving off bubbles, high-spirited
예문 Mineral water can often be **effervescent**.
미네랄워터는 종종 거품이 생길 수 있다.

04 flabbergast
/ flǽbərgæ̀st /

동 소스라쳐 놀라게 하다

syn amaze, astonish, astound

영영 cause to be overcome with astonishment

예문 His accession to the top spot in the company **flabbergasted** everyone who knew him.
그가 그 회사의 최고지위로 승진한 것은 그를 아는 모든 사람들을 놀라게 했다.

05 flagrant
/ fléigrənt /

형 악명 높은, 극악한

syn notorious, outrageous, shameless

영영 conspicuously offensive

예문 We cannot condone such **flagrant** violations of the rules.
우리는 그런 심각한 규칙 위반을 묵과할 수 없다.

06 guile
/ gáil /

명 교활, 간계

syn artfulness, cunning, deceit

영영 the clever use of dishonest behaviour

예문 Now is the time for guts and **guile**.
지금은 배짱과 술책이 필요한 때입니다.

07 implicate
/ ímplikèit /

동 관련시키다, 휩쓸려들게 하다

syn embroil

영영 involve or connect intimately or incriminatingly

예문 The letter that **implicates** him in the bribery case is the key evidence for the case.
그가 뇌물수수 사건에 관여했음을 시사하는 그 편지는 사건의 핵심 증거이다.

day 15

08 jaded

/ dʒéidid /

동 지친

syn fatigue, tire, wear down

영영 exhausted or dissipated

예문 They were **jaded** after the long drive from Manchester city.
맨체스터로부터의 오랜 운전 후에 그들은 몹시 피곤했다.

09 jaunty

/ dʒɔ́:nti /

형 쾌활한, 근심 없는

syn buoyant, carefree, debonair

영영 having a buoyant or self-confident air

예문 Jazz began as popular music with **jaunty** rhythm in early 20C of American history.
재즈는 20세기 초 미국에서 시작된 경쾌한 리듬의 대중음악이다.

10 lambaste

/ læmbéist /

동 몹시 때리다, 비난하다

syn thrash, beat, rebuke, scold

영영 give a thrashing

예문 Atheists don't **lambaste** gods.
무신론자들은 신을 비난하지 않는다.

11 larceny

/ lá:rsəni /

명 절도죄

syn burglary, robbery, stealing, theft

영영 the unlawful taking of others' personal property

예문 The police finally uncovered a criminal operation that engaged in **larceny** and extortion.
경찰은 마침내 절도와 강도 사건이 연루된 한 범행의 전모를 밝혔다.

12 manifold
/ mǽnəfòuld /

형 다양한

syn multifarious

영영 of many different kinds

예문 It was a good opportunity for Darwin to become acquainted with the **manifold** variations of animal life.
동물들의 다양한 변이에 익숙해진 것은 다윈으로서는 좋은 기회였다.

13 obfuscate
/ ábfəskèit /

동 (판단 등을) 흐리게 하다

syn cloud, complicate, confuse

영영 make confused or opaque to perceive

예문 My boss **obfuscated** me by asking irrelevant questions.
상관은 엉뚱한 질문을 하여 나를 당황케 했다.

14 oblivious
/ əblíviəs /

형 염두에 없는, 기억하지 않는

syn inattentive, insensible, unaware, unconscious

영영 lacking conscious awareness

예문 I was **oblivious** that he had any complaints.
그가 어떤 불평이 있는지는 염두에 두지 않았다.

15 ostentatious
/ àstentéiʃəs /

형 과시하는, 겉보기를 꾸미는

syn affected, conspicuous, pretentious

영영 characterized by pretentious, showy, or vulgar display

예문 A real hero is never **ostentatious**.
진정한 영웅은 결코 과시하지 않는다.

Day 16

01 disaffect / dìsəfékt /
동 불평을 품게 하다
syn distance, estrange, separate

영영 cause to lose affection or loyalty

예문 His regal bearing impressed even those **disaffected** with monarchy.
그의 당당한 태도는 군주정에 불만 품은 사람들에게조차 강한 인상을 주었다.

02 disavow / dìsəváu /
동 부인하다
syn abjure, deny

영영 disclaim knowledge or association with something

예문 Every year, American leaders **disavow** partisan politics.
매년 미국의 지도자들은 당파적 정치를 하지 않는다고 부인한다.

03 embellish / imbéliʃ /
동 아름답게 하다, 꾸미다
syn adorn, decorate

영영 make beautiful by ornamentation

예문 She usually **embellishes** her hair with brightly colored ribbons.
그녀는 보통 밝은 색의 리본으로 머리를 장식한다.

04 flout
/ fláut /

동 비웃다, 조롱하다

syn defy, disdain, mock

영영 treat without respect

예문 The headstrong youth **flouted** all authority.
그 고집 센 젊은이는 모든 권위를 비웃었다.

05 heed
/ híːd /

동 주의하다, 마음에 두다

syn obey, consider

영영 pay attention

예문 He did not **heed** my warning at all.
그는 나의 경고에 유의하지 않았다.

06 inarticulate
/ ìnɑːrtíkjulət /

형 발음이 분명치 않은, 모호한

syn incomprehensible, indistinct, muffled, dumb

영영 uttered without the use of normal words or syllables

예문 He becomes **inarticulate** when angry.
그는 성이 나면 (흥분되어) 말을 못 한다.

07 jaundice
/ dʒɔ́ːndis /

동 황달 걸리게 하다, 편견 갖게 하다

syn bias, influence, predispose

영영 cause an illness that makes skin and eyes become yellow

예문 She **jaundiced** her claim by asking too much.
그녀는 부당한 청구를 하여 오히려 요구를 불리하게 만들었다.

08 jeremiad
/ dʒèrəmáiəd /
명 비탄, 하소연
syn lament, deploration

영영 a very long sad complaint or list of complaints

예문 At her father's funeral Jane's heart was numbed with **jeremiad**.
그녀의 아버지 장례식에서 그녀의 마음은 비탄에 짓눌렸다.

09 lurid
/ lúərid /
형 전율적인, 무시무시한
syn ghastly, grisly, gruesome, horrifying

영영 shocking and violent in a way that is deliberate

예문 The **lurid** stories he told shocked his listeners.
그의 무시무시한 이야기들은 듣는 사람들에게 충격을 주었다.

10 mores
/ mɔ́:reiz /
명 사회적 관행, 관습
syn ethics, ideals, morality

영영 the customs and behaviour that are considered typical of a particular social group or community

예문 Many of the old **mores** of the Tohoku region are slowly disappearing.
일본 동북지방의 많은 옛 관습은 천천히 사라지고 있다.

11 obsequious
/ əbsí:kwiəs /
형 아첨하는, 비굴한
syn fawning, groveling, obeisant

영영 full of or exhibiting servile compliance

예문 I hate his **obsequious** smile.
나는 그의 비굴한 웃음이 싫다.

12 ostracism
/ ástrəsìzm /

명 추방, 배척

syn banishment, deportation, exclusion

영영 the act of banishing or excluding

예문 Foreign visitors had better adopt the practice if he is to avoid social **ostracism**.
외국 방문객들이 사회적 배척을 피하기 위해서는 그 관행을 받아들이는 것이 좋다.

13 profane
/ prouféin /

형 모독적인, 불경스런

syn blasphemous, impious, irreverent

영영 having or showing a lack of respect for holy things

예문 He imposed the "Sedition Act," which made it a crime for anyone to say or write anything "disloyal, **profane**, or abusive language" against the government.
그는 이른바 '선동법'을 강요했는데 정부에 대해서 불성실하거나 모독적이고 부정적인 언어를 사용하는 누구라도 죄가 되었다.

14 profligate
/ práfligət /

형 방탕한, 품행이 나쁜

syn depraved, dissolute, lascivious, licentious

영영 using money or time in a careless way

예문 He was considered rather **profligate**, spending half his inheritance while in college.
그는 학창시절에 물려받은 재산의 절반을 소비하는 등 품행이 나쁜 것으로 알려졌다.

15 qualm
/ kwá:m /

명 불안한 마음, 주저함

syn doubt, misgiving, reservation, scruple

영영 a feeling of doubt or worry

예문 He felt **qualms** about letting her go alone.
그는 그녀를 혼자 보내는 것이 불안하였다.

Day 17

01 exasperate
/ igzǽspərèit /

동 노하게 하다, 약 오르게 하다

syn anger, infuriate, madden

영영 make someone very angry or impatient

예문 He was **exasperated** at his wife's dishonesty.
그는 부인의 부정직함에 화가 났다.

02 exculpate
/ ékskʌlpèit /

동 무죄로 하다, 죄를 벗기다

syn acquit, exonerate, pardon

영영 clear someone of guilt or blame

예문 The police **exculpated** Tom from a charge of murder.
경찰은 Tom의 억울한 살인혐의를 벗겨주었다.

03 forage
/ fɔ́:ridʒ /

동 식량을 찾아다니다, 약탈하다

syn hunt, rummage, scrounge

영영 wander in search of food or provisions

예문 Cows are allowed to **forage** about for food.
소는 먹을 풀을 찾아 돌아다닐 수 있게 되어 있다.

04 garner
/ gá:rnər /
동 모으다, 축적하다
syn attain, earn, accumulate

영영 gather into storage

예문 I went to the library to **garner** as much information as I could on the topic.
그 주제에 관하여 최대한 많은 정보를 모으기 위해 도서관으로 갔다.

05 hiatus
/ haiéitəs /
명 벌어진 틈, (연속된 것의) 중단
syn break, gap

영영 a break in the continuity of a work

예문 Nixon's overture to China interrupted a long **hiatus** in American-Chinese relations.
닉슨이 중국과의 교섭을 제안하여 중미 관계의 오랜 단절이 막을 내렸다.

06 incarnate
/ inká:rnət /
동 육체를 갖게 하다, 구체화하다
syn actualize, embody, manifest

영영 give a definite or human form

예문 His ideals were **incarnated** in his poems.
그의 이상은 그의 시 속에서 구체화되었다.

07 incendiary
/ inséndièri /
형 불나게 하는, 선동적인
syn combustible, flammable, ignitable

영영 tending to create strife, violence, etc

예문 Cowell's fellow judges were also unanimous in their approval of her **incendiary** performance, sending her into the semifinals.
카우웰의 동료 심사위원들 또한 그녀를 준결선에 올리고 그녀의 열정적 연주에 대해 만장일치의 찬사를 보냈다.

08 incisive

/ insáisiv /

형 날카로운, 통렬한

syn astute, keen, penetrating

영영 clear and sharp as in operation or expression

예문 I was impressed with my student's *incisive* analysis of the problem.
나는 그 문제에 대한 나의 학생의 날카로운 분석에 감명을 받았다.

09 jocular

/ dʒákjulər /

형 익살맞은, 우스운, 농담의

syn comical, droll, humorous

영영 characterized by joking and good humor

예문 He is so *jocular* he is very popular at parties.
그는 너무나 익살맞아서 파티에서 매우 인기가 높다.

10 kismet

/ kízmit /

명 운명, 천명

syn destiny, doom, fate

영영 the idea that everything in your life is already decided

예문 He has worked out one's own *kismet*.
그는 자신의 혼자 힘으로 제 운명을 개척해왔다.

11 morose

/ məróus /

형 기분이 언짢은, 침울한

syn melancholy, somber

영영 ill-tempered or gloomy

예문 The recent death of both grandparents has made him pensive and *morose*.
조부모의 최근의 사망은 그를 시름에 잠기고 침울하게 만들었다.

12
omnipresent

/ àmniprézənt /

형 두루 편재하는

syn ubiquitous, present

영영 present everywhere simultaneously

예문 On Christmas Eve, Santa Claus is **omnipresent**.
크리스마스이브에 산타클로스는 어디에도 있다.

13
pathology

/ pəθálədʒi /

명 병리학, 병리

syn pathobiology

영영 the scientific study of the nature of disease

예문 This report charts a course for future work in forensic **pathology** and identifies areas for immediate action.
이 보고서는 법의병리학 분야의 차후 연구 과정을 도표화하였고, 즉각적 조처가 필요한 분야를 표시하고 있다.

14
raucous

/ rɔ́:kəs /

형 쉰 목소리의, 소란한

syn harsh, loud, piercing, shrill

영영 rough-sounding and harsh

예문 The **raucous** cries of the crows awoke me early every morning.
까마귀의 쉰 울음소리가 이른 아침 나를 깨웠다.

15
sanctimonious

/ sæ̀ŋktəmóuniəs /

형 신성한 체 하는

syn holier-than-thou, pharisaic

영영 affecting piety or making a display of holiness

예문 You do not have to be so **sanctimonious** to prove that you are devout.
네가 신앙이 독실하다는 것을 입증하려고 신성한 척 할 필요는 없다.

day 17

day by day II 279

Day 18

01 forestall /fɔːrstɔ́ːl/
동 앞지르다, 기선 제압하다
syn avert, circumvent, deter
영영 prevent or defeat by acting first
예문 A result like that is hard to **forestall**.
그와 같은 결과를 막기는 힘들다.

02 genteel /dʒentíːl/
형 품위 있는, 고상한
syn aristocratic, cultured, patrician, refined
영영 refined in manner, well-bred and polite
예문 The young man impressed everyone with his refined, **genteel** manners.
그 젊은 남자는 그의 고상하고 품위 있는 매너로 인해 모든 사람들에게 감명을 주었다.

03 hideous /hídiəs/
형 무시무시한, 소름 끼치는
syn abhorrent, frightful, ghastly
영영 offensive to moral sensibilities
예문 Every day we hear of some **hideous** crime.
매일 우리는 끔찍한 범죄 소식을 접한다.

04 homage
/ hámidʒ /

명 경의, 충성의 맹세

syn honor, respect, veneration

영영 ceremonial acknowledgment showing respect

예문 Many people came to pay **homage** to the dead man.
많은 사람들이 고인에게 경의를 표하러 왔다.

05 inane
/ inéin /

형 어리석은, 무의미한

syn idiotic, ludicrous, moronic

영영 devoid of intelligence

예문 His ideas were so **inane**, I didn't bother to refute them.
그의 아이디어는 너무 어리석어서 나는 그들의 주장에 애써 논박하지 않았다.

06 obscene
/ əbsí:n /

형 외설의

syn indecent, lewd, pornographic

영영 offensive to accepted standards of decency or modesty

예문 Shakespeare's Falstaff is an **obscene**, jolly, fat man who is also a thief.
셰익스피어의 작품 캐릭터 폴스타프는 도둑인 동시에 음탕하고, 명랑하고 뚱뚱한 사람이다.

07 paucity
/ pɔ́:səti /

명 소수, 결핍

syn lack, need, poverty, scarcity

영영 smallness of number or quantity

예문 I would like to travel after retirement, but I may be limited by a **paucity** of funds.
나는 은퇴 후에 여행을 하고 싶지만 금전 제약을 받을 것 같다.

08 pejorative
/ pidʒɔ́ːrətiv /

형 가치를 떨어뜨리는, 경멸적인

syn belittling, degrading, derisive

영영 tending to make or become worse

예문 His use of **pejorative** language indicated his contempt for the audience.
그의 경멸적 언어 사용은 그가 청중들을 멸시하고 있음을 방증했다.

09 pellucid
/ pəlúːsid /

형 투명한, 명료한

syn pure, clear, transparent

영영 admitting the passage of light

예문 Your scheme is so **pellucid** that it will fool no one.
당신의 계획은 다 드러나 보이는 내용이어서 아무도 속일 수 없을 것이다.

10 sanguine
/ sǽŋgwin /

형 쾌활한, 자신만만한

syn buoyant, cheerful, hopeful, optimistic

영영 cheerfully optimistic

예문 He's **sanguine** about getting the work finished on time.
그 일을 제 시간에 마칠 것에 대해 그는 자신한다.

11 satiate
/ séiʃièit /

동 물리게 하다, 물릴 정도로 주다

syn glut, sate, stuff, surfeit

영영 satisfy an appetite or desire fully

예문 My mother always cooks enough food to **satiate** an army.
나의 어머니는 한 무리의 군대에게 먹일 만큼 충분한 음식을 하신다.

12 scathing
/ skéiðiŋ /

형 냉혹한, 가차 없는

syn biting, brutal, caustic, cutting

영영 harshly critical

예문 War had broken out between the colonies and Great Britain, a war for independence that lasted for six **scathing** years.
식민지와 영국 사이에 전쟁이 발발했는데 그것은 냉혹함으로 점철된 6년간의 독립 전쟁이었다.

13 uncanny
/ ʌnkǽni /

형 엄청난, 무시무시하게 기분 나쁜

syn curious, odd, strange, unnatural

영영 peculiarly unsettling, as if of supernatural origin

예문 Her ability to know what people are seemed to be **uncanny**.
그녀의 사람 알아보는 능력은 무시무시해 보였다.

14 undulate
/ ʌ́ndʒulèit /

동 물결이 일다, 파동 치다

syn flow, gush, stream

영영 cause to move in a smooth wavelike motion

예문 The waves **undulated** beneath the boat.
파도가 보트 밑에서 파동 쳤다.

15 vapid
/ vǽpid /

형 맛이 없는, 활기가 없는

syn insipid, senseless

영영 not giving an interest and point

예문 She made a **vapid** comment about the weather.
그녀는 날씨에 대해 김빠진 말을 했다.

day 18

Day 19

01

gorge
/ gó:rdʒ /

동 게걸스레 먹다

syn cram, glut, gormandize

영영 devour greedily

예문 If you exercise a bunch but then **gorge** yourself, you will be more fit but still will not lose fat.
운동을 열심히 하지만 많이 먹는다면, 더 건강할 수는 있어도 여전히 살을 뺄 수는 없을 것이다.

02

granulate
/ grǽnjulèit /

동 (작은) 알갱이로 만들다

syn bashful, modest, reserved

영영 make into minute grain

예문 If fresh food is unavailable, the best artificial food for discussion is a high quality **granulated** food.
만약 신선한 음식을 구할 수 없다면, 가능한 최고의 인공 음식은 고급 미립 음식이다.

03

grisly
/ grízli /

형 섬뜩한, 소름끼치는

syn dreadful, ghastly, gory

영영 extremely frightening and usually connected with death

예문 They found the **grisly** scene in the kitchen.
그들은 부엌에서 끔찍한 광경을 목격했다.

284 SAving Time SAT Vocabulary

04 jest
/ dʒést /

명 농담, 익살

syn gag, joke, prank

영영 something said or done to amuse people

예문 That's a mere matter of **jest**.
그것은 농담에 불과하다.

05 jibe
/ dʒáib /

동 조화하다, 일치하다

syn agree, concur, correspond

영영 be in accord

예문 His story doesn't **jibe** with what I told you about.
그녀의 이야기는 내가 너에게 얘기했던 것과 일치하지 않는다.

06 jut
/ dʒʌ́t /

동 돌출하다, 불룩 내밀다

syn extend, extrude, project

영영 stick out above or beyond a surface

예문 A row of small windows **jutted** out from the roof.
일련의 작은 창들이 지붕에서 돌출되어 나와 있다.

07 carping
/ ká:rpiŋ /

형 흠잡는, 시끄럽게 구는

syn fault-finding

영영 tending to make petty complaints

예문 Peter was perfectly satisfied, so nobody cast any blight on his happiness by **carping** criticism.
피터는 완벽히 만족했고 헐뜯는 비판으로써 그의 행복을 망치는 사람은 없었다.

day 19

08

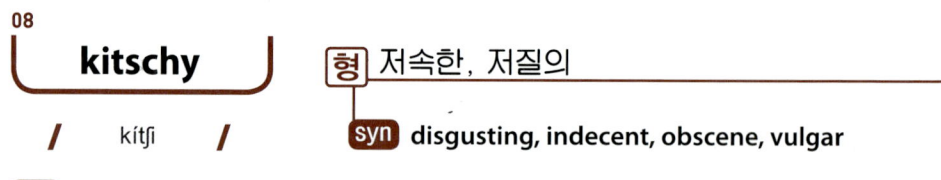

kitschy

/ kítʃi /

형 저속한, 저질의

syn disgusting, indecent, obscene, vulgar

영영 of bad taste, especially in the arts

예문 This book has a bad **kitschy** cover but otherwise it would be a good populist book.
이 책은 저급한 표지를 갖고 있는데 그렇지 않다면 인기 있는 책이 되었을 것이다.

09

lackey

/ lǽki /

명 (제복을 입은) 종복

syn attendant, hireling, minion

영영 a liveried male servant

예문 So we arrived together at the door where the **lackey** stood.
그래서 우리는 종복이 서 있는 문에 같이 도착했다.

10

laggard

/ lǽgərd /

명 탈락자

syn dawdler, lag, loafer, loiterer

영영 a slow and lazy person

예문 You may be a communications **laggard**, though you are a professional in other work areas.
당신은 다른 업무분야에서는 잘하고 있지만 의사소통이 답답한 사람일 수 있다.

11

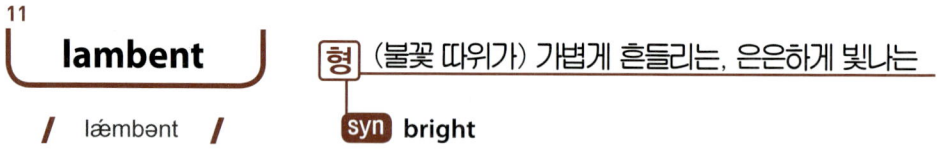

lambent

/ lǽmbənt /

형 (불꽃 따위가) 가볍게 흔들리는, 은은하게 빛나는

syn bright

영영 flickering softly over a surface

예문 Ruth lifted her eyes to his, and their **lambent** fires were suddenly rekindled.
루스는 그의 눈을 올려다보았고 그들의 은은하게 빛나는 눈빛은 갑자기 다시 불붙었다.

12. meritorious
/ mèritɔ́:riəs /

형 공적 있는, 가치 있는

syn commendable, creditable, laudable

영영 deserving reward or praise

예문 The soldier was honored specific reference for **meritorious** conduct.
그 군인은 공적을 세워 특별한 칭송을 받았다.

13. methodical
/ məθádikəl /

형 질서 있는, 조직적인

syn systematic, orderly

영영 arranged or proceeding in systematic order

예문 You need to take a **methodical** approach in solving each problem.
너는 각 문제들을 해결하기 위해 조직적 접근을 해야 한다.

14. notary
/ nóutəri /

명 공증인

syn a notary public

영영 a clerk licensed to prepare legal documents

예문 And the **notary** can be here at 7:30, too?
공증인도 7시 30분까지 이곳에 올 수 있는 건가요?

15. penultimate
/ pinʌ́ltəmət /

형 끝에서 둘째의

syn penult

영영 of anything that is next to the last

예문 The **penultimate** round starts at Dodger Stadium, on Sunday.
다저 스타디움에서 일요일에 준결승이 열린다.

Day 20

01 abscond / æbskánd /
동 도망하다
syn bolt, disappear, escape
영영 leave secretly and hide oneself, often to avoid arrest
예문 The teller **absconded** with the bonds issued by his predecessor.
은행출납계원은 선임자가 발행한 채권을 가지고 도망쳤다.

02 acquiescent / æ̀kwiésnt /
형 묵묵히 따르는, 묵인하는
syn assenting, compliant, consenting, dutiful
영영 willing to do what somebody wants
예문 He was **acquiescent** and ready to go along with his friend's desires.
그는 묵묵히 따랐으며 그의 친구의 열망에 부응할 준비가 되어 있었다.

03 bemuse / bimjú:z /
동 멍하게 하다, 곤혹케 하다
syn confuse, daze
영영 cause to be confused emotionally
예문 Her beautiful image **bemused** his eyes.
그녀의 아름다운 자태가 그의 눈을 멀게 했다.

04 besiege

/ bisíːdʒ /

동 에워싸다, 공세를 퍼붓다

syn harass, plague, provoke, torment

영영 surround with hostile forces

예문 For years, the Greeks **besieged** the city of Troy.
다년간 그리스군은 트로이를 포위하였다.

05 bewitch

/ biwítʃ /

동 마법을 걸다, 호리다

syn curse, enchant, hex

영영 place under one's power as if by magic

예문 He was **bewitched** by the princess' beauty.
그는 그 공주의 미모에 매혹되었다.

06 captious

/ kǽpʃəs /

형 헐뜯는, 흠잡기 좋아하는

syn fault-finding, carping

영영 marked by a disposition to find trivial faults

예문 The famous actress disliked **captious** questions from the press.
그 유명한 여배우는 기자들의 흠잡는 듯한 질문을 싫어했다.

07 knavery

/ néivəri /

명 속임수, 부정행위

syn miscreant, rogue

영영 acts of lying, cheating or stealing

예문 We'd be crushed if we faced the truth of our own **knavery**.
만약 우리가 저지른 부정에 대한 진실과 마주한다면, 우리는 무너질 것이다.

08 cascade

/ kæskéid /

명 (작은) 폭포

syn cataract, fall, rapids

영영 a steep and small waterfall

예문 So now Della's beautiful hair fell about her, shining like a **cascade** of brown waters.
델라의 아름다운 머리카락이 흐트러지며 갈색 폭포처럼 빛났다.

09 deification

/ dìːəfikéiʃən /

명 신으로 섬기기, 신성시

syn reverence, veneration, worship

영영 the act of treating or worshiping as a god

예문 Thus even love, which is the **deification** of persons, must become more impersonal every day.
사람들을 신성시하는 마음인 사랑조차 분명 매일 더 비인격적이 되어간다.

10 emphatic

/ imfǽtik /

형 강조된, 뚜렷한

syn assertive, forceful, insistent

영영 expressed or performed with emphasis

예문 "I couldn't disagree more," another surgeon said an **emphatic** answer.
'나는 완전 동감이오.'라고 다른 외과의사가 강한 어조로 말했다.

11 enamor

/ inǽmər /

동 호리다, 매혹하다

syn charm, enchant, enthrall

영영 inspire with love

예문 He is **enamored** with the girl.
그는 그 소녀에 반해 있다.

12. finicky
/fíniki/

형 (외양 등에) 몹시 신경을 쓰는, 까다로운

syn overfastidious

영영 difficult to please

예문 Alligators are **finicky** eaters.
악어 식성은 좀 까다롭다.

13. gloat
/glóut/

동 흡족한 듯이 바라보다

syn boast, brag, flaunt, strut

영영 feel or express pleasure or self-satisfaction

예문 Not only did our arch rivals win the football game, they **gloated** after wards.
우리의 교활한 라이벌들이 축구게임에 이겼을 뿐 아니라, 이후 그들은 고소한 듯 쳐다보기까지 했다.

14. litany
/lítni/

명 탄원, 장황한 이야기

syn petition

영영 a repetitive or incantatory recital

예문 Remember the prayer of our holy **litany**, where we implore the Divine Power.
우리가 신성한 힘을 달라고 비는 성스러운 청원의 기도를 기억하라.

15. marauder
/mərɔ́:dər/

동 약탈하다, 습격하다

syn pillage, plunder, ransack

영영 rove and raid in search of plunder

예문 The house was **maraudered** of all its valuables.
집 안의 귀중품을 전부 약탈당했다.

Day 21

01 bereft / biréft /
형 빼앗긴, 잃은
syn minus
영영 lacking in something needed or expected
예문 He is **bereft** of all happiness.
그는 모든 행복을 빼앗기고 있다.

02 bestial / béstʃəl /
형 흉포한, 야만스런
syn barbaric, brutal, cruel, fierce
영영 marked by brutality or depravity
예문 Due to the **bestial** punishment, he died.
그 잔인한 벌로 그는 죽었다.

03 blithe / bláið /
형 즐거운, 유쾌한
syn cheerful, content, delighted
영영 very happy or cheerful
예문 She seems to go through life with a positive and **blithe** outlook.
그녀는 긍정적이고 유쾌한 관념을 갖고 인생을 사는 것처럼 보인다.

04 canard

/ kəná:rd /

명 허위 보도, 와전

syn misrepresentation

영영 false telling

예문 It is almost impossible to protect oneself from such a base **canard**.
그런 비열한 허위보도를 막기란 거의 불가능하다.

05 carnage

/ ká:rnidʒ /

명 살육, 대량 학살

syn bloodshed, butchery, slaughter

영영 the killing or wounding large numbers of people

예문 At the school, I learned about the **carnage** in Jeju Island.
학창 시절에 나는 제주 대학살에 대해 배웠다.

06 cataclasm

/ kǽtəklæ̀zm /

명 파열, 분열

syn agitation, breakup

영영 a division into smaller parts

예문 I need not say that we were strangers to any species of **cataclasm**.
우리는 어떤 부류의 분열도 생소해 보인다는 것을 굳이 말할 필요가 없다.

07 eclat

/ eikláː /

명 대성공, 명성

syn splendid result

영영 great success

예문 The movie was an **eclat**.
그 영화는 대성공이었다.

08 embroil
/ imbróil /

동 (사태를) 혼란케 하다, 번거롭게 하다

syn enmesh, entangle, implicate, involve

영영 throw into confusion or strife

예문 He was **embroiled** in difficulties at that time.
그 당시 그는 곤란한 상황에 말려들었다.

09 fawning
/ fɔ́:niŋ /

형 아양 부리는

syn groveling, obsequious, servile, subservient

영영 attempting to win favor from people by flattery

예문 He refused to be **fawning** to anyone.
그는 어느 누구에게도 아첨하기를 거부했다.

10 febrile
/ fí:brail /

형 열병의, 열로 생기는

syn feverish

영영 relating to or characterized by fever

예문 He went on in a **febrile** and feminine agitation.
그는 계속 열병 기운으로 나약한 동요 상태였다.

11 gainsay
/ gèinséi /

동 부정하다, 반박하다

syn contradict, counter, deny, dispute

영영 declare false

예문 There is no **gainsaying** his honesty.
그가 정직하다는 점은 부인할 수 없다.

12. gazette
/ gəzét /

명 신문, (시사 문제 등의) 정기 간행물, 관보
syn newspaper, official report

영영 an official journal

예문 Having been indicted for being party to a crime, he was **gazetted** out.
그가 범죄 사건에의 연루로 기소된 후에, 그의 사직발령이 관보에 실렸다.

13. gentry
/ dʒéntri /

명 신사계급, 상류 사회
syn upper class

영영 people of high social position

예문 The people in it are landed **gentry**.
그곳에 속한 그 사람들은 땅을 가진 상류층이다.

14. homeopathy
/ hòumiápəθi /

명 유사 동종 요법
syn homeotherapy

영영 treating based on a drug having symptoms similar to those of the disease itself

예문 He had been assured that cigars were excellent for the health but he knew as little about tobacco as about **homeopathy**.
그는 담배가 건강에 좋다는 것을 확신했지만 유사요법만큼이나 담배 자체에 대해서도 아는 것이 없었다.

15. impious
/ ímpiəs /

형 경건치 않은, 불경한
syn blasphemous, disrespectful, irreverent, profane

영영 lacking reverence

예문 The worshippers resented her **impious** remarks about their faith.
숭배자들은 그들의 믿음에 대한 그녀의 부적절한 발언에 대해 분개했다.

Day 22

01 commodious / kəmóudiəs /
형 넓은, 널찍한
syn ample, roomy, spacious
영영 large and roomy
예문 After sleeping in small roadside cabins, they found their hotel suite **commodious**.
그들이 노변의 작은 오두막에서 자보니, 호텔방이 넓다는 것을 알게 되었다.

02 deft / déft /
형 (일의) 솜씨가 좋은, 능란한
syn adroit, dexterous, skillful
영영 quick and neat in movement
예문 He is **deft** at skiing.
그는 스키를 잘 탄다.

03 educe / idjú:s /
동 추론하다, 연역하다
syn deduce, infer, presume
영영 draw or bring out
예문 From this we **educe** a method for the construction.
이것을 기초로 하여 그 건조 방법을 추론해낸다.

04 encumber
/ inkʌ́mbər /

동 방해하다, 거치적거리게 하다

syn burden, hinder, impede

영영 put a heavy load

예문 Heavy armor **encumbered** him in the water.
수중에서 중장비가 그에게 거치적거렸다.

05 figment
/ fígmənt /

명 가공적인 일, 허구

syn fabrication, fiction, concoction

영영 something invented, made up, or fabricated

예문 The technology to clone endangered species doesn't belong in science **figment**.
멸종의 위기에 있는 종들을 복제하는 기술은 과학적 허구가 아니다.

06 high-strung
/ hái-strʌ́ŋ /

형 신경질적인, 흥분하기 쉬운

syn delicate, nervous, jittery

영영 tending to be very nervous and easily excited

예문 Many people became very **high-strung** about the reports of a homicidal maniac.
많은 사람들은 살인마에 대한 보도에 매우 과민해졌다.

07 lascivious
/ ləsíviəs /

형 음탕한, 호색의, 외설적인

syn carnal, lecherous, lewd, libidinous, lustful

영영 given to or expressing lust

예문 His **lascivious** glance made the young lady feel uncomfortable.
그의 음탕한 눈길은 그 젊은 여자를 불편하게 했다.

08 lesion
/ líːʒən /
명 외상, 손상, 정신적 상해
syn damage, hurt, injury

영영 any localized abnormal structural change in a bodily part

예문 He had a minor **lesion** on the elbow.
그는 팔꿈치에 가벼운 부상을 입었다.

09 niggardly
/ nígərdli /
형 인색한, 쩨쩨하게 구는
syn begrudging, cheap, miserly, stingy

영영 grudging and petty in giving or spending

예문 Billionaire Howard Hughes is both generous and **niggardly**.
억만장자 하워드 휴즈는 관대하면서도 때로 인색하다.

10 officious
/ əfíʃəs /
형 (쓸데없이) 참견하는
syn intrusive, meddlesome, nosy, obtrusive

영영 marked by excessive eagerness

예문 We all thought she was rather **officious** but we ignored it.
우리 모두는 그녀가 쓸데없이 참견한다고 여기고 그것을 무시했다.

11 onus
/ óunəs /
명 부담, 무거운 짐, 의무
syn liability, responsibility, load

영영 a difficult responsibility or necessity

예문 The emperor was spared the **onus** of signing the surrender papers.
황제는 항복 문서에 서명하는 부담을 덜었다.

12. patriarch
/ péitriɑ:rk /

명 가장, 족장, 로마 교황

syn matriarch, Pope

영영 the head of a family, the chief of a tribe

예문 In many primitive tribes, the leader was the **patriarch**.
많은 원시 부족에서 지도자는 족장이었다.

13. pliant
/ pláiənt /

형 휘기 쉬운, 유연한, 고분고분한

syn acquiescent, agreeable, flexible

영영 yielding readily to influence or domination

예문 The connections in the raft are slack and **pliant**.
뗏목 목재들의 연결이 느슨해서 뒤틀리기 쉽다.

14. ravenous
/ rǽvənəs /

형 게걸스럽게 먹는, 탐욕스러운

syn gluttonous, hungry, insatiable

영영 greedy for gratification

예문 His empty feeling had become hunger, and the hunger grew bigger, until soon he was as **ravenous** as a bear.
그의 공복감은 허기로 바뀌고 그 허기가 더 커져서 그는 곰 같이 게걸스럽게 되었다.

15. sedentary
/ sédntèri /

형 앉은 채 있는, 정주하는

syn fixed, immobile, inactive, stationary

영영 characterized by or requiring much sitting

예문 Because he had a **sedentary** occupation, he decided to visit a gymnasium weekly.
그는 앉아서 일하는 직업을 가지고 있기 때문에, 매주 체육관에 가기로 결심했다.

Day 23

01
adamant

/ ǽdəmənt /

형 요지부동의, 단호한

syn **impervious, immovable, unyielding**

영영 not giving in or unyielding in a situation

예문 Although the pressure from the opposition party was intense, the President remained **adamant** about his decision to go ahead with the project.
야당으로부터의 압력이 거셌지만 대통령은 그 프로젝트를 진행하려는 결정을 바꾸지 않았다.

02
betroth

/ bitróuð /

동 약혼시키다

syn **engage**

영영 get someone engaged formally before the wedding

예문 Believing that he is rich, she **betrothed** her daughter to him.
그가 돈이 많다고 믿고 그녀는 자기 딸을 그에게 약혼시켰다.

03
circumvent

/ sə́:rkəmvént /

동 우회하다, 피하다

syn **skirt, circle**

영영 avoid restriction in a clever way

예문 The Japanese army was known to **circumvent** their enemies to attack, but it did not work well for them against Americans in the pacific.
일본군은 공격을 위해 적을 우회하는 것으로 유명했지만 태평양에서 미국인들에 대항해서는 잘 먹혀 들지 않았다.

04 clamor
/ klǽmər /

명 시끄러운 외침, 떠들썩함

syn uproar

영영 making a loud noise by insisting on something

예문 The mayor blocked the square as he wanted to stop people **clamoring** against the government.
그 시장은 사람들이 정부에 대항하여 반대할 수 없게 광장을 막았다.

05 denigrate
/ dénigrèit /

동 폄하하다

syn belittle

영영 If you denigrate someone or something, you cast aspersions on or defame the person or the object

예문 The record company insists the reporter **denigrated** the company on false assumption.
그 음반 회사는 그 기자가 잘못된 추정으로 회사의 명예를 실추시켰다고 주장한다.

06 enigmatic
/ ènigmǽtik /

형 애매한, 불가사의한

syn mystifying, cryptic

영영 being obscure, puzzling and difficult to understand

예문 As the English teacher didn't tell much about himself, many students thought he was **enigmatic**.
그 영어 선생님이 자신의 이야기를 그다지 하지 않기 때문에 많은 학생들은 그를 불가사의한 존재로 여겼다.

07 enmity
/ énməti /

명 원한, 증오, 적대감

syn ill will, hatred, hostility

영영 a feeling of strong hatred towards someone

예문 My father's hot temper earned him the **enmity** of his business partners.
나의 아버지는 다혈질적인 기질로 사업 파트너들에게 적대감을 샀다.

08 fortuitous
/ fɔːrtjúːətəs /
형 우연한, 행운의
syn lucky, fortunate

영영 regarded as lucky or fortunate

예문 It is extremely **fortuitous** to win the lottery.
복권에 당첨되는 것은 굉장한 행운이다.

09 gingerly
/ dʒíndʒərli /
부 신중히, 지극히 조심스럽게
syn attentively, carefully

영영 very carefully because of danger or difficulty

예문 They walked **gingerly** on the icy street.
그들은 빙판길에서 조심스럽게 걸었다.

10 glossary
/ glásəri /
명 소사전, 용어집
syn list

영영 a list of special or technical terms, usually in an alphabetical order

예문 It took them over a month to prepare the **glossary** of the new physics textbook.
새 물리 교과서의 용어집을 준비하는 것은 한 달 이상이나 걸렸다.

11 heterogeneous
/ hètərədʒíːniəs /
형 이종의, 이질의
syn miscellaneous

영영 varied and diverse in character

예문 The government is actively encouraging people to accept the **heterogeneous** population in society.
정부는 다문화 인구를 사회에 수용하도록 적극 장려하고 있다.

12 hidebound

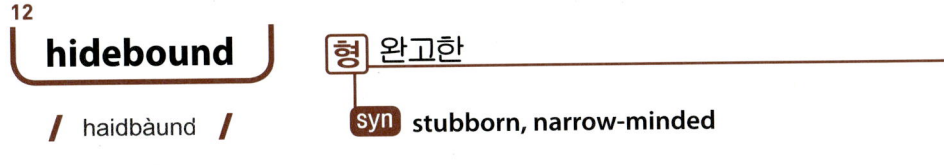

/ haidbàund /

형 완고한

syn **stubborn, narrow-minded**

영영 criticized for being stubborn and unwilling to change

예문 Some people say that a man gets to be **hidebound** and old fashioned when he becomes a middle aged person.
남자가 중년의 나이가 되면 고집이 세어지고 보수적으로 변한다고들 한다.

13 inchoate

/ inkóuət /

형 시작하기 직전의, 시작 단계인

syn **beginning, starting, infancy**

영영 quite recent, therefore not being properly developed

예문 The project is in **inchoate** stage and needs time to be completed.
그 프로젝트는 막 시작하는 단계에 있고 완성되기 위해서는 시간을 필요로 한다.

14 incorrigible

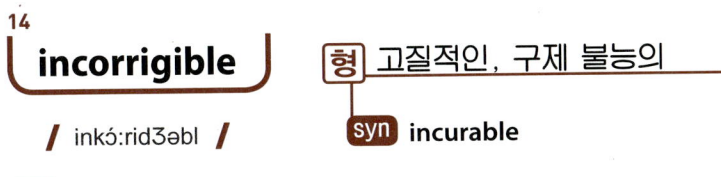

/ inkɔ́:ridʒəbl /

형 고질적인, 구제 불능의

syn **incurable**

영영 making some mistakes but being unlikely to change it

예문 The court found the criminal **incorrigible**, and, therefore, sentenced him to life imprisonment.
법원은 그 범죄자를 구제불능이라 여겨 그에게 종신형을 언도했다.

15 indefatigable

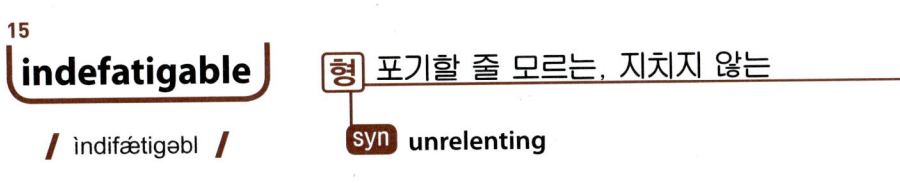

/ ìndifǽtigəbl /

형 포기할 줄 모르는, 지치지 않는

syn **unrelenting**

영영 not getting tired of doing something

예문 With **indefatigable** zeal, he has searched for information about the spice trade in the South Pacific.
포기하지 않고 남태평양의 향신료 무역에 관한 정보를 찾아왔다.

Day 24

01 brazen
/ bréizn /
형 시끄러운, 뻔뻔스러운
syn bold, shameless

영영 very bold and not caring what other people think

예문 The loyal princess of Monaco became known for being **brazen** even as a small girl.
그 모나코의 공주는 어려서부터 뻔뻔스러운 것으로 유명했다.

02 circumlocution
/ sə̀ːrkəmloukjúːʃən /
명 완곡한 표현, 수다
syn digression, rambling

영영 a way of expressing words by not being clear

예문 The professor's **circumlocutions** in his lecture were refreshing and stimulating.
그 교수가 수업에서 구사하는 완곡한 표현들은 신선하고 자극적이었다.

03 clemency
/ klémənsi /
명 관용, 관대한 처분
syn mercy

영영 a willingness to punish less severely

예문 The government gives **clemency** to the convicted criminals on Independence Day.
정부는 독립기념일마다 죄수들을 사면한다.

04 cloying

/ klɔ́iiŋ /   형 지나치게 감상적인, 너무 감미로운

syn sweet, cowed

영영 too kind or sentimental

예문 She didn't realize that her **cloying** kindness made others to shy away from her.
그녀는 지나친 친절로 인해 다른 사람들이 그녀를 멀리함을 깨닫지 못했다.

05 desecrate

/ désikrèit /   동 (신성하게 여기는 것을) 훼손하다

syn violate, insult

영영 damage or insult something considered as sacred

예문 Native American Indians were shocked to find their sacred burial ground **desecrated** by white settlers.
미국 원주민들은 백인 정착민들에 의해 자신들의 신성한 묘가 훼손된 것을 알고 충격을 받았다.

06 desegregate

/ di:ségrigèit /   동 인종차별대우를 폐지하다

syn abolish, repeal

영영 abolish an institution meant to discriminate people of different race

예문 The apartheid policy was **desegregated** when Nelson Mandela became the president.
인종 분리 정책은 넬슨 만델라가 대통령이 되었을 때 폐지되었다.

07 epitome

/ ipítəmi /   명 본보기, 전형

syn abstract, summary, embodiment

영영 the best possible example

예문 I believe that my wife is the **epitome** of what a good wife is supposed to be.
나는 나의 아내가 좋은 아내란 무엇인지를 보여주는 완벽한 본보기라 믿는다.

day 24

08 indolent
/índələnt/
형 게으른, 나태한
syn lazy

영영 wanting to avoid activity

예문 In public schools, teachers can be disgusted with apathetic and **indolent** students.
공립학교에서는 선생님들이 무관심하고 게으른 학생들을 싫어할 수 있다.

09 multifarious
/mʌltəféəriəs/
형 여러 부분으로 된
syn various, multitude

영영 consisting of numerous aspects

예문 One common trait that the nations of Singapore and US share is the mix of **multifarious** cultures.
싱가포르와 미국의 공통점은 다양한 문화가 조합됐다는 것이다.

10 parsimony
/pá:rsəmòuni/
형 (금전적으로) 인색한
syn frugality, stinginess

영영 not spending money for others

예문 Some people think that the rich must be **parsimony** people, but it is not true.
부자들이 인색하다고들 생각하지만 사실은 그렇지 않다.

11 penurious
/pənjúəriəs/
형 궁핍한
syn destitute, penniless

영영 not just being poor but lacking in all basic necessities

예문 The miserable part of my life was when I went **penurious** and not being able to buy my son any milk.
인생에서 가장 불행했던 때는 내가 궁핍해져서 아들에게 우유를 조금이라도 사줄 수 없을 때였다.

12 rapture
/ ræptʃər /

명 환희, 기쁨

syn delight, ecstasy

영영 a feeling of extreme happiness and joy

예문 When I saw my son for the first time in my life, my mind was filled with **rapture**.
아들을 처음으로 보았을 때 나의 마음은 기쁨으로 가득 채워졌다.

13 repudiate
/ ripjú:dièit /

동 거절하다, 부인하다

syn reject, deny, disown

영영 deny others' request or an allegation

예문 The speaker of White House **repudiated** the claim that America has something to do with the sinking of a naval vessel.
백악관 대변인은 미국이 군함 침몰과 관련 있다는 주장을 반박했다.

14 serendipity
/ sèrəndípəti /

명 뜻밖의 기쁨

syn luck, surprise

영영 something luckily and unexpected

예문 It was a **serendipity** that I found my long lost friend from junior high school on a website.
오랫동안 못 봤던 중학교 동창을 인터넷에서 발견한 것은 뜻밖의 기쁨이었다.

15 sinuous
/ sínjuəs /

형 선회하는, 물결 모양의, 구불구불한

syn lithe, serpentine

영영 having smooth twists and turns

예문 A sea snake swims in **sinuous** motion in the water.
바다뱀은 물속에서 구불구불한 움직임으로 수영한다.

Day 25

01 coagulate
/ kouǽgjulèit /

동 (용액을) 응고시키다, 굳어지다
syn solidify, thicken

영영 change to a solid or semi-solid state

예문 The investigators at the murder scene discovered that the blood had already **coagulated**.
살인 장소에서 조사관들은 혈흔이 이미 굳었음을 발견했다.

02 alacrity
/ əlǽkrəti /

명 민활, 민첩함, 경쾌
syn eagerness, speed

영영 brisk and cheerful readiness

예문 He moved with such an **alacrity** that I could barely keep up with him.
그가 너무 민첩하게 움직여서 그를 따르는 것이 힘들었다.

03 delinquency
/ dilíŋkwənsi /

명 태만, 청소년 비행
syn wrongdoing, misconduct

영영 minor crime, especially that committed by young people

예문 **Delinquency** is often an expression of frustration felt against school.
청소년 비행은 종종 학교에 대한 좌절의 표현이다.

04 evanescent

/ èvənésnt /

형 사라져가는, 덧없는

syn fleeting, momentary

영영 vanishing or slowly fading away

예문 As many TV celebrities think that their fame will be **evanescent**, they run their own business in case of no work.
많은 TV 연예인들은 인기가 순간이라 생각하기 때문에 일이 더 이상 없을 경우를 대비하여 자체 사업을 운영한다.

05 exacerbate

/ igzǽsərbèit /

형 (상황을) 악화시키다

syn aggravate

영영 make a situation get even worse

예문 Her attempts at helping her friend construct a model airplane **exacerbated** the situation.
친구의 모형 비행기 만들기를 도우려는 그 여자의 시도는 그 상황을 악화시켰다.

06 inexorable

/ inéksərəbl /

형 멈출 수 없는, 거침없는

syn relentless

영영 not stopping and keeping going

예문 The price of oil has been on **inexorable** increase due to ever growing Chinese economy.
석유의 가격은 계속해서 커가는 중국 경제 때문에 거침없이 오르고 있었다.

07 infatuate

/ infǽtʃuèit /

동 판단력을 흐리게 하다, 얼빠지게 하다

syn daze, stun

영영 inspire someone with an intense but short-lived passion

예문 When I saw my wife for the first time at a cafe, I was completely **infatuated** with her.
내가 어느 카페에서 나의 아내를 처음 보았을 때 나는 그녀에게 완전히 빠져 버렸다.

08

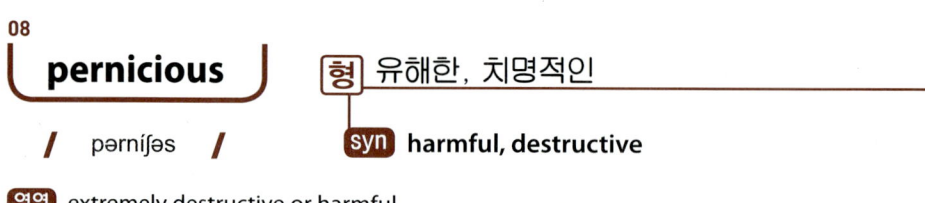

pernicious 형 유해한, 치명적인

/ pərníʃəs / syn **harmful, destructive**

영영 extremely destructive or harmful

예문 Many people are not aware that tuberculosis is a ***pernicious*** disease that can affect much of the population.
결핵이 다수 인구에 영향을 끼칠 수 있는 치명적 질병이라는 것을 많은 사람들이 알지 못하고 있다.

09

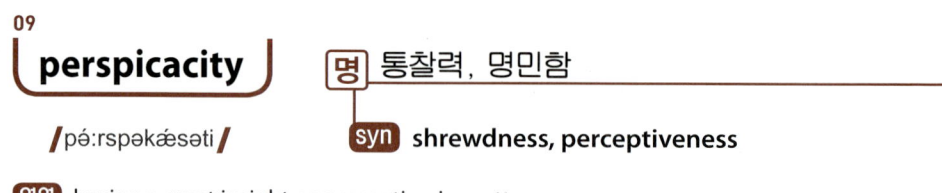

perspicacity 명 통찰력, 명민함

/ pə́:rspəkǽsəti / syn **shrewdness, perceptiveness**

영영 having a great insight or perception in matters

예문 ***Perspicacity*** is required of students who aspire to be the future scientists.
미래의 과학자가 되기를 열망하는 학생들에게는 통찰력이 요구되어진다.

10

requisition 명 요구, 징발

/ rèkwəzíʃən / syn **demand, call**

영영 a formally written request that allows an institution to obtain goods

예문 There has been an ongoing ***requisition*** from North Korea to negotiate with US regarding nuclear weapon issue.
핵무기 문제에 관해 미국과 협상하려는 북한의 계속되는 요구가 있었다.

11

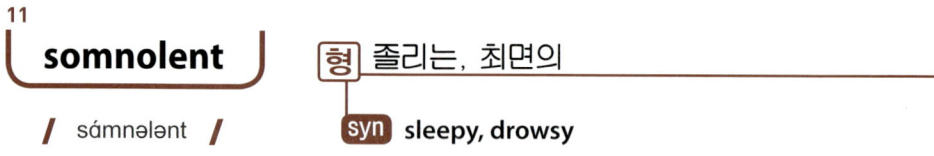

somnolent 형 졸리는, 최면의

/ sámnələnt / syn **sleepy, drowsy**

영영 causing or suggestive of drowsiness

예문 The ***somnolent*** kindergarteners kept falling asleep and couldn't follow what their teacher was saying.
잠이 오는 유치원생들은 계속 잠에 빠졌고 그들의 선생님이 말하는 것을 이해할 수 없었다.

12. sophomoric
/ sàfəmɔ́:rik /
형 (대학) 2년생의, 미숙한
syn immature, uninformed

영영 not yet mature and often acting with arrogant attitude

예문 Teenagers do not realize that their judgements can look **sophomoric** to the adults.
십대들은 그들의 판단력이 어른들에게는 미숙해 보일 수 있다는 것을 깨닫지 못한다.

13. travesty
/ trǽvəsti /
명 졸렬한 모방, 모조품
syn parody

영영 a very bad representation of another thing

예문 Many who witnessed the trial regarded its decision to be a **travesty** of justice.
그 재판을 목격한 많은 사람들은 법원의 결정이 정의의 졸렬한 모방품이라고 여겼다.

14. variegated
/ vέəriəgèitid /
형 다양성이 많은, 잡색의
syn mottled, dappled

영영 exhibiting different colors

예문 Since I like simplicity, I do not like a necktie that is **variegated** in colors.
나는 단순함을 좋아하기 때문에 다양한 색의 얼룩덜룩한 넥타이를 좋아하지 않는다.

15. veneer
/ vəníər /
명 덧붙이는 판자, 겉치장
syn facade

영영 a surface appearance that hides what is below

예문 I was deceived by his **veneer** of sophistication and held him with utmost respect.
나는 그의 겉치장에 불과한 섬세함에 속아서 그를 크게 존중해주었다.

day 25

Day 26

01 agile / ǽdʒəl /
형 기민한, 몸이 재빠른
syn quick, nimble
영영 very quick at doing something or moving
예문 One should be very **agile** to be a running back in American football.
미식축구에서 러닝 백이 되기 위해서는 굉장히 민첩해야 한다.

02 cognizant / kágnəzənt /
형 인식하고 있는
syn aware, mindful
영영 having knowledge or awareness
예문 The politician is not **cognizant** of the negative impression he has with the public.
그 정치가는 그에게 가지는 대중들의 부정적 인상을 인식하지 못한다.

03 burnish / bə́ːrniʃ /
동 갈다, 닦다, 광내다
syn brighten, polish
영영 do something to make something look better and improved
예문 The manager had the waitresses **burnish** all the silverware in the restaurant.
매니저는 웨이트리스들이 식당 안에 있는 모든 식기류들을 닦아서 광내게 만들었다.

04 buttress
/ bʌ́tris /

동 지지하다

syn supports, support

영영 give strength to something or hold it up

예문 Castles or cathedrals in the west couldn't be built without **buttresses**.
서양의 성들이나 성당들은 부벽들이 없이는 세워질 수 없었다.

05 chide
/ tʃáid /

동 책망하다, 꾸짖다

syn disparage, censure

영영 blame or criticise

예문 My wife sometimes **chides** our son for watching too much television.
나의 아내는 가끔 아들이 TV를 너무 많이 보는 것을 꾸짖는다.

06 collateral
/ kəlǽtərəl /

형 평행한, 부차적인

syn subsidiary

영영 not important but secondary

예문 The scientists investigated the **collateral** effect of their experiment.
과학자들은 그들의 실험의 부차적 효과를 조사했다.

07 despondent
/ dispándənt /

형 낙담한, 실의에 빠진

syn dejected, discouraged

영영 feeling depressed, discouraged or hopeless

예문 If you are seriously **despondent** and don't engage in anything, you may need some psychiatric help.
만약 당신이 크게 낙담해서 아무 일도 손에 안 잡히면 정신과 도움이 필요할 수 있다.

day by day II 313

08 excavate
/ ékskəvèit /

동 발굴하다

syn burrow

영영 dig out something from the ground

예문 Archaeologists *excavated* 12,000-year-old artifacts from the sea in southern Peru.
고고학자들은 페루 남부의 바다에서 12,000 년이나 된 유물들을 발굴했다.

09 excursion
/ ikskə́:rʒən /

명 (짧은) 여행, 소풍

syn trip, tour, journey

영영 a pleasure trip that only lasts for a short time

예문 The students will go on a school *excursion* to an amusement park near Seoul.
학교 소풍을 서울 가까이 있는 놀이공원으로 갈 것이다.

10 execrate
/ éksəkrèit /

동 (통렬히) 비판하다, 비난하다

syn criticize

영영 strongly criticize someone for their misdeeds

예문 The spokesman of White House vehemently *execrated* Iran for their violation of a UN resolution.
백악관 대변인은 유엔 조약의 위반에 대해 이란을 맹렬히 비난했다.

11 exigent
/ éksədʒənt /

형 위급한, 급박한

syn urgent, critical

영영 urgent and requiring immediate action and attention

예문 I saw some police and emergency units heading towards me in *exigent* manner.
나는 몇몇 경찰과 응급 차량이 내가 있는 쪽으로 급히 오는 것을 보았다.

12 inimical
/ inímikəl /

형 적대감의, 불리한

syn antagonistic, hostile

영영 acting hostile and making a situation difficult

예문 I still can not understand why my superior acts **inimical** towards me.
나는 왜 상관이 나에게 적대적으로 행동하는지 모르겠다.

13 iniquitous
/ iníkwətəs /

형 부정의, 사악한

syn evil, immoral

영영 very unfair or morally bad

예문 Sometimes, religious leaders warn their followers against the **iniquitous** influence of nonbelievers.
가끔 종교 지도자들은 신자들에게 비신자들의 부정적 영향을 경고한다.

14 perusal
/ pərú:zəl /

명 정밀조사, 숙독, 정독

syn inspection, review

영영 a careful screening of documents for preventing leakage of information

예문 After a careful **perusal** by the review board, the science magazine has decided to publish his thesis.
검토 위원회의 면밀한 조사 이후 그 과학 잡지측은 그의 논문을 출간하기로 했다.

15 rendezvous
/ rá:ndəvù: /

명 회합, 집합, 랑데부

syn meeting, appointment

영영 a secret meeting that will gather people who try to pursue a matter

예문 The teachers chose a spot for their **rendezvous** where they will meet to discuss the project.
선생님들은 만나서 그 프로젝트를 의논할 회합 장소를 선택했다.

Day 27

01 fetter
/ fétər /

동 구속하다

syn shackle, chain, restrain

영영 put a chain or place shackle on one's feet

예문 Slaves shipped from Ivory Coast to America were **fettered** to iron chains throughout their journey.
코트디부아르로부터 미국으로 보내진 노예들은 그들의 여행 내내 쇠사슬에 묶여 있었다.

02 inextricable
/ inékstrikəbl /

형 얽힌, 떼려 해도 뗄 수 없는

syn entangled

영영 not getting separated from one another

예문 The history of Korea and Japan is **inextricable** from one another whether people like it or not.
한국과 일본의 역사는 좋든 싫든 서로에게서 떼어낼 수 없다.

03 injunction
/ indʒʌ́ŋkʃən /

명 명령, 지령

syn order, ruling, command

영영 an official order from a court

예문 When a court issues you an **injunction**, you must keep up to it or face stiff penalties.
법원이 당신에게 명령을 내리면 당신은 그것을 따르거나 아니면 엄벌을 받아야 한다.

04 innuendo
/ ìnjuéndou /

명 빗대는 말, 빈정거림

syn insinuation

영영 an indirect reference addressing something in rude ways

예문 My wife doesn't like it when I make sexual **innuendos**.
나의 아내는 내가 성적인 농담을 하면 좋아하지 않는다.

05 scurrilous
/ skə́:rələs /

형 천박한, 악의적인

syn vulgar, coarse

영영 meant to hurt or damage one's reputation

예문 I invented **scurrilous** stories about Eric in his absence and told them to his students.
나는 에릭이 없는 동안 그에 대한 악의적 이야기를 만들어 그의 제자들에게 얘기했다.

06 seminal
/ sémənl /

형 중대한, 영향력이 큰

syn vital, influential

영영 having a strong influence on later

예문 The **seminal** document of German people who helped Jews to escape persecution still moves people to this date.
유태인들이 박해를 피하도록 도와준 독일인들의 중대한 기록은 오늘날까지도 감명을 준다.

07 temerity
/ təmérəti /

명 무모함, 저돌

syn audacity, recklessness

영영 excessive confidence or boldness

예문 The student had the **temerity** to challenge his math teacher on a mathematical problem.
그 학생은 한 수학 문제를 놓고 수학 선생님에게 도전하는 무모함을 보였다.

08 tenable
/ ténəbl /
형 (비판, 공격에) 견딜 수 있는
syn bearable

영영 able to be maintained against difficulties

예문 It was his **tenable** nature that helped to see him through a difficult time.
어려운 시기에 그를 견딜 수 있게 해준 것은 그의 참을성이었다.

09 venial
/ ví:niəl /
형 가벼운, 용서할 수 있는
syn tolerable

영영 slight and pardonable

예문 Police do not press serious charge but give warning to those who committed a **venial** offense.
경찰은 경범죄를 저지른 사람들을 법적 조치하지 않고 경고만 준다.

10 wallow
/ wálou /
동 허우적거리다, 밀어닥치다
syn roll, pushing

영영 roll about or lie in dust and water

예문 Though I minded my son to be careful, he went about **wallowing** himself in the mud.
나는 아들에게 조심하라고 주의를 줬지만 진흙탕에서 뒹굴고 말았다.

11 wedge
/ wédʒ /
동 끼워 넣다, 고정시키다
syn lodge, squeeze

영영 squeeze something through a narrow gap

예문 I **wedged** myself through a jam packed bus.
나는 만원 버스 사이로 비집고 들어갔다.

12. welter

/ wéltər /

명 혼란, 엉망진창

syn rush, chaos

영영 a rush of information or things hard to accept

예문 Existing **welter** of books on TOEFL makes it hard for students to pick a right book for them.
토플 책들이 현재 쏟아져 나와 있는 와중에 학생들은 자신에게 적합한 책을 찾기가 어렵다.

13. winsome

/ wínsəm /

형 유쾌한, 매력 있는

syn charming, engaging

영영 having an attractive value that everyone is drawn into

예문 People prefer to be around a **winsome** person because of his or her cheerful attitude.
사람들은 발랄한 태도 때문에 매력적인 사람과 같이 있기를 선호한다.

14. writhe

/ ráið /

동 (고통으로) 몸을 비틀다

syn squirm, wriggle

영영 turn and twist body in great pain

예문 When I attacked Sean's side, he let out a cry and **writhed** in great pain.
내가 숀의 옆구리를 공격했을 때 그는 비명을 질렀고 고통으로 몸부림쳤다.

15. zany

/ zéini /

형 바보 같은, 엉뚱한

syn wacky, silly

영영 describing a silly or foolish person

예문 I sometimes got into the habit of telling **zany** stories that my students didn't like.
나는 학생들이 좋아하지도 않는 엉뚱한 이야기를 하는 습관이 있었다.

Day 28

01 **abeyance**
/ əbéiəns /

명 중지, 정지
syn intermission

영영 a condition of suspended activity

예문 Since the clash in Eastern Sea, the trade and cultural exchanges between North and South Korea have been in **abeyance**.
동해에서의 충돌 후 남북한의 무역과 문화 교류가 중단된 상태다.

02 **belabor**
/ biléibər /

동 논의하다, (말로) 공격하다
syn preach, assault

영영 argue or discuss in excessive detail

예문 I do not want to **belabor** you on the issue as I have already discussed it earlier.
나는 전에 그 문제에 대해 이야기했기 때문에 그것으로 당신과 길게 입씨름하고 싶지 않다.

03 **beseech**
/ bisíːtʃ /

동 애원하다, 간청하다
syn implore, plead, beg

영영 ask someone desperately and anxiously

예문 The public is **beseeching** the government not to go ahead with the project as they see it waste of budget.
대중들은 그것이 예산 낭비라고 생각해서 그 프로젝트를 진행하지 않도록 정부에게 간청하고 있다.

04

caddish
/ kǽdiʃ /

형 (여자에 대해) 야비한

syn rascal, scoundrel

영영 behaving ungentlemanly

예문 I saw a man who was arguing with a woman driver and he seemed to be very **caddish** toward her.
나는 여성 운전자와 말싸움하고 있는 남자를 봤는데 그는 여자에게 아주 무례한 것 같았다.

05

cant
/ kǽnt /

형 (점잔빼는) 위선적인 말투, 은어

syn hypocrisy, lingo

영영 statements that are not sincere

예문 The main reason why many people choose not to vote is because they are sick of politicians' **cant** speech.
사람들이 투표를 안 하는 주된 이유는 그들이 정치가들의 위선적 말에 질렸기 때문이다.

06

causality
/ kɔːzǽləti /

명 인과관계

syn cause-and-effect

영영 the relation between causes and effects

예문 The researchers have been investigating the **causality** of declining population and came up with a gloomy result.
연구가들은 줄고 있는 인구의 역학 관계를 조사해 왔고 우울한 결과를 내놓았다.

07

decency
/ díːsnsi /

명 예절 바름, 관대

syn propriety, correctness

영영 the quality or state of being decent

예문 His bad behavior made me wonder if he had any sense of **decency**.
그의 나쁜 행동은 그가 상식적인 체면이 있는지 궁금하게 만들었다.

day by day II 321

08 emend

/ iménd /

동 교정하다

syn correct, edit

영영 edit or rewrite a written material

예문 Just when Mike thought all his work was over, another author asked him to **emend** what he wrote.
마이크가 일이 끝났다고 생각했을 찰나 다른 저자가 자신의 글을 교정해 달라고 했다.

09 encapsulate

/ inkǽpsjulèit /

동 (말의 의미를) 요약하다

syn sum up

영영 sum up important aspects into a simple expression

예문 It is very hard to **encapsulate** the ideas of Sigmund Freud, the most famous German psychologist.
가장 유명한 독일 의학자, 지그문트 포로이트의 생각을 요약하는 것은 매우 어렵다.

10 inoculate

/ inákjulèit /

동 접종하다, 예방 주사 놓다

syn vaccinate

영영 introduce vaccine into a body in order to increase its immunity

예문 In Korea, most children are **inoculated** against certain childhood diseases.
한국의 아이들 대부분은 유아 질환에 대한 예방 접종들을 맞는다.

11 incapacitate

/ ìnkəpǽsətèit /

동 무능력하게 하다

syn disable, cripple

영영 make someone unable to live normally

예문 **Incapacitated** people often fall to poverty as they are not provided with enough support.
불구가 된 사람들은 충분한 지원을 못 받기 때문에 종종 가난에 허덕인다.

12. incarcerate
/ inkáːrsərèit /

동 감금하다, 투옥하다

syn imprison

영영 put someone in prison

예문 The Thai government **incarcerated** many protesters demanding the resignation of prime minister and his cabinet.
태국 정부는 총리와 내각의 사퇴를 요구하는 많은 시위자들을 투옥했다.

13. pert
/ pə́ːrt /

형 버릇 없는, 건방진

syn brash, impudent

영영 showing a lack of respect

예문 I could not tolerate my brother's **pert** behavior and remarks anymore.
나는 내 동생의 버릇 없는 행동과 언행들을 더 이상 참을 수 없었다.

14. petulance
/ pétʃuləns /

명 무례한 태도, 건방진 언동

syn rudeness, irritability

영영 a rude remark or childish behavior

예문 I can not tolerate his **petulance** any longer.
나는 그의 건방진 태도를 더 이상 용납할 수 없다.

15. realm
/ rélm /

명 왕국, 범위

syn field, world, area

영영 an area of study or thought

예문 The online game takes its players into the **realm** of fantasy and excitement.
그 온라인 게임은 플레이어들을 환상과 흥분의 세계로 빠지게 한다.

Day 29

01 adulation
/ ædʒuléiʃən /

명 아첨, 알랑거림
syn flattery, cajolery

영영 admiration and praise greater than is necessary

예문 Running candidates often receive tremendous **adulation** from their supporters.
출마 후보들은 종종 그의 지지자들로부터 많은 찬사를 받는다.

02 barren
/ bǽrən /

형 불모의, 메마른
syn arid, desolate, empty

영영 an area of land unsuitable for sustaining any lives

예문 The **barren** landscapes of Australian Outback now represents the country and attracts many visitors.
호주 오지의 메마른 땅은 이제 나라를 대표하고 많은 관광객들을 끌어들인다.

03 charlatan
/ ʃáːrlətn /

명 협잡꾼, 사기꾼
syn fake, fraud

영영 someone who falsely claims to have skills

예문 Although he sounded quite intelligent and professional, it soon beame clear that he was a **charlatan**.
그가 매우 똑똑하고 전문가인 듯 들렸지만 실은 사기꾼이라는 것이 곧 명백해졌다.

04 circumnavigate

/sə́ːrkəmnǽvəgèit/

동 우회하다, (세계) 일주하다

syn bypass, detour

영영 sail all the way around something

예문 The pilot was asked to **circumnavigate** the usual route and approach the runway from different direction.
그 조종사는 일상 루트를 우회하여 다른 방향에서 활주로에 접근해 달라는 요청을 받았다.

05 emollient

/imáljənt/

형 진정시키는

syn soothing

영영 making something calmer

예문 You will experience the **emollient** effect once you take this pill.
당신이 이 약을 먹자마자 진정 효과를 경험할 것이다.

06 endearment

/indíərmənt/

명 친애, 애정의 표시

syn love, affection

영영 an expression of affectionate words for the loved ones

예문 The lovers sitting on the bench were exchanging words of **endearment**.
벤치에 앉아있는 연인들은 애정 어린 말들을 주고받고 있었다.

07 ferment

/fə́ːrmənt/

명 대소동, 효소

syn agitation, commotion

영영 excitement among a group of people

예문 The whole nation seems to be in **ferment** over upcoming local elections.
나라 전체가 다가오는 지방 선거로 떠들썩한 것처럼 보인다.

08 fester

/ féstər /

동 상처 따위가 곪다, 아프다

syn spoil, rot

영영 exist in a state of progressive deterioration

예문 I don't want to **fester** our relationship.
나는 우리의 관계를 악화시키기 싫다.

09 genuflect

/ dʒénjuflèk /

동 무릎을 꿇다, 추종하다

syn kneel, obey

영영 kneel down in defeat or show obedience

예문 In Catholic churches, you can see many worshippers **genuflecting** when they are praying.
천주교 성당에서는 신도들이 기도할 때 무릎을 꿇고 있는 모습을 볼 수 있다.

10 glitter

/ glítər /

명 동 빛남, 빛나다

syn flash, sparkle, twinkle

영영 shine very brightly or reflect the light off its surface

예문 The stars I saw in the night sky of a camping day were so **glittering**.
야영하는 날 밤 하늘에서 본 별들은 매우 빛나고 있었다.

11 gnarled

/ na:rld /

형 옹이투성이의, 비뚤어진

syn contorted, deformed

영영 rough and twisted with age

예문 I feel guilty whenever I look at my wife's **gnarled** hands.
나는 아내의 울퉁불퉁한 손을 볼 때마다 죄책감이 든다.

12. hindsight
/ háindsàit /

명 뒤늦은 묘안

syn foresight

영영 understanding of a situation only after its happening

예문 I realized that there are many mistakes in my work on **hindsight**.
나중에 알고 보니 나의 작품에 많은 실수가 있다는 것을 깨달았다.

13. impound
/ impáund /

동 가두다, 압수하다

syn confiscate

영영 take one's possession with force

예문 The police sent me a notice that shows where I can claim my **impounded** car.
경찰은 어디서 압수된 내 차를 찾을 수 있는지 알려주는 통지서를 보냈다.

14. imprecate
/ ímprikèit /

동 저주하다

syn curse

영영 utter against someone

예문 I **imprecated** a curse on my former boss for firing me once, but I hold no grudge against him now.
나를 해고한 것 때문에 한때 예전의 사장을 저주했지만 이제는 아무런 원한이 없다.

15. luscious
/ lʌ́ʃəs /

형 맛있는, 기분이 좋은

syn rich, delicious

영영 sweet and delicious

예문 The Australian honey dew melon my uncle gave me yesterday was so **luscious**.
나의 삼촌이 어제 주신 호주산 참외는 너무 맛있었다.

day 29

Day 30

01 condescend
/ kàndəsénd /
동 겸손하게 굴다
syn deign, stoop

영영 act humbly but not out of free will

예문 After some time passed, the queen of England **condescended** to visit the grave of Princess Diana.
시간이 흐른 후에는 영국 여왕도 숙연해져서 다이애나비의 무덤을 방문했다.

02 condolence
/ kəndóuləns /
명 조상, 애도
syn solace, compassion

영영 an expression of sympathy in sorrow, especially in funeral

예문 It was a pity to see only few people coming to offer their **condolence** at the send-off ceremony of the sailors.
그 선원들의 영결식에 소수만이 애도하러 온 것을 보고 안타까웠다.

03 conformity
/ kənfɔ́:rməti /
명 유사, 부합
syn acquiescence, compliance

영영 a correspondence in form or appearance

예문 They stayed in the **conformity** with standards of basic human rights.
그들은 기본적 인권 사항을 준수했다.

04 consolidate
/ kənsálədèit /

동 통합하다

syn combine, incorporate, merge

영영 gather the fractions to unite them as a whole

예문 She is going to give public speech aimed at **consolidating** the divided opinions.
그녀는 분열된 의견들을 통합하기 위해 대중 연설을 할 예정이다.

05 demoralize
/ dimɔ́:rəlàiz /

동 사기를 꺾다, 혼란시키다

syn dishearten

영영 cause someone to lose confidence

예문 When the chairman was indicted for tax evasion, some employees were so **demoralized** that they resigned themselves from the company.
사장이 탈세 때문에 기소되었을 때 몇몇 직원들은 너무 사기가 꺾여 회사를 사임했다.

06 emeritus
/ imérətəs /

형 명예퇴직의

syn honorary

영영 retired from an active duty, but still keeping the honorary title

예문 It gave me a great inspiration to see the pictures of professors **emeritus** in the school president's office.
대학 학장의 사무실에서 명예교수들의 사진들을 보는 것은 나에게 큰 영감을 주었다.

07 enchant
/ intʃǽnt /

동 매혹하다

syn fascinate, charm

영영 attract someone strongly

예문 I was so **enchanted** by her kind personality that I couldn't stop thinking about her.
나는 그녀의 친절한 성격에 매혹되어 그녀를 계속 생각하지 않을 수 없었다.

day by day II 329

08 enfeeble

/ infíːbl /   동 약화시키다
syn weaken, compromise

영영 make something very weak

예문 The swine flu can **enfeeble** any man for two days with high fever.
신종 독감은 고열이 동반되며 어떤 사람이든 2일 동안은 무기력하게 만들 수 있다.

09 exquisite

/ ikskwízit /   형 아름다운, 절묘한
syn elegant, graceful

영영 very beautiful and delicate

예문 Korean traditional clothes are known for their **exquisite** design and quality.
한국 전통 복장은 아름다운 디자인과 품질로 알려져 있다.

10 fraternize

/ frǽtərnàiz /   동 친하게 사귀다
syn mingle

영영 behave in a friendly manner

예문 When a flight attendant **fraternizes** with you, you might get the impression that she likes you.
한 비행기 승무원이 당신에게 친근히 대한다면 그녀가 당신을 좋아한다는 인상을 받을 수 있다.

11 fraudulent

/ frɔ́ːdʒulənt /   형 사기의, 부정의
syn cheating, deceitful

영영 based on or done by fraud

예문 Anyone who is found guilty of doing something **fraudulent** should be disassociated.
어떤 부정을 저지른 혐의가 있는 사람은 사회에서 격리되어야 한다.

12 frivolous

/ frívələs /

형 경솔한, 들뜬

syn **careless, hasty, rash**

영영 carefree and superficial

예문 Visiting Las Vegas, they sometimes get so **frivolous** that they want to play some betting machines.
라스베가스를 방문할 때 그들은 가끔 너무 들떠 기계 도박을 하기 원합니다.

13 impulsive

/ impʌ́lsiv /

형 충동적인

syn **spontaneous**

영영 acting without forethought

예문 Jessica is an **impulsive** buyer and would spend quite a bit of fortunes.
제시카는 충동 구매자이고 꽤 많은 돈을 쓰기도 한다.

14 indemnity

/ indémnəti /

명 보증

syn **guarantee**

영영 protection against damage or loss

예문 When I went to the bank to get a loan, they asked me to put my house up as an **indemnity**.
내가 대출 받으러 은행에 갔을 때 그들은 내 집을 보증으로 놓도록 요청했다.

15 infringe

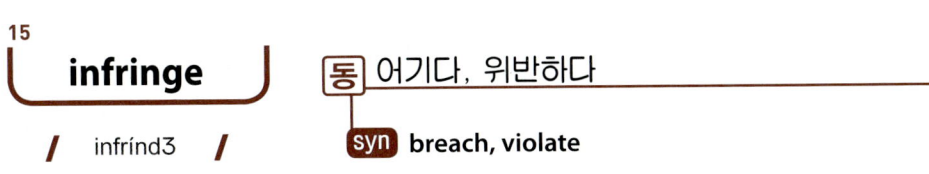

/ infríndʒ /

동 어기다, 위반하다

syn **breach, violate**

영영 break a law or rule

예문 It is believed that past governments under military dictatorships used to **infringe** on basic human rights.
과거의 군부 독재 하의 정부들이 기본 인권을 유린해 왔다고 믿어진다.

SAving Time
SAT Vocabulary

외연과 내포

외연과 내포

01 감시

- **guard** — 대상에 대한 호위 (외부와의 격리에 초점)
- **surveillance** — 감시라는 행위 자체
- **watch** — 지속적으로 지켜보는 것

- The wise dog always guarded his lazy and sleeping baby.
  그 영리한 개는 나른해서 잠자고 있는 아기를 항상 지키고 있었다.
- They should have gone to avert the surveillance of the enemy.
  그들은 적의 감시를 피하기 위해 떠났어야 했는데.
- He got very bored and felt monotony as he watched their life.
  그는 그들 생활을 감시하면서 상당한 지루함과 단조로움을 느꼈다.

02 공범

- **abettor** — 범행 교사자, 선동자
- **accomplice** — 범행 연루자
- **conspirator** — 음모나 반역의 공모자

- The abettor of a crime was sentenced to 3 years.
  그 범죄의 선동자는 3년형을 선고 받았다.
- The accomplice of robbery is wanted by the police.
  그 강도 공범자가 경찰에 수배되었다.
- A group of conspirators planned to kill the dictator.
  공모자 집단은 그 독재자를 암살할 계획을 세웠다.

03 보존

- **conserve** — 현상 유지하다
- **maintain** — 표준 상태를 유지하다
- **preserve** — 본래의 상태를 지키다 (자연보호 등)

- The nationalists are very keen to conserve their language.
  민족주의자들은 자신들의 언어를 보존하는 데 매우 열심이다.
- unable to maintain the shop any more, she shut it up.
  그녀는 점포를 더 이상 지탱할 수 없어서 폐업했다.
- They have made an agreement to preserve the swamp.
  그들은 늪지를 보존하려는 것에 동의를 했다.

04 바꾸다

- **alter** — 일부지만 핵심을 고치다
- **convert** — 목적에 맞게 개조하다
- **transmute** — 고급의 것으로 바꾸다

- My grandma altered her will without telling us beforehand.
  할머니는 우리에게 미리 말하지 않고 그녀의 유언장을 고쳤다.
- Converting ice into cold water requires heat energy.
  얼음을 찬물로 변환시키는 데 열에너지가 필요하다.
- Alchemists tried to transmute lead into gold.
  연금술사들은 납을 금으로 바꾸기 위해 노력했다.

05 맞바꾸다

- **exchange** 주고받다
- **barter** 물물교역하다
- **swap** 동종의 것들 중 대체 목적으로 바꾸다

- We will exchange our phone numbers.
  우리는 전화번호를 주고받을 것이다.
- I want to barter my car off with your old yacht.
  내 차와 당신의 오래 된 요트를 바꿔 처분하고 싶다.
- Never swap horses while crossing the stream.
  어려울 때 조직을 바꾸지 마라.

06 가까이

- **almost** 거의
- **close** 일어나지 않을 일이 유사 상태로 일어날 때
- **near** 물리적으로 가까운

- Almost all the people came out.
  거의 모든 사람들이 밖으로 나왔다.
- These five lines close together in a center.
  이들 다섯 개의 선은 중심에서 만날 듯 말 듯하다.
- The summer vacation is drawing near.
  여름 방학이 다가오고 있다.

07 계단

- **step** 계단이나 사다리에서의 한 단
- **stair** 주로 옥내 일직선 계단, 층과 층 사이의 한 계단 전체
- **ramp** floor를 포함한 'ㄷ'자 계단이나 step이 없는 우회도로

- A man is standing on the middle step of a ladder he climbs.
  한 남자가 자신이 오르고 있는 사다리의 중간 단에 서 있다.
- The elevator was full, so I took the stairs.
  엘리베이터에 사람이 꽉 차서 계단으로 올라왔다.
- Ramps should be made for wheelchair users.
  휠체어 사용자들을 위해 경사로가 설치되어야 한다.

08 비싼

- **dear** (일반적 의미의) 값비싼
- **costly** 원가가 비싼
- **expensive** 부가가치가 커서 값이 비싸게 매겨진

- This book is dear in price.
  이 책은 값이 비싸다.
- I would buy a computer if it were cheaper. It is very costly nowadays.
  컴퓨터가 가격이 비싸지 않으면 하나를 살 텐데. 요즘은 워낙 비싸다.
- The saleswoman showed me some, but all were too expensive.
  그 판매원은 나에게 몇몇을 보여줬는데, 전부 다 너무 비쌌다.

09 고객

- **customer** — 상점 고객
- **client** — 전문인에게 의뢰 맡긴 고객, 단골손님
- **guest** — 숙박 손님, 이벤트 초대 손님

- The firm has excellent customer relations.
  그 회사는 고객 관리를 잘 한다.
- I have built up a loyal satisfied client for European clothes.
  나는 유럽식의 의류를 원하는 한 사람을 충실한 단골로 만들었다.
- I would like you to be my guest tonight.
  오늘밤은 편하게 대접을 받으세요.

10 끌다

- **pull** — (일반적 의미의) 당기다
- **drag** — 무거운 것을 질질 끌다
- **draw** — 많은 힘 들이지 않고 잡아당기다
- **haul** — 무거운 물체를 도구로 서서히 끌다
- **trail** — 자신의 몸 뒤에서 물건을 끌고 가다
- **tug** — 견인하다

- A performer who pulls large crowds
  많은 관중을 끌어 모으는 연주자
- He dragged the heavy box.
  그는 무거운 상자를 질질 끌었다.
- He drew the chair closer to the table.
  그는 테이블에 가까이 의자를 끌었다.
- The dentist hauled the tooth.
  치과의사는 (기계로) 이를 뽑았다.

- The dog ran off, trailing its leash.
  그 개가 가죽끈을 땅에 끌며 도망갔다.
- She tugged at her tight boots.
  그녀는 그녀의 꽉 끼는 부츠를 당겨 신었다.

11 방사하다

- **eject**   퇴거시키다
- **emit**   빛, 열, 향기를 발산하다
- **spew**   (연기, 용암 등을) 대량으로 방출하다
- **radiate**   빛, 열 등을 방사하다

- He ejected the guys who started the fight.
  그는 싸움을 시작했던 이들을 몰아냈다.
- A stove was emitting heat.
  한 난로가 열을 발산하고 있었다.
- A volcano that spewed molten lava destroyed the small town.
  용암을 분출한 화산은 그 조그만 마을을 파괴했다.
- Heat radiates from the stove.
  열이 난로에서 발산된다.

12 냄새

- **aroma**   방향, 강렬한 향취
- **fragrance**   향기, 향수
- **odor**   다소 부정적 냄새

- The Westerners hate the aroma of garlic.
  서구인들은 마늘의 독특한 냄새를 싫어한다.

- The poet was allured by the fragrance of lilacs.
  그 시인은 라일락 향기에 매료되었다.
- an odor of cigar smoke
  담배 연기 냄새

13

냉정

- apathetic   무관심하여 냉담한
- impassive   (일반적 의미의) 냉담한
- phlegmatic   기질적으로 차분한
- stoical   쾌락과 고통에 의연한
- stolid   둔감한

- The apathetic electorates don't support the irrational candidate no more.
  그 냉정한 유권자는 그 불합리한 지원자를 더 이상 지원하지 않았다.
- People think he is cold-blooded because of his impassive face.
  사람들은 차가운 인상 때문에 그가 냉정할 것이라고 생각한다.
- The judge was a phlegmatic person.
  그 재판관은 냉정을 잃지 않는 사람이었다.
- I had to be a stoical person during the business hours though I had extreme toothache.
  나는 근무시간에 참기 힘든 치통이 와도 (일할 수 있을 정도로) 참을성 있는 사람이어야만 했다.
- He was a rather stolid type, so his girlfriend got angry with him.
  그가 다소 둔감한 타입이어서 그의 여자 친구는 그에 대해 화가 났다.

14

논문

- thesis   졸업 논문
- treatise   장문의 학술 논문
- dissertation   박사 학위 논문

- This thesis is well constructed.
  그의 졸업논문은 훌륭했다.
- His scientific treatise has been awarded to the first prize.
  우리의 과학논문은 대상을 받았다.
- We need to submit a dissertation to a university before the due date.
  우리는 지정 날짜 전에 대학 논문을 제출해야 한다.

15 늘이다

- **elongate**   (초기 물량의 변화 없이) 잡아 늘이다
- **expand**   크기나 수 등을 확장하다
- **prolong**   (특히, 시간상) 연장하다

- The dough has an elongated shape.
  반죽이 납작하게 늘여진 모양이다.
- She expanded her store by adding another room.
  그녀는 방을 추가하여 상점을 넓혔다.
- We prolonged our stay.
  우리는 체류 기간을 연장했다.

16 도전하다

- **challenge**   해볼 만한 과제로서의 도전
- **dare**   과감한 도전

- He challenged me to a game of chess.
  그는 나에게 체스 게임하자고 도전했다.
- The boy dared a jump into the water.
  그 소년은 용감히 물속에 뛰어들었다.

17 주조하다

- **coin**   화폐나 신조어를 만들다
- **mold**   거푸집에 넣어서 특정 형태를 만들다

- They coined silver dollars.
  그들은 은화를 만들었다.
- It was an effort to mold their character into an ideal self image.
  이것은 이상적 자아상에 가깝도록 인성을 도야하려는 노력이었다.

18 말하다

- **say**   단순히 말한다는 의미
- **speak**   발화하다, 특정 언어를 구사하다
- **tell**   어떤 대상에게 정보를 전달하다
- **talk**   협의하다, 언외로 의사 전달하다

- Don't say a single word.
  한 마디도 하지 마.
- Can you speak Cantonese?
  광동어를 할 줄 아십니까?
- I told him the truth.
  나는 그에게 진실을 말했다.
- Money talks.
  돈은 효력이 있다.

19 힘

- **power**   (일반적 의미의) 힘
- **might**   큰 완력
- **momentum**   추진력, 여세
- **strength**   강도, 강점
- **potency**   잠재력, 유효성

- I don't have enough power to pass it through without any evidence.
  나는 어떤 증거 없이는 그것을 감히 통과할 여력이 없다.
- I feel God's might.
  신의 힘을 받은 것 같다.
- The rise in interest rates finally appears to be losing momentum.
  금리의 상승으로 경기부양력마저 상실되는 것 같다.
- What is your strength in the class?
  그 수업에서 당신의 강점은 무엇입니까?
- If you keep a medicine too long, it may lose its potency.
  약을 너무 오래 보관하면 효능이 떨어질 수도 있다.

20 보수

- **pay**   일반적 지불금
- **wage**   일반적 노동의 임금 및 그 수준
- **salary**   사무직 근로자들의 정액 급여
- **stipend**   교사 및 성직자 급료, 연구원 보조금

- I drew my full pay.
  나는 봉급 전액을 인출했다.
- What is his wage? Does he deserve that amount?
  그의 임금은 얼마죠? 그는 그만한 돈을 받을 자격이 있습니까?

외연과 내포 343

- The average monthly salary paid by the company was not reported.
  그 업체의 월평균 급여는 발표되지 않았다.
- He has received stipends from the government.
  그는 정부 보조금을 받아왔다.

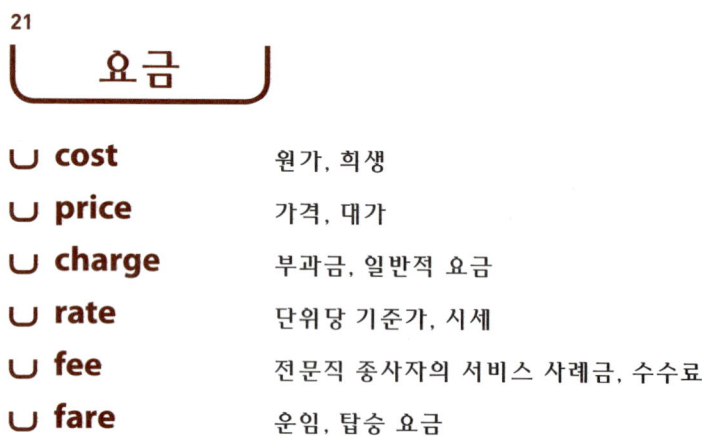

21 요금

- cost   원가, 희생
- price   가격, 대가
- charge   부과금, 일반적 요금
- rate   단위당 기준가, 시세
- fee   전문직 종사자의 서비스 사례금, 수수료
- fare   운임, 탑승 요금

- The cost of the government project is astronomical.
  그 정부 기획 프로그램에 들 비용이 엄청나다.
- The prestige class will double the price.
  일등석은 요금이 두 배로 들 거야.
- He gives used clothes free of charge to the very poor.
  그는 입던 옷들을 극빈자들에게 무상으로 나눠준다.
- The rate is 1100 won to the dollar.
  환율이 달러당 1000원이다.
- His consulting fee is not fairly charged.
  그의 상담료는 제대로 책정되어 있지 않다.
- How much is the fare to LA?
  LA까지 요금이 얼마죠?

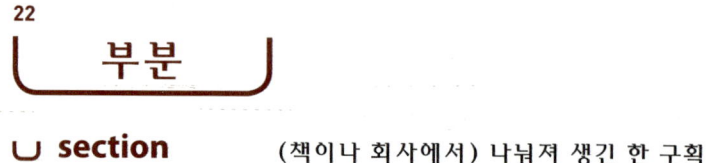

22 부분

- section   (책이나 회사에서) 나눠져 생긴 한 구획

- portion　　　한 개체에 할당된 부분
- compartment　(운송수단이나 수납장 등의) 칸막이된 한 구획
- piece　　　전체에서 나온 한 부분이지만 그 자체로 완전한 것

- The company elevated him to the section chief.
  회사에서 그를 과장으로 승진시켰다.
- The best portion of a good life is the little nameless acts of kindness.
  삶을 이루는 국면들 중 잊지 못할 것은 익명으로 베풀어진 친절이다.
- Please, put your bag into the compartment in the plane.
  그 비행기에서는 가방을 칸막이 안에 넣도록 하십시오.
- Would you like to have a piece of chocolate cake?
  초콜릿 케이크 좀 드시겠습니까?

23 빌리다

- debt　　일반적 부채, 채무 상태
- lease　　(일정기간) 임대, 임차
- loan　　금융기관 대출금

- He borrowed $1,000 from the bank, and he never paid back his debt.
  그는 은행에서 1000달러를 대출하였으나 빚을 다 청산하지는 못했다.
- This office is not for sale, but for lease.
  그 사무실은 팔려는 것이 아니라 임대용이다.
- The loan restriction on apartments also cut demand.
  아파트의 대부 자격 제한으로 대출자가 줄었다.

24 빠르다

- abrupt　　갑작스럽다는 의미
- brisk　　행동이 재빠르다는 의미

☐ **prompt**   적절히 신속하게

- People were scared by the abrupt change in the weather.
  사람들은 날씨의 갑작스런 변화에 놀랐다.
- She had a brisk walk in the park and disappeared all of a sudden.
  그녀는 공원에서 재빠르게 움직였고, 갑자기 사라졌다.
- The guard was prompt to go back and investigate the noise.
  그 경호원은 즉각 그 소음을 추적해 조사하였다.

25 상금

☐ **award**   (긍정적 수행에 대한) 상
☐ **bounty**   정부 하사금, 현상금
☐ **tribute**   높은 사람에게 바치는 공물

- Michael received an award for the best actor.
  마이클이 최고의 남자 배우 부문으로 이 상을 받았다.
- The company received a bounty on export from the government.
  그 회사는 정부로부터 수출 촉진 장려금을 받았다.
- The tribe renders tribute to our great king.
  그 부족은 우리의 대왕에게 공물을 바친다.

26 생각하다

☐ **think**   (일반적 의미의) 생각하다
☐ **conceive**   어떤 개념을 마음에 그리다
☐ **find**   의견을 가지다, ~라고 생각하다
☐ **consider**   (사전에) 신중하게 고려하다
☐ **suppose**   나름대로의 근거로 가정하다

- ∪ **speculate**   세부적 근거 없이 추측하다
- ∪ **reflect**   주로 과거의 일을 곰곰이 생각하다
- ∪ **meditate**   묵상하다, 속으로 계획하다
- ∪ **deliberate**   결단 내리기 전 신중히 검토하다

- I think you are a handsome boy.
  나는 네가 잘생겼다고 생각한다.
- We conceived a plan to increase profits.
  우리는 이익을 증진할 수 있는 계획을 생각해냈다.
- I found the book entertaining.
  나는 그 책이 흥미진진하다는 것을 알게 됐다.
- Her success is not surprising considering her training.
  그녀의 연습량을 고려한다면 그녀의 성공은 놀랄 만한 것이 아니다.
- Suppose you are the kid who just lost his mom. How could you do that?
  만약 네가 엄마를 잃은 아이라고 가정한다면 어떻게 할 거니?
- The lawyer speculated that high cholesterol was a contributing factor to the patient's health problems
  그 변호사는 높은 수치의 콜레스테롤이 그 사람의 건강 문제를 일으킨 주요소라고 추정했다.
- He reflected that it was difficult to solve the problem.
  그는 그 문제를 힘들게 풀었다고 생각했다.
- She meditated a visit to her daughter.
  그녀는 딸을 방문할까 하고 생각했다.
- They deliberated on the problem which they needed to solve ASAP.
  그들은 그 해결할 문제에 대해 가능한 빨리 검토했다.

27 길

- ∪ **lane**   차선 단위, 좁은 길
- ∪ **mall**   가로수길, 산책로
- ∪ **path**   (밟아서 생긴) 길, 행로

- The Seoul City Government introduced an exclusive bus lane, and it works!
  서울시청이 버스전용차선을 도입했는데 효과가 있다.
- They are tired of hanging around the mall.
  사람들이 쇼핑몰을 돌아다니는 것에 싫증이 나 있다.
- The path ascends here. Prepare yourself to sweat!
  여기부터 오르막이야. 땀 흘릴 준비해!

28 성격

- **property** 특성
- **attribute** 고유의 속성, 자질
- **character** 한 개체의 종합적 특성
- **individuality** 개성
- **personality** 인품, 개성
- **temperament** 타고난 성미, 기질

- Elasticity is a property of rubber.
  탄력은 고무 특유의 속성이다.
- Omnipotence is the attribute of God.
  전지전능함은 신만이 가질 수 있는 속성이다.
- Humanity is the character of our nation.
  인간성은 우리 민족의 특성이다.
- His writings are marked by his strong individuality.
  그의 작품은 그의 뚜렷한 개성이 한 축을 이룬다.
- She has personality plus.
  그녀에게는 개성 이상의 뭔가가 있다.
- They are not congenial in temperament with each other.
  그들은 서로 성미가 안 맞는다.

29 시대

- **period**   일반적인 기간의 의미
- **age**   특정 인물이나 사물이 관여된 한 시대
- **era**   사건이나 기타 속성으로 구분된 한 시대
- **epoch**   획기적 변화로 주목되는 시간대, (지질학에서) 세, 기

- He was arrested as a spy in the period of social unrest.
  그는 사회적으로 불안한 시기에 스파이로 체포되었다.
- The writer lived in the Elizabethan Age.
  그 작가는 엘리자베스 시대에 살았다.
- This is an era of mass communication.
  지금은 매스컴의 시대다.
- His invention made a new epoch.
  그의 발명은 신기원을 이루어냈다.

30 이야기

- **story**   일반적인 이야기의 의미, 줄거리
- **narrative**   서술체 담화
- **anecdote**   일화, 기담
- **tale**   설화, 지어낸 이야기
- **lore**   민족의 구전 이야기
- **myth**   신화, 널리 믿어지지만 허구인 통념
- **legend**   전설
- **fable**   교훈적 우화

- He outlined the story of a movie.
  그는 한 영화의 줄거리를 말했다.

- He will only allow poetry using a simple narrative style.
  그는 간단한 서술식의 시만을 허락할 것이다.
- An amusing anecdote is told of him.
  그에 얽힌 재미있는 일화가 있다
- Each tale has the timeless quality of fables.
  각각의 설화는 우화가 가지는 항구적 특성을 갖추고 있다.
- In Chinese lore the bat is an emblem of good fortune.
  중국설화에서는 박쥐가 행운의 상징이다.
- There is a famous Greek Myth about flying to the Sun.
  태양으로의 비행과 관련된 한 유명한 그리스 신화가 있다.
- The play was based on Irish legend.
  그 연극은 아일랜드 전설에 기반을 두었다.
- She has told me fables that she heard from her grandmother.
  그녀는 할머니에게서 들은 우화들을 나에게 들려주었다.

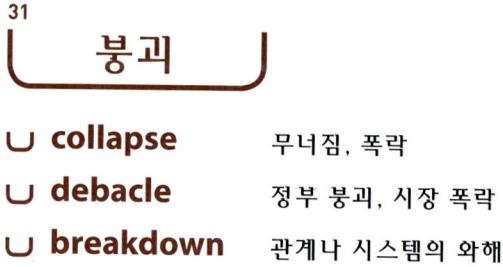

31 붕괴

∪ **collapse**   무너짐, 폭락
∪ **debacle**   정부 붕괴, 시장 폭락
∪ **breakdown**   관계나 시스템의 와해

- Sampoong Department Store was collapsed in 1990s.
  삼풍백화점은 1990년대에 무너졌다.
- After the debacle of the Soviet Union, many Russian teachers converted to English teachers through English teaching training program.
  소비에트 연방의 해체 후, 많은 러시아어 교사들은 영어 교수 트레이닝 프로그램을 통해 영어 교사가 되었다.
- He has been suffering from nervous breakdown of the worst kind.
  그는 심각한 신경쇠약으로 고생하고 있었다.

32 어울림

- **match**   조화되다
- **fit**   사이즈나 형태 등이 잘 맞다
- **suit**   색깔과 스타일이 잘 어울리다

- The trimming does not match the silk hat.
  그 장식은 그 정장 모자에 어울리지 않는다.
- This jumper doesn't fit on me.
  이 점퍼의 사이즈가 나에게 맞지 않다.
- This tie suits on you! You look great, man!
  이 넥타이는 너에게 잘 어울린다. 매우 멋지구나.

33 용서하다

- **forgive**   죄, 사람을 용서하다
- **exonerate**   무죄 입증하다, 면제하다
- **acquit**   재판을 통해 무죄 방면하다
- **amnesty**   (정치적) 사면하다
- **condone**   묵과하다

- Your father will forgive you if you regret from your heart.
  진심으로 뉘우친다면 당신의 아버지는 당신을 용서할 것이다.
- The attorney exonerated him from an accusation at the trial.
  그 변호인은 고소공판을 통해 그를 무죄로 하였다.
- He is acquitted of murder with the help of a competent attorney.
  그는 유능한 변호인의 도움으로 살인 무죄 방면되었다.
- The president amnestied many political prisoners in honoring the Independence Day of Korea.
  대통령은 광복절을 맞아 많은 정치사범들을 사면했다.
- She condoned her husband's infidelity.
  그녀는 남편의 배신을 용서했다.

34 울다

- cry (주로 소리 내어) 울다
- weep 눈물을 흘리다
- sob 북받쳐 흐느껴 울다
- wail 고통 등으로 울부짖다
- whimper (동정심을 바라고) 낑낑대고 울다

- A shrill cry awoke me from my sleep.
  날카로운 고함 소리에 잠이 깼다.
- I am a soldier and unapt to weep.
  나는 군인이라 우는 일 따위는 하지 않는다.
- He sobbed his heart out.
  그는 가슴이 터지도록 흐느껴 울었다.
- Jane wailed in an ominously sorrowful manner.
  제인은 청승맞게 울었다.
- They obeyed without a whimper to the boss.
  그들은 사장에게 앓는 소리 하지 않고 순종했다.

35 웃다

- laugh (일반적 의미의) 웃다
- giggle 뭔가를 보거나 듣고 킬킬 웃다
- chuckle 싱긋이 혼자 재미있어 하다
- grin (이를 드러내고) 씩 웃다

- We would laugh about it when it's all over.
  우리는 나중에 이 일에 대해 웃게 될 것이다.
- Don't just giggle. Tell me what it's about.
  킥킥대지만 말고 뭐가 그렇게 재미있는지 말해줘.

- He often chuckles while he reads comic books.
  그는 종종 만화를 보며 씩 웃는다.
- I didn't like the job, but I had to grin and bear it.
  나는 그 일이 안 내켰지만 울며 겨자 먹기로 해야 했다.

36 이기다

- beat   물리치다, 능가하다
- defeat   상대를 격퇴시키다
- win   게임 등에서 이기다

- I beat him down to a lower price
  결국 나는 더 낮은 가격으로 협상에서 그를 이겼다.
- She defeated the opponent team in the first set.
  그녀는 첫 세트에서 상대방 팀을 제압했다.
- I won the lottery.
  나는 복권에 당첨되었다.

37 인식

- identify   신원확인하다
- perceive   (감각으로) 지각하다, 간파하다
- recognize   분간하다, 보고 곧 알아보다
- realize   상황에 대하여 깨닫다
- catch   알아듣다

- Can you identify who was in the murder scene?
  당신은 누가 살인 현장에 있었는지 알아낼 수 있습니까?
- Nobody perceived me entering the room.
  누구도 내가 방에 들어가는 것을 인지하지 못했다.

- Look at this photo. Can you recognize him? He is my son.
  이 사진을 봐. 그가 누군지 알겠니? 그는 내 아들이야.
- You get him to realize that we will be in the trouble unless we pay him.
  우리가 그에게 돈을 지불하지 않으면 문제에 봉착할 것을 네가 그로 하여금 깨닫도록 해라.
- Can you catch his meaning?
  너는 그가 의미하는 바를 알겠니?

38 인접

- **adjacent**   (접촉하지 않고) 부근에 있는
- **adjoining**   점, 선에 접속해 있는
- **contiguous**   연속으로 닿아 있는
- **tangent**   다른 곡선과 교차하지 않고 접하는

- The families who live in adjacent farmhouses help each other.
  인근 농가 사람들끼리 서로를 도와준다.
- My French friend lives an adjoining room in my boarding house.
  나의 프랑스인 친구는 기숙사에서 내 옆방에 지내고 있다.
- In ancient time, a region contiguous to other countries suffered from frequent war.
  고대에 여러 나라와 접경한 지역은 빈번히 전쟁을 치렀다.
- The line from the center of the circle and the line tangent to a circle meet an angle of 90 degrees.
  반지름과 접선은 90°의 각으로 만난다.

39 전달

- **carry**   (일반적 의미의) 운반하다
- **transmit**   통과시키다
- **convey**   일정한 경로 및 수단으로 전달하다

- They carry something heavy on their back.
  그들은 등에 무거운 것을 지고 간다.
- Glass transmits light well.
  유리는 빛을 잘 통과시킨다.
- Air conveys sound.
  공기는 (매질로서) 소리를 전달한다.

40 정상

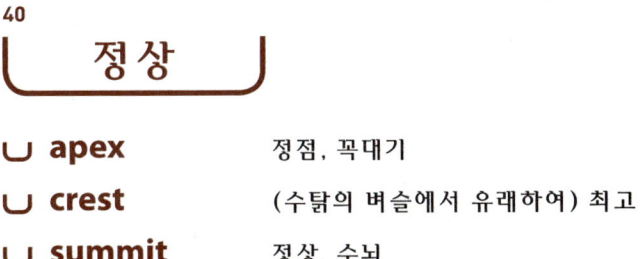

⎵ **apex**	정점, 꼭대기
⎵ **crest**	(수탉의 벼슬에서 유래하여) 최고
⎵ **summit**	정상, 수뇌

- He studied the solar apex last night.
  그는 지난밤 태양 향점을 연구했다.
- A desperate fight between an elephant and a lion is on its crest.
  코끼리와 사자의 사투가 절정에 이르고 있다
- The summit talks blew up over the nuclear test ban.
  핵실험 금지 문제를 논하는 정상 회담이 결렬되었다.

41 주시

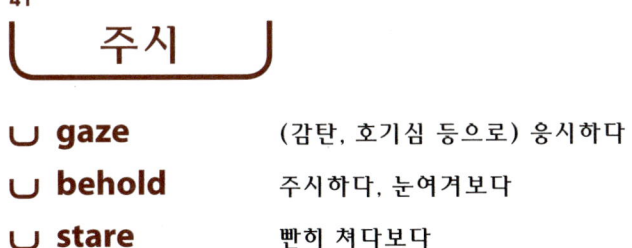

⎵ **gaze**	(감탄, 호기심 등으로) 응시하다
⎵ **behold**	주시하다, 눈여겨보다
⎵ **stare**	빤히 쳐다보다

- They are gazing at each other. They must be in love.
  그들은 서로를 응시했다. 그들은 사랑에 빠졌다.
- The fight is a spectacle sight to behold.
  그 격투는 대단한 볼거리이다.

- It's hardly the thing to stare at people.
  사람들을 빤히 쳐다보는 것은 예의가 아니다.

42 표명

- **assert**   신념에 입각하여 주장하다
- **affirm**   증거에 입각하여 주장하다
- **claim**   당연한 권리로서 요구하다
- **declare**   공공연하게 선언하다

- She continued to assert her innocence.
  그녀는 계속 자기 결백을 주장했다.
- The suspect affirmed he had been at home all evening.
  그 용의자는 저녁 내내 집에 있었다고 알리바이를 주장했다.
- They claimed a full refund on the defective products.
  그들은 결점이 있는 상품에 대하여 전액 환불해줄 것을 요구했다.
- I guess we have to declare bankruptcy.
  파산 신고를 해야겠다.

43 중립

- **neutral**   중립의
- **unbiased**   기울지 않은, 편견이 없는
- **nonchalant**   무편무당의, 냉담한

- Journalists are supposed to be politically neutral.
  언론관계자들은 정치적으로 중립을 지켜야 한다.
- I am unbiased when I am in the forum.
  나는 편견 없이 그 토론에 임한다.

- He is a nonchalant fellow. That's why he got no friend.
  그는 냉담한 친구다. 그 때문에 그는 친구가 없다.

44 증오

- ⌴ hate   몹시 싫어하다
- ⌴ detest   몹시 경멸하다
- ⌴ abhor   질색하다

- I hate cold weather, so I go other countries every winter.
  나는 추운 날씨를 싫어한다. 그래서 겨울마다 다른 지역에 간다.
- I detest dishonest people.
  나는 정직하지 않은 사람들을 싫어한다.
- People abhor cockroaches.
  사람들은 바퀴벌레를 매우 혐오한다.

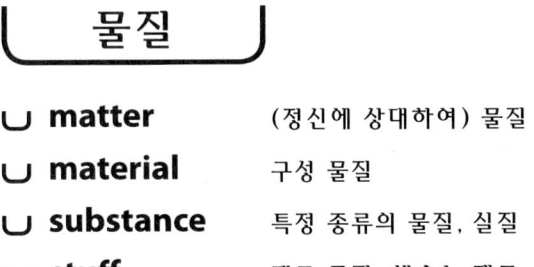

45 물질

- ⌴ matter   (정신에 상대하여) 물질
- ⌴ material   구성 물질
- ⌴ substance 특정 종류의 물질, 실질
- ⌴ stuff   재료 물질, 채우는 재료

- Manure is made of animal droppings and rotting plant matter.
  거름은 동물의 배설물과 썩어가는 식물체로 만들어진다.
- The suit is of flexible material.
  그 한 벌 옷은 유연한 소재로 되어 있다.
- This substance consists of one element.
  이 물질은 단원소분자이다.

- What was that barbecue stuff your mom cooked?
  너의 어머니가 해 주셨던 그 바비큐 요리가 뭐였지?

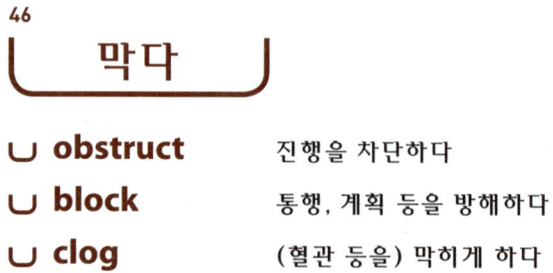

46 막다

⊔ **obstruct** 진행을 차단하다
⊔ **block** 통행, 계획 등을 방해하다
⊔ **clog** (혈관 등을) 막히게 하다

- The crowd obstructed the police in the discharge of their duties.
  군중은 그들의 의무를 이행하기 위해 경찰들의 길을 막았다.
- It blocks out harmful ultraviolet rays like colored-glass lenses .
  그것은 유해한 자외선을 색유리 렌즈처럼 잘 차단한다.
- Heavy traffic clogged the freeways.
  교통량이 많아 고속도로가 막혔다.

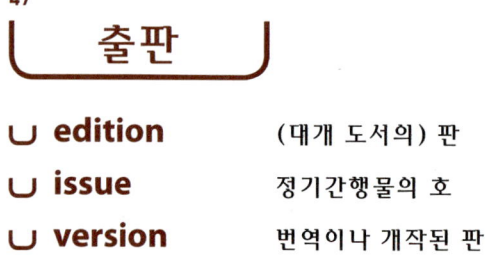

47 출판

⊔ **edition** (대개 도서의) 판
⊔ **issue** 정기간행물의 호
⊔ **version** 번역이나 개작된 판

- This is the first edition of the book.
  이것은 그 책의 초판본이다.
- Bring the 7th issue on the newsletter.
  그 회보의 제7호를 가져와라.
- The English version of the novel is due for publication.
  그 소설의 영어판이 출간될 예정이다.

48 피로

- **tired**   (일반적 의미의) 피곤한
- **exhausted**   정력을 거의 다 소모한, 고갈된
- **fatigued**   심신이 지친
- **weary**   오래 작업 후에 지친

- I'm cold and tired. I'm going home.
  춥고 지쳐서 그만 집에 가려 한다.
- I am so exhausted. I can't work any more.
  나는 매우 지쳐서 더 이상 일을 할 수 없다.
- I went to bed fatigued.
  나는 (하루 일과를 마치고) 지쳐서 잠자리에 들었다.
- She was weary after a long journey
  그는 오랜 여행으로 매우 지쳐 있었다.

49 확인

- **confirm**   예약 등의 사실을 확인하다
- **verify**   진위 등을 입증하다
- **certificate**   공식 인증하다

- Would you mind calling us to confirm your reservation?
  예약한 것을 확인하려면 전화 주세요.
- I need to verify your documents first before I can confirm your pass.
  당신의 합격을 확증 짓기 전에 제출 서류의 진위부터 확인해야겠습니다.
- It will be certificated as a qualification in its own right.
  그것은 그 자체로 하나의 자격증으로 공인될 것이다.

50 회전

- **turn** — 원형을 그리면서 돌다 (1회전이 아닌 경우에도 씀)
- **revolve** — 공전하다
- **rotate** — 자전하다
- **spin** — 반복적으로 급히 돌다
- **circulate** — 순환/유통하다

- Please, turn left at the next corner.
  다음 코너에서 왼쪽으로 돌아가십시오.
- The door revolves so that it prevents cold wind getting inside.
  차가운 바람을 막기 위해 그 문은 회전식으로 작동한다.
- Rotate the handle to open the door.
  문을 열려면 손잡이를 돌리시오.
- Just seeing the sight makes my head spin.
  그 장면을 보는 것만으로 눈앞이 빙빙 돈다.
- Hot water circulates through these pipes.
  뜨거운 물이 이 파이프를 통해 순환한다.

SAving Time
SAT Vocabulary

부록

전문 용어 100선

01	abdomen	n.	배, 복부
02	ablation	n.	(일부의) 제거, 절개
03	abortive	a.	실패한, 낙태의
04	abscess	n.	농양, 종기
05	acrophobia	n.	고소공포증
06	acupuncture	n.	침술, 침술요법
07	acute	a.	예리한, 날카로운
08	ailing	a.	병든, 괴로워하는
09	ailment	n.	질병, 질환
10	alchemy	n.	연금술, 연단술
11	alimentary	a.	영양의, 소화의
12	allergic	a.	알레르기 (체질)의
13	alleviate	v.	(심신의 고통을) 덜다, 완화하다
14	alluvium	n.	충적층, 충적토
15	amentia	n.	정신박약
16	amnesia	n.	기억상실
17	amphibian	n.	양서류, 수륙양용차량
18	anabatic	a.	(기상) 상승 기류의

19	analeptic	n.	강장제
20	analgesia	n.	무통증, 통각 상실
21	anatomy	n.	해부
22	anemia	n.	빈혈
23	anesthetize	v.	마취시키다
24	anthrophobia	n.	대인공포증
25	anthropoid	a.	사람을 닮은, 유인원 무리의
26	antitoxin	n.	항독소, 면역소
27	aphasia	n.	실어증
28	apoplexy	n.	졸도, 뇌일혈
29	autopsy	n.	부검, 검시
30	axiom	n.	이치, 원리
31	bacterium	n.	박테리아 (pl. bacteria)
32	capillary	a.	털 모양의; 모세관 현상의
33	catabolism	n.	이화 작용
34	cathartic	a.	배변의, 변이 통하는
35	centrifugal	a.	원심성의, 원심분리기
36	cerebral	a.	대뇌의, 반전음
37	clavicle	n.	쇄골
38	contraception	n.	피임
39	convulsion	n.	경련

40	declivity	n.	경사
41	denominator	n.	분모, 공통점
42	depilation	n.	탈모
43	dermatologist	n.	피부과 전문의사
44	diabetes	n.	당뇨병
45	diaphragm	n.	횡격막
46	dorsal	a.	등(쪽)의
47	dyspepsia	n.	소화불량
48	emasculate	v.	거세하다, 약하게 하다
49	embolism	n.	색전증, 혈관폐색증
50	embryo	n.	배아, 애벌레
51	entomologist	n.	곤충학자
52	epilepsy	n.	간질
53	epileptic	n.	간질환자
54	equilibrium	n.	균형, 평형
55	ergatocracy	n.	노동자 정치
56	euthanasia	n.	안락사
57	fauna	n.	동물군
58	fetus	n.	태아
59	gallstone	n.	담석
60	gastrointerstinal	a.	위장의, 위장 내의

61	**genital**	n.	생식기(의)
62	**geometry**	n.	기하학, 결합구조
63	**granite**	n.	화강암
64	**gynecologist**	n.	부인과 의사
65	**hominoid**	n.	유인원
66	**horticulture**	n.	원예
67	**hypertension**	n.	고혈압, 과도한 긴장
68	**hypnosis**	n.	최면
69	**hypochondria**	n.	건강 염려증
70	**hypotension**	n.	저혈압
71	**hypothermia**	n.	저체온증
72	**innervation**	n.	신경 자극 전달
73	**insulin**	n.	인슐린
74	**intravenous**	a.	정맥 내의
75	**invertebrate**	a.	척추가 없는
76	**ionosphere**	n.	전리층
77	**iris**	n.	홍채, 붓꽃
78	**isotope**	n.	동위 원소
79	**labyrinth**	n.	미궁, 미로
80	**leucocyte**	n.	백혈구
81	**leukemia**	n.	백혈병

82	lexicon	n.	어휘
83	lineage	n.	혈통, 계통
84	logistics	n.	병참, 물류 관리
85	malnutrition	n.	영양실조, 영양장애
86	marsupial	a.	주머니가 있는, 유대 동물의
87	membrane	n.	(세포)막, 양피지
88	metathesis	n.	치환, 복분해
89	microbe	n.	세균, 미생물
90	microorganism	n.	미세 구조
91	monoxide	n.	일산화물
92	morphology	n.	형태학
93	neurology	n.	신경학
94	nostrum	n.	엉터리 약
95	numerator	n.	분자
96	ornithology	n.	조류학
97	pathogen	n.	병원균, 병원체
98	pediatrician	n.	소아과 의사
99	postmortem	a.	사후의, 죽은 뒤의
100	topography	n.	지형학, 지지학

연습문제 정답

day 1
/ I /
1. naive
2. feign
3. obligated
4. facet
5. pacify

/ II /
1. fad
2. bait
3. cacophony
4. maladroit
5. antagonize

day 2
/ I /
1. tantalize
2. ramble
3. connote
4. quaint
5. wafer

/ II /
1. unilateral
2. salient
3. wane
4. wakeful
5. ramble

day 3
/ I /
1. fallacy
2. abashed
3. daunt
4. galvanize
5. illicit

/ II /
1. abhor
2. decadence
3. aberrant
4. callous
5. fecund

day 4
/ I /
1. tailored
2. paleolithic
3. validate
4. laconic
5. vain

/ II /
1. taboo
2. valor
3. undue
4. magnanimity
5. sage

day 5

/ I /
1. dazzled   2. debilitates   3. abjure   4. abducted   5. abbreviate

/ II /
1. bashful   2. illimitable   3. famish   4. eccentric   5. jovial

day 6

/ I /
1. humility   2. rectify   3. abate   4. deface   5. hypocrite

/ II /
1. immoderate   2. quadruple   3. decipher   4. hindrance   5. scrutinize

day 7

/ I /
1. elicit   2. imperative   3. laudable   4. hypothetical   5. eloquent

/ II /
1. flamboyant   2. lethargic   3. impertinent   4. hypothetical   5. delusion

day 8

/ I /
1. capricious   2. defame   3. impending   4. negated   5. elucidated

/ II /
1. immeasurable   2. fervor   3. normative   4. jubilant   5. officiate

day 9
/ I /
1. transcend 2. wretched 3. voracious 4. sequestered 5. primeval
/ II /
1. severity 2. trifle 3. volition 4. sinister 5. zeal

day 10
/ I /
1. empowered 2. delude 3. meticulous 4. grudge 5. obstinate
/ II /
1. nonchalant 2. impede 3. fleeting 4. abstinent 5. abrasive

day 11
/ I /
1. efficacious 2. debase 3. fabricate 4. impassive 5. abide
/ II /
1. idiosyncratic 2. goad 3. abject 4. gluttony 5. edict

day 12
/ I /
1. malevolent 2. ignominious 3. aberration 4. abdicated 5. beguile
/ II /
1. candor 2. fastidious 3. decry 4. beguile 5. languid

day 13

/ I /
1. nourished 2. hierarchy 3. fathom 4. noisome 5. obtuse

/ II /
1. hypocrisy 2. maxim 3. odious 4. defer 5. impecunious

day 14

/ I /
1. censure 2. eminent 3. negligent 4. gregarious 5. delegates

/ II /
1. gregarious 2. caustic 3. panacea 4. luminous 5. fetid

day 15

/ I /
1. denounced 2. implicit 3. manifested 4. hereditary 5. mandate

/ II /
1. implacable 2. jeopardy 3. nurture 4. enervate 5. partisan

day 16

/ I /
1. imputes 2. mollify 3. obsolete 4. diminutive 5. modulate

/ II /
1. empirical 2. haphazard 3. impudent 4. nuance 5. quarantine

day 17

/ I /
1. lavish   2. lax   3. razed   4. generic   5. salutation

/ II /
1. incessant   2. amiable   3. pathos   4. exhort   5. extol

day 18

/ I /
1. legitimate   2. reconciled   3. temperance   4. foretells   5. reclusive

/ II /
1. forbearance   2. genesis   3. tedious   4. incontrovertible   5. lenient

day 19

/ I /
1. implication   2. hale   3. implored   4. metamorphosis   5. implement

/ II /
1. militant   2. hallmark   3. imperturbable   4. hail   5. penitent

day 20

/ I /
1. miscellaneous   2. accentuate   3. egomania   4. gist   5. dejected

/ II /
1. abstain   2. fictitious   3. abrasion   4. deduce   5. imperceptible

day 21

/ I /
1. falterd   2. abstract   3. defaults   4. embody   5. absolve

/ II /
1. accolade   2. falter   3. defiant   4. homogeneous 5. imperil

day 22

/ I /
1. endowed   2. elevated   3. degraded   4. commemorate 5. gerrymandering

/ II /
1. decentralize 2. levy   3. fervid   4. endeavor   5. ratify

day 23

/ I /
1. chronicles 2. fortitude   3. genuine   4. adhering   5. increment

/ II /
1. bestow   2. blunder   3. entail   4. captivate   5. acquit

day 24

/ I /
1. ephemeral   2. notorious   3. serene   4. forlorn   5. bizarre

/ II /
1. boisterous 2. indomitable 3. clandestine 4. fluctuate   5. effuse

day 25

/ I /
1. deprecate   2. transient   3. codified   4. solidarity   5. perplexed

/ II /
1. ineffable   2. solicitous   3. inequitable   4. coerce   5. laborious

day 26

/ I /
1. deter   2. initiated   3. revoked   4. agnostic   5. combustion

/ II /
1. deteriorate   2. inhibit   3. pertinacious   4. ostensible   5. colloquial

day 27

/ I /
1. scrupulous   2. yearn   3. lethal   4. innate   5. ventilate

/ II /
1. enthrall   2. xenophobia   3. wrongful   4. entice   5. zealot

day 28

/ I /
1. absurd   2. anguish   3. beckoned   4. benevolence   5. discomfit

/ II /
1. discrete   2. philanthropic   3. perturb   4. benevolence   5. accomplice

day 29

/ I /
1. hallucination 2. adulterated 3. clarify 4. hastening 5. inclusive

/ II /
1. clarify 2. bias 3. adroit 4. impose 5. encompass

day 30

/ I /
1. condone 2. detest 3. ensue 4. feasibility 5. formidable

/ II /
1. ferocious 2. industrious 3. confine 4. impair 5. dawdle

핵심 고급 단어
SAving **T**ime
SAT Vocabulary

1판 1쇄 인쇄 2011년 5월 20일
1판 1쇄 발행 2011년 5월 25일

저자 박기혁, 박종범, 송승룡
발행인 이미옥
발행처 디지털북스
정가 15,000원
등록일 1999년 9월 3일
등록번호 220-90-18139

| 저자 합의 |
| 인지 생략 |

주소 서울 광진구 능동 253-21 (우편번호 143-849)
전화번호 (02) 447-3157~8
팩스번호 (02) 447-3159

www.ithinkbook.co.kr

ISBN\978-89-956910-8-3 (13740)
Copyright ⓒ 2011 Digital Books Publishing Co.,Ltd